Lecture Notes in Computer Science

Edited by G. Goos, J. Hartmanis and J. van Leeuwen

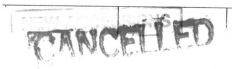

Springer
Berlin
Heidelberg
New York
Barcelona
Budapest
Hong Kong
London
Milan
Paris
Santa Clara
Singapore
Tokyo

Dhabaleswar K. Panda   Craig B. Stunkel (Eds.)

Network-Based Parallel Computing

Communication, Architecture, and Applications

Second International Workshop, CANPC '98
Las Vegas, Nevada, USA
January 31 - February 1, 1998
Proceedings

 Springer

Series Editors

Gerhard Goos, Karlsruhe University, Germany
Juris Hartmanis, Cornell University, NY, USA
Jan van Leeuwen, Utrecht University, The Netherlands

Volume Editors

Dhabaleswar K. Panda
The Ohio State University, Department of Computer and Information Science
Columbus, OH 43210-1277, USA
E-mail: panda@cis.ohio-state.edu

Craig B. Stunkel
IBM T.J. Watson Research Center
P.O. Box 218, Yorktown Heights, NY 10598, USA
E-mail: stunkel@watson.ibm.com

Cataloging-in-Publication data applied for

Die Deutsche Bibliothek - CIP-Einheitsaufnahme

Network based parallel computing : communication, architecture, and
applications ; second international workshop ; proceedings / CANPC '98, Las
Vegas, Nevada, USA, January, February 1998. Dhabaleswar K. Panda ; Craig B.
Stunkel (ed.). - Berlin ; Heidelberg ; New York ; Barcelona ; Budapest ; Hong
Kong ; London ; Milan ; Paris ; Santa Clara ; Singapore ; Tokyo : Springer,
1998
  (Lecture notes in computer science ; Vol. 1362)
  ISBN 3-540-64140-8

CR Subject Classification (1991): C.2, D.1.3, F.1.2, D.4.4

ISSN 0302-9743
ISBN 3-540-64140-8 Springer-Verlag Berlin Heidelberg New York

© Springer-Verlag Berlin Heidelberg 1998
Printed in Germany

Typesetting: Camera-ready by author
SPIN 10631803   06/3142 – 5 4 3 2 1 0   Printed on acid-free paper

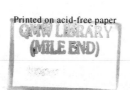

Preface

Clusters of workstations connected by local area networks (LANs) have gained popularity as a platform for cost-effective parallel processing, establishing the paradigm of *network-based parallel computing*. Hardware and software LAN technology was not initially developed for parallel processing, and thus the communication overhead between workstations can be quite high. This has forced severe constraints on maximizing parallel performance in workstation clusters.

A large number of research groups from academia, industry, and research labs are currently engaged in deriving novel hardware and software solutions to alleviate these bottlenecks. Many new interconnection technologies (such as Fast Ethernet, ATM, Myrinet [1], Fibre Channel), software schemes (such as Fast Messages [4], U-Net [3], Active Messages [6]), and standards (such as PacketWay [2]) are being developed to provide low-latency and high-bandwidth interconnection for network-based parallel computing. These developments are facilitating the migration of many parallel applications to network-based platforms consisting of PCs/Workstations.

The first international workshop [5] focusing on these issues was held last year in conjunction with HPCA-3, the 3rd International Symposium on High-Performance Computer Architecture. This year, the 1998 Workshop on Communication, Architecture, and Applications for Network-Based Parallel Computing (CANPC '98) continues to examine and address these concerns further. Potential authors submitted 10-page extended abstracts which were typically reviewed by 4–5 referees, including at least two program committee members. We were able to accept 18 papers out of a total of 38 submissions. We believe that the resulting selections comprise an important compilation of state-of-the-art solutions for network-based parallel computing systems. This CANPC workshop was sponsored by the IEEE Computer Society, and was held in conjunction with HPCA-4, the 4th International Symposium on High-Performance Computer Architecture, held in Las Vegas on Jan. 31–Feb. 4, 1998. The workshop itself took place on Jan. 31–Feb. 1.

We would like to thank all of the authors who submitted papers to this workshop. Special thanks go to the program committee and the other referees for providing us with high-quality reviews under tight deadlines. We thank Jean-Loup Baer, Program Chair for HPCA-4, for his support of this workshop. Many thanks to Lionel Ni for allowing us to use his Web-based review software which made our jobs considerably easier. Thanks to Rajeev Sivaram for maintaining and upgrading this software. Lastly, we thank the editorial staff of Springer-Verlag for agreeing to an extremely tight publication schedule in order to provide the workshop attendees with these proceedings as they registered.

January/February 1998   Dhabaleswar K. Panda and Craig B. Stunkel

References

1. N. J. Boden, D. Cohen, and et al. Myrinet: A Gigabit-per-Second Local Area Network. *IEEE Micro*, pages 29–35, Feb 1995.
2. D. Cohen, C. Lund, T. Skjellum, T. McMahon, and R. George. The End-to-End (EEP) PacketWay Protocol for High-Performance Interconnection of Computer Clusters, Oct 1997. http://WWW.ERC.MsState.Edu/labs/hpcl/packetway/.
3. T. V. Eicken, A. Basu, V. Buch, and W. Vogels. U-Net: A User-level Network Interface for Parallel and Distributed Computing. In *ACM Symposium on Operating Systems Principles*, 1995.
4. M. Lauria and A. Chien. MPI-FM: High Performance MPI on Workstation Clusters. *Journal of Parallel and Distributed Computing*, pages 4–18, Jan 1997.
5. D. K. Panda and Craig Stunkel, editors. *Communication and Architectural Support for Network-Based Parallel Computing (CANPC), Lecture Notes in Computer Science, Volume 1199*. Springer-Verlag, 1997.
6. T. von Eicken, D. E. Culler, S. C. Goldstein, and K. E. Schauser. Active Messages: A Mechanism for Integrated Communication and Computation. In *International Symposium on Computer Architecture*, pages 256–266, 1992.

CANPC '98 Program Committee

Dhabaleswar K. Panda, *Ohio State University* (co-chair)
Craig B. Stunkel, *IBM T.J. Watson Research Center* (co-chair)

Henri Bal, *Vrije University, The Netherlands*
Prith Banerjee, *Northwestern University, USA*
Debashis Basak, *Fore Systems, USA*
Jehoshua Bruck, *Caltech, USA*
Andrew Chien, *Univ. of Illinois, USA*
Al Davis, *University of Utah, USA*
Jose Duato, *Universidad Politécnica de Valencia, Spain*
Sandhya Dwarkadas, *University of Rochester, USA*
Thorsten von Eicken, *Cornell University, USA*
Michael Foster, *National Science Foundation, USA*
Mike Galles, *Silicon Graphics, Inc., USA*
Kourosh Gharachorloo, *DEC WRL, USA*
Bob Horst, *Tandem Computers, USA*
Vipin Kumar, *University of Minnesota, USA*
Andreas Nowatzyk, *DEC WRL, USA*
Greg Pfister, *IBM, USA*
Vernon Rego, *Purdue University, USA*
Jaswinder Pal Singh, *Princeton University, USA*
Marc Snir, *IBM T.J. Watson Research Center, USA*
Per Stenstrom, *Chalmers University, Sweden*
Anand Tripathi, *University of Minnesota, USA*
Wolf-Dietrich Weber, *HAL Computers, USA*
Sudhakar Yalamanchili, *Georgia Tech, USA*

Referees

Table of Contents

The Remote Enqueue Operation on Networks of Workstations

Evangelos P. Markatos and Manolis G.H. Katevenis and Penny Vatsolaki*

Institute of Computer Science (ICS)
Foundation for Research & Technology – Hellas (FORTH), Crete
P.O.Box 1385 Heraklio, Crete, GR-711-10 GREECE
markatos@ics.forth.gr
http://www.ics.forth.gr/proj/avg/telegraphos.html

Abstract. Modern networks of workstations connected by Gigabit networks have the ability to run high-performance computing applications at a reasonable performance, but at a significantly lower cost. The performance of these applications is usually dominated by their efficiency of the underlying communication mechanisms. However, efficient communication requires that not only messages themselves are sent fast, but also notification about message arrival should be fast as well. For example, a message that has arrived at its destination is worthless until the recipient is alerted to the message arrival.

In this paper we describe a new operation, the *remote-enqueue* atomic operation, which can be used in multiprocessors, and workstation clusters. This operation atomically inserts a data element in a queue that physically resides in a remote processor's memory. This operation can be used for fast notification of message arrival, and for fast passing of small messages. Compared to other software and hardware queueing alternatives, remote-enqueue provides high speed at a low implementation cost without compromising protection in a general-purpose computing environment.

1 Introduction

Popular contemporary computing environments are comprised of powerful workstations connected via a network which, in many cases, may have a high throughput, giving rise to systems called *workstation clusters* or Networks of Workstations (NOWs) [1]. The availability of such computing and communication power gives rise to new applications like multimedia, high performance scientific computing, real-time applications, engineering design and simulation, and so on. Up to recently, only high performance parallel processors and supercomputers were able to satisfy the computing requirements that these applications need. Fortunately, modern networks of workstations connected by Gigabit networks have the ability to run most applications that run on supercomputers, at a reasonable

---

* The authors are also with the University of Crete.

performance, but at a significantly lower cost. This is because most modern Gigabit interconnection networks provide both low latency and high throughput. However, efficient communication requires that not only messages themselves are sent fast, but also notification about message arrival should be fast as well. For example, a message that has arrived at its destination is worthless until the recipient is alerted to the message arrival.

In this paper we present the *Remote Enqueue* atomic operation, which allows user-level processes to enqueue (short) data in remote queues that reside in various workstations in a cluster, with no need for prior synchronization. This operation was developed within the Telegraphos project [18], in order to provide a fast message arrival notification mechanism. The Telegraphos network interface provides user applications with the ability to read/write remote memory locations, using regular load/store instructions to remote memory addresses. Sending (short) messages in Telegraphos can be done by issuing one or more remote write operation, which eliminates traditional operating system overheads that used to dominate message passing. Thus, sending (short) messages can be done from user-level by issuing a few store assembly instructions. Although sending a message can be done fast, notifying the recipient of the message arrival may take significant overhead. For example, one might use a shared flag in which the sender writes the memory location (in the recipient's memory) where the message was written. When the recipient checks for messages, it reads this shared flag and finds out if there is an arrived message and where it is. However, if two or more senders attempt to send a message at about the same time, only one of them will manage to update the flag, and the other's update will be lost. A solution would be to have a separate flag for each possible sender. However, if there are several potential senders, this solution may result in significant overhead for the receiver, who would be required to poll too many flags. Arranging the flags in hierarchical (scalable) data structures might reduce the polling overhead, but it would increase the message notification arrival overhead.

Our solution to the message arrival notification problem is to create a remote queue of message arrival notifications. A remote queue is a data structure that resides in the remote node's main memory. After writing their message to the receiver's main memory, senders enqueue their message arrival notifications in the remote queue. Receivers poll their notification queues to learn about arrived messages. Although enqueueing notifications in remote queues can be done completely in software, we propose a hardware *remote enqueue* operation that *atomically* enqueues a message notification in a remote queue. The benefits of our approach are:

- *Atomicity at low cost*: to prevent race conditions, all software-implemented enqueue operations are based on locking (or on `fetch_and_`ϕ) operations that appropriately serialize concurrent accesses to the queue. These operations incur the overhead of at least one network round-trip delay. Our hardware-implemented remote enqueue operation serializes concurrent enqueue operations at the receiver's network interface, alleviating the need for round-trip messages.

– *Low-latency flow control:* Most software-implemented enqueue operations may delay (block) the enqueing process if the queue is full. For this reason, most software-implemented enqueue operations need to read some metadata associated with the remote queue in order to make sure that the remote queue is not full. Unfortunately, reading remote data may take at least one round-trip network delay. In our approach, the enqueueing process *always* succeeds; if the queue fills up after an enqueue operation, a software handler is invoked (at the remote node) to allocate more space for the queue. Since our remote enqueue operation is non-blocking, and does not need to read remote data, it can return control to its calling processes, as soon as the data to be enqueued have been entered in the sender's network interface, that is the remote enqueue operation may return control within a few (network interface) clock cycles - usually a fraction of a microsecond.

The rest of the paper is organized as follows: Section 2 surveys previous work. Section 3 presents a summary of the Telegraphos workstation cluster. Section 4 presents the remote enqueue operation, and section 5 summarizes this paper.

2 Related Work

Although networks of workstations may have an (aggregate) computing power comparable to that of supercomputers (while costing significantly less), they have rarely been used to support high-performance computing, because communication on them has traditionally been very expensive. There have been several projects to provide efficient communication primitives in networks of workstations via a combination of hardware and software: Dolphin's SCI interface [19], PRAM [24], Memory Channel [13], Myrinet [6], ServerNet [26], Active Messages [12], Fast Messages [17], Galactica Net [16], Hamlyn [9], U-Net [27], NOW [1], Parastation [28], StarT Jt [15], Avalanche [10], Panda [2], and SHRIMP [4] provide efficient message passing on networks of workstations based on memory-mapped interfaces. We view our work as complimentary to these projects, in the sense that we propose a fast message notification mechanism that can improve the performance of all these message passing systems.

Brewer *et. al* proposed *Remote Queues,* a communication model that is based on enqueueing and dequeuing information in queues in remote processors [8]. Although their model is mostly software based, it can be tuned to exploit any existing hardware mechanisms (e.g. hardware queues) that may exist in a parallel machine. Although their work is related to ours we see two major differences:

– *Remote queues* combine message transfer with message notification: the message itself is enqueued in the remote queue. The receiver reads the message from the queue and (if appropriate) copies the message to its final destination in its local memory. In our approach we assume that the message has been posted directly in its final destination in the receiver's memory, and only the notification of the message arrival need to be put in the queue - our approach results in less message copy operations. Suppose for example that the sender and the receiver share a common data structure (e.g. a graph). Using out approach, the sender deposits its information directly in the remote graph, where the receiver will read it from. On the contrary, in the remote queues approach, the messages are first placed in a queue, and the receiver will have to copy the messages from the queue and put their information on the common graph, resulting in one extra copy operation. Recent commercial network interfaces like the Memory Channel and the PCI-SCI efficiently support our approach of the direct deposit of data in the receiver's memory.

- *Remote Queues* have been designed and implemented in commercial and experimental massively parallel processors that run parallel applications in a controlled environment, supporting little or no multiprogramming. Our approach has been designed for low-cost Networks of Workstations that support sequential and parallel applications at the same time.

In single-address-space multiprocessors, our remote enqueue operation can be completely implemented in software using any standard queue library. Brewer *et. al* propose such an implementation on top of the Cray T3D shared-memory multiprocessor [8]. Any such implementation (including the one in [8]) suffers from software overhead that includes at least one atomic operation (to atomically get an empty slot in the queue), plus several remote memory accesses (to place the data in the remote queue and update the remote pointers). This overhead is bound to be significant in a Network of Workstations.

In many multiprocessors, nodes have a network co-processor. Then, the remote enqueue operation can be implemented with the help of this co-processor. The co-processor implements sophisticated forms of communication with the processes running on the host processor. For example, a process that wants to enqueue a message in a remote queue, sends the message to the co-processor, which forwards it to the co-processor in the remote node, which in turn places the message in the remote queue. Although the existence co-processors improves the communication abilities of a node, it may result (i) in software overhead (after all they are regular microprocessors executing a software protocol), and (ii) in increased end-system cost.

3 The Telegraphos NOW

The Remote enqueue operation described in this paper is developed within the Telegraphos project [22]. *Telegraphos* is a distributed system that consists of network interfaces and switches for efficient support of parallel and distributed applications on a workstation cluster. We call this project Telegraphos or $T\eta\lambda\acute{e}\gamma\rho\alpha\phi o\varsigma$ from the greek words $T\eta\lambda\acute{e}$ meaning remote, and $\gamma\rho\acute{\alpha}\phi\omega$ meaning write, because the *central* operation on Telegraphos is the remote write operation. A remote write operation is triggered by a simple `store` assembly instruction, whose argument is a (virtual) memory address mapped on the physical memory of another workstation. The remote write operation makes possible the (user-to-user, fully protected) sending of short messages with a *single* instruction. For comparison, traditional workstation clusters connected via FDDI and ATM take several thousands of instructions to send even the shortest message across the network. Telegraphos also provides remote read operations, DMA operations, atomic operations (like fetch_and_increment) on remote memory locations, and a non-blocking fetch(remote,local) operation that copies a remote memory location into a local one. Finally, Telegraphos also provides an eager-update multicast mechanism which can be used to support both multicasted message-passing, and update-based coherent shared memory.

Telegraphos provides a variety of hardware primitives which, when combined with appropriate software will result in efficient support for shared-memory applications. These primitives include:

- *Single remote memory access*: On a *remote* memory access, traditional systems require the help of the operating system, which either replicates locally the remote page and makes a local memory access, or makes the single remote access on behalf of the requesting process. To avoid this operating system overhead, Telegraphos provides the processor with the ability to make a read or write operation to a remote memory location without replicating the page locally and without any software intervention; just like shared-memory multiprocessors do [3].
- *Access counters:* If a page is accessed by a processor frequently, it may be worthwhile to replicate the page and make all accesses to it locally. To allow informed decisions, Telegraphos provides access counters for each remotely-mapped page. Each time the processor accesses a remote page, the counter is decremented, and when it reaches zero an interrupt is sent to the processor which should probably replicate the page locally [7, 20, 21].
- *Hardware multicasting:* Telegraphos provides a write multicast mechanism in hardware which can be used to implement one-to-many message passing operations, as well as an update-based memory coherence protocol. This multicast mechanism uses a novel memory coherency protocol that makes sure that even when several processors try to update the same data and multicast their updates at the same time, they will all see a consistent view of the updated data; details about the protocol can be found at [22].
- *User-level DMA:* To facilitate efficient message passing, Telegraphos allows user-level initiation of all shared-memory operations including DMA. Thus, Telegraphos does not need the involvement of the Operating System to transfer information from one workstation to another [23].

The Telegraphos network interface has been prototyped using FPGA's; it plugs into the TurboChannel I/O bus of DEC Alpha 3000 model 300 (Pelican) workstations.

4   Remote Enqueue

We propose a new atomic operation, the *remote enqueue (REQ)* atomic operation. The REQ atomic operation is invoked with two arguments:,

- *REQ(vaddr, data)*, where *vaddr* is the virtual address that uniquely identifies a remote queue (a remote queue always resides on the physical memory of a different processor from the one invoking the REQ operation), and *data* is a single word of information to be inserted in the queue. This information is most usually a virtual address (pointer) that identifies the message body that the processor invoking the REQ operation has just sent to the processor that hosts the queue in its memory. [2].

We define a *remote queue* to be a portion of a remote processor's memory that is managed as a FIFO queue. This FIFO queue is a linked list of buffers which are physically allocated in the remote processor's memory. Data are placed in this FIFO queue by the *remote enqueue (REQ)* operation, implemented in hardware. Data are removed from this FIFO queue with a *dequeue* operation which is implemented in user-level software.

The following limitations are imposed to the buffers of a remote queue, for the hardware remote enqueue operation to be efficient:

- The starting address of each buffer should be an integer multiple of the buffer size, which is a power of two.
- The maximum buffer size is 64KB (for a 32-bit word processor).
- If the buffer size is larger than the page size, each buffer should be allocated in contiguous physical pages.

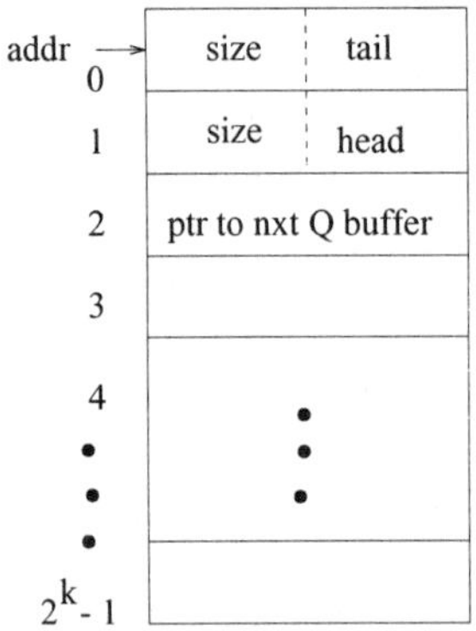

Fig. 1. Layout of a data buffer. A remote queue is just a linked list of such buffers. The first three words of the buffer are reserved to store the size, the tail, the head, and the pointer to the next Q buffer.

The layout of the buffer is shown in figure 1. The *head* and *tail* are indices in the *data buffer*. A queue is a linked list of such data buffers. For a 32-bit-word processor, both *tail*, and *head* are 16 bit quantities, and not full memory

---

[2] The Telegraphos network always delivers remote data *in-order* from a given source to a given destination node. Thus, data can never arrive before the corresponding REQ operation is posted

addresses. The reason is that, in traditional systems (where *tail* and *head* are full addresses), we calculate the pointer to the head (or the tail) of the queue by adding *addr* with *head* (or *tail*), meaning that we need to pay the hardware cost of an extra adder, and the performance cost of a word-length addition. In our system instead, where the *addr* is a multiple of a power of two, and both *head* and *tail* are always less than this power of two, we calculate the pointer to the head (or the tail) of the queue by performing an inexpensive OR operation instead of an expensive addition.

4.1   The Enqueue Operation

When processor A wants to enqueue some *data* in the remote queue *vaddr* that physically resides on processor B's memory, it invokes the $REQ(vaddr,data)$ atomic operation. A portion of this operation in implemented on the sender node's network interface, and another portion of this operation is implemented on the receiver node's network interface.

The Sender Node: When the software issues a REQ(vaddr,data) atomic operation, the local network interface takes the following actions:

- It prepares a *remote-enqueue-request* packet to be sent to the remote node that contains *paddr* (the physical address that corresponds to virtual address *vaddr*), and *data*, and
- It releases the issuing processor, which is able to continue with the rest of its program, without having to wait for the remote enqueue operation to complete.

The Receiver Node: When the destination node receives a *remote-enqueue-request* packet it extracts the *paddr* and *data* arguments from the packet and performs the remote-enqueue operation as the following atomic sequence of steps:

- Writes the *data* to the buffer entry pointed by the *tail* index (the address of the entry is calculated as *(paddr OR tail)*.
- Increments the *tail* by 1 modulo buffer *size* (If the *tail* equals the *size* of the buffer, then *tail* gets the value of the first available buffer location: 3 (see figure 1)).
- If the buffer overflows *(tail = head)*, the network interface stops accepting incoming network requests, and sends an interrupt to the (destination) processor.

The hardware finite state machine (FSM) of the destination HIB for the remote enqueue operation "req(addr, data)" is shown in table 1.

Hardware Diagram: The Telegraphos datapath for the remote enqueue operation (at the receiver side) is shown in figure 2. The whole operation is controlled by five control signals: LD0, RD0, WR0, RD1, and WR1, that are generated by a simple Finite State Machine in the above order.

```
1.   read  (addr)            -> (size, tail) // read tail and size of Q
2.   write (addr OR tail)<- (data)  // insert new element in Q
     // Note: (addr OR tail) points to the first free element in the Q
     // thus: no adder is needed
3.   tmp                      <- (tail + 1) // increment tail modulo size
     // if (tmp == size) then tail = 3
4.   if (tmp & size)     then
          tail <- 3
     else
          tail <- tmp
     // Note: if (tmp == size) then (tmp & size) == 1
     // else  (tmp & size) == 0,
     // thus the comparison can be implemented with AND
     // gates instead of a general purpose comparator
5.   read  (addr+1)        -> (size,head) // read head of Q
6.   if (head == tail) then
          stop_accepting_network_requests()
          interrupt host (overflow)
     else
          write (addr)  <- (size,tail)
```

Table 1. Finite State Machine for the Remote Enqueue Operation.

- LD0 loads the ADDRESS and DATA registers with the address and data that are the arguments of the remote enqueue operation.
- RD0 starts the reading of the $(size, tail)$ pair from $address$.
- WR0 starts the writing of the $data$ into the remote queue at address $addr\ OR\ tail$
- RD1 starts the reading of the $(size, head)$ pair from $(address + 1)$.
- Finally, WR1 writes the new $(size, tail)$ pair into $address$

4.2   Handling Buffer Overflow

When the current buffer fills up, an interrupt is sent to the processor which starts executing the operating system. The actions that the operating system should take are:

- Copy the contents of the full buffer into an empty one. Mark the previously overflowed buffer as empty.
- Link the new buffer into a queue of buffers associated with this queue. The $next$ field in the queue is used for this purpose.
- Enable the Network Interface to handle all requests.

4.3   Dequeuing and Queue Handling in the Receiver Software

In this section we outline how the dequeue operation can be efficiently implemented in software at user-level. A straightforward implementation of the dequeue operation would be:

```
deq(queue)
{
    buffer = find_last_buffer_following_the_next_pointers() ;
    if (is_empty(buffer) {
        if (is_first(buffer, queue))
            return EMPTY_QUEUE ;
        else {
            deallocate(buffer) ;
            buffer = find_last_buffer_following_the_next_pointers() ;
        }
    }
    result =  buffer[head] ;   head ++ ;
    if (head == size)
        head = 3 ;
    return result
}
```

Unfortunately, the above solution does not always work, because it is executed in user-space, and as such, it may be interrupted at any time. For example, consider the following scenario:

– A dequeue operation starts executing, taking an element from the head buffer (say A) of the queue.
– Before the operation completes, it is interrupted.
– In the meanwhile, the head buffer overflows, the operating system takes control, copies the buffer A into an empty one (say B), resetting the previously full buffer A.
– Some more remote enqueue operations are executed, completely overwriting the previous data on A (which are safely copied into the recently allocated buffer B).
– The dequeue operation eventually resumes execution trying to dequeue elements from buffer A, which does not have the elements the dequeue operation expects to find, which are now in buffer B!

Fortunately, on the Alpha processor there is a special mode the *PAL mode* which enables (super) users to write their own code (of limited size) and run it uninterrupted [25]. Thus, if the above code is turned into PAL code, it will run uninterrupted. PAL code is invoked via the special *cal_pal* routine, that the DEC Alpha processor provides. Although any user is allowed to call a PAL function, only the super user is allowed to install new PAL functions, thereby protecting the integrity of the system. Thus, the above mentioned race conditions disappear because the dequeue operation runs uninterrupted in PAL mode.

Although PAL calls are an elegant way of executing short sequences of instructions uninterrupted, they are specific to the Alpha processor. Moreover, interrupt disabling (and of course PAL calls) is an effective way of synchronization only in uniprocessors. Disabling interrupts in symmetric multiprocessing

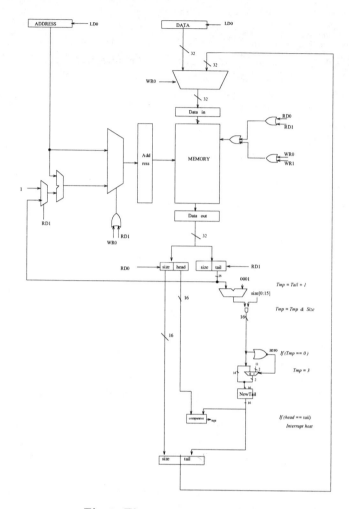

Fig. 2. The enqueue hardware.

systems that share a common network interface does not necessarily guarantee the absence of race conditions. For this reason, we have developed a more general solution that allows dequeue operations to proceed at user-level without the need to invoke PAL calls. Our solution is based on the collaboration between the operating system and the library that implements the dequeue operation. We assume the existence of a "do-not-preempt-me" bit (per queue) that is shared by the user application and the kernel. [3] When the application is about to execute a dequeue operation, it sets the "do-not-preempt-me" bit. When the dequeue operation completes, it resets the "do-not-preempt-me" bit. If the queue becomes full while an application is dequeuing something from the queue, the operating

---

[3] Similar mechanisms has been used to avoid preempting a user-level thread while executing in a critical section [11].

system driver that handles the buffer overflow interrupt, does not allocate a new buffer but sets a "full-queue" flag. When the interrupt handler returns, the application will resume execution, and it will complete the dequeue operation. When the dequeue operation completes, it checks the "full-queue" flag. If the flag is set, the application will invoke the network interface driver (e.g. through an ioctl call) to allocate more space for the queue and to enable the network interface to handle further enqueue operations. This solution works even in multiprocessor workstations that share a single network interface, with only one additional requirement: threads that execute concurrent dequeue operations (from the same queue) have to synchronize through a lock variable (associated with the queue). The first instruction of a dequeue operation is to acquire the lock, and the last instruction is to release the lock. Thus, while a thread is dequeuing data from a queue, no other thread is allowed to do the same, and thus no other thread can access shared information like the "do-not-preempt-me" bit and the "full-queue" flag. In case of buffer overflow, user-level threads should keep the lock up till the time the operating system allocates more space for the queue. If the queue fills up while at the same time a thread is executing a dequeue operation, the operating system allows the dequeue operation to complete; after the operation completes it invokes the operating system to allocate more space for the queue and to enable further network transactions.

4.4   Issuing an Enqueue Operation

An enqueue operation is invoked as: *enq(vaddress, data)* (where *vaddress* is the virtual address of the base of the first queue buffer and *data* are the data to be enqueued). In order to create a valid *remote enqueue request* packet, the network interface needs to know the *physical* address *paddr* that corresponds to virtual address *vaddr*, as well as the *data* argument. However, users are not allowed to communicate physical addresses to the network interface, because (i) they do not know the mapping between virtual and physical pages, and (ii) malicious or ignorant users may request enqueue operations to physical addresses on which they do not have read/write access. To alleviate this problem we use the mechanism of *shadow-addressing* [5, 14, 23]. The method of shadow addressing is used to securely translate virtual to physical addresses and pass them to the network interface from user-level processes. For each virtual address vaddr that is mapped in the physical address paddr, there is also a shadow address shadow(vaddr), which is mapped in the shadow physical address shadow(paddr).[4] The shadow function is simple and known to the network interface. One simple shadow function is to concatenate each address with an extra shadow bit. When the shadow bit is set, then the address is a shadow one. For example, 0x0FFFFFFFF is a regular 33-bit address, while 0x1FFFFFFFF is its shadow address.

An access to a shadow address is always interpreted by the network interface as a special argument passing operation. For example, suppose that virtual

---

[4] The Operating System is responsible for creating both mappings at memory allocation (initialization) time.

address `vaddr` is mapped to physical address `paddr`, and that the virtual address `shadow(vaddr)` is mapped into `shadow(paddr)`. Normally, a load (store) operation to virtual address `vaddr` by a user application is translated by the TLB (page-table) into a load (store) operation to physical address `paddr` and is performed by the appropriate memory controller. Similarly, a load (store) operation to virtual address `shadow(vaddr)` is translated by the TLB into a load (store) operation to physical address `shadow(paddr)`. When, however, this operation reaches the network interface it will be treated as an argument passing operation, and neither a load nor a store operation will be performed to physical address `shadow(paddr)`. Thus, when the user application wants to pass to the network interface the physical address `paddr`, it makes a store operation to virtual address `shadow(vaddr)`. Eventually the physical address `shadow(paddr)` reaches the network interface, which recognizes the shadow address and takes the physical address `paddr` by applying function $shadow^{-1}$ to physical address `shadow(paddr)`. [5]

Thus, a remote enqueue atomic operation is issued using a single assembly instruction as follows:

REQ (vaddr, data)
  /* pass physical address shadow(paddr) to the
  ** network interface */
  STORE data **TO** shadow(vaddr)

5 Summary

In this paper we describe a new operation, the *remote-enqueue* atomic operation, which can be used in multiprocessors, and workstation clusters. This operation atomically inserts a data element in a queue that physically resides in a remote processor's memory. This operation can be used for fast notification of message arrival, and for fast passing of small messages. Both enqueue and dequeue operations can be issued from user-level processes without any need to call the operating system. Both operations enforce standard virtual memory protection when accessing remote queues, and thus they provide full protection in a general-purposed multiprogrammed environment. Compared to other software and hardware queueing alternatives, remote-enqueue provides high speed at a low implementation cost without compromising protection in a general-purpose computing environment.

Acknowledgments

This work was supported in part by ESPRIT project 6253 "Supercomputer Highly Parallel System" (SHIPS), funded by the European Union, through DG

---

[5] All shadow addresses should be within the physical address range of the network interface, and distinct from the normal physical addresses used by that network interface.

III of its Commission, HPCN Unit. We deeply appreciate this financial support, without which this work would have not existed. A patent application for the above work has been filed: E. Markatos, M Katevenis, and P. Vatsolaki: "Notification of message arrival in a parallel computer system", Patent application number 97410036.4, (Europe) March 19th 1997.

References

1. T.E. Anderson, D.E. Culler, and D.A. Patterson. A Case for NOW (Networks of Workstations). *IEEE Micro*, 15(1):54–64, February 1995.
2. H. Bal, R. Hofman, and K. Verstoep. A Comparison of Three High Speed Networks for Parallel Cluster Computing. In *Proc. 1st International Workshop on Communication and Arch. Support for Network-Based Parallel Computing*, pages 184–197, 1997.
3. BBN Advanced Computers Inc. *Inside the TC2000^{TM} Computer*. Cambridge, Massachusetts, February 1990.
4. M. Blumrich, K. Li, R. Alpert, C. Dubnicki, E. Felten, and J. Sandberg. Virtual Memory Mapped Network Interface for the SHRIMP Multicomputer. In *Proc. 21-th International Symposium on Comp. Arch.*, pages 142–153, Chicago, IL, April 1994.
5. M.A. Blumrich, C.Dubnicki, E.W. Felten, and K. Li. Protected, User-level DMA for the SHRIMP Network Interface. In *Proc. of the 2nd International Symposium on High Performance Computer Architecture*, pages 154–165, San Jose, CA, February 1996.
6. N.J. Boden, D. Cohen, and W.-K. Su. Myrinet: A Gigabit-per-Second Local Area Network. *IEEE Micro*, 15(1):29, February 1995.
7. William J. Bolosky, Michael L. Scott, Robert P. Fitzgerald, Robert J. Fowler, and Alan L. Cox. NUMA Policies and Their Relation to Memory Architecture. In *Proceedings of the Fourth International Conference on Architectural Support for Programming Languages and Operating Systems*, pages 212–221, Santa Clara, CA, April 1991.
8. E.A. Brewer, F.T. Chong, L.Tl Liu, S.D. Sharma, and J.D. Kubiatowicz. Remote Queues: Exposing Message Queues for Optimization and Atomicity. In *Symp. on Parallel Algorithms and Architecures*, 1995.
9. G. Buzzard, D. Jacobson, S. Marovich, and J. Wilkes. Hamlyn: a High-performance Network Interface, with Sender-Based Memory Management. In *Proceedings of the Hot Interconnects III Symposium*, August 1995.
10. A. Davis, M. Swanson, and M. Parker. Efficient Communication Mechanisms for Cluster Based Parallel Computing. Technical report, University of Utah, Dept. of Computer Science, 1996.
11. J. Edler, J. Lipkis, and E. Schonberg. Process Management for Highly Parallel UNIX Systems. Technical Report Ultracomputer Note 136, Ultracomputer Research Laboratory, New York University, April 1988.
12. T. von Eicken, D. E. Culler, S. C. Goldstein, and K. E. Schauser. Active Messages: A Mechanism for Integrated Communication and Computation. In *Proc. 19-th International Symposium on Comp. Arch.*, pages 256–266, Gold Coast, Australia, May 1992.
13. R. Gillett. Memory Channel Network for PCI. *IEEE Micro*, 16(1):12, February 1996.

14

14. J. Heinlein, K. Gharachorloo, S. Dresser, and A. Gupta. Integration of Message Passing and Shared Memory in the Stanford FLASH Multiprocessor. In *Proc. of the 6-th International Conference on Architectural Support for Programming Languages and Operating Systems*, pages 38–50, 1994.
15. James C. Hoe and Mike Ehrlich. StarT-JR: A Parallel System from Commodity Technology. In *Proceedings of the 7th Transputer/Occam International Conference*, November 1995. Tokyo, Japan.
16. Andrew W. Wilson Jr., Richard P. LaRowe Jr., and Marc J. Teller. Hardware Assist for Distributed Shared Memory. In *Proc. 13-th Int. Conf. on Distr. Comp. Syst.*, pages 246–255, Pittsburgh, PA, May 1993.
17. V. Karamcheti, S. Pakin, and A. Chien. High Performance Messaging on Workstations: Illinois Fast Messages (FM) for Myrinet. In *Supercomputing 95*, 1995.
18. Manolis G. H. Katevenis, Evangelos P. Markatos, George Kalokerinos, and Apostolos Dollas. Telegraphos: A Substrate for High-Performance Computing on Workstation Clusters. *Journal of Parallel and Distributed Computing*, 43(2):94–108, June 1997.
19. O. Lysne, S. Gjessing, and K. Lochsen. Running the SCI Protocol over HIC Networks. In *Proceedings of the Second International Workshop on SCI-based Low-cost/High-perfocmance Computing (SCIzzL-2)*, March 1995. Santa Barbara, CA.
20. E.P. Markatos. Using Remote Memory to avoid Disk Thrashing: A Simulation Study. In *Proceedings of the ACM International Workshop on Modeling, Analysis, and Simulation of Computer and Telecommunication Systems (MASCOTS '96)*, pages 69–73, February 1996.
21. E.P. Markatos and C.E. Chronaki. Trace-Driven Simulations of Data-Alignment and Other Factors affecting Update and Invalidate Based Coherent Memory. In *Proceedings of the ACM International Workshop on Modeling, Analysis, and Simulation of Computer and Telecommunication Systems (MASCOTS '94)*, pages 44–52, January 1994.
22. E.P. Markatos and M. G.H. Katevenis. Telegraphos: High-Performance Networking for Parallel Processing on Workstation Clusters. In *Proc. of the 2nd International Symposium on High Performance Computer Architecture*, pages 144–153, Feb 1996. URL: http://www.csi.forth.gr/ proj/arch-vlsi/papers/ 1996.HPCA96.Telegraphos.ps.gz.
23. E.P. Markatos and M. G.H. Katevenis. User-Level DMA without Operating System Kernel Modification. In *Proc. of the 3rd International Symposium on High Performance Computer Architecture*, pages 322–331, Feb 1997. URL: http://www.csi.forth.gr/proj/aavg/papers/ 1997.HPCA97.user_level_dma.ps.gz.
24. D. Serpanos. *Scalable Shared-Memory Interconnections*. PhD thesis, Princeton University, Dept. of Computer Science, October 1990.
25. R. Sites. Alpha AXP Architecture. *Communications of the ACM*, 36(2):33–44, February 1993.
26. Tandem Computers Inc. ServerNet Technology: Introducing the Worlds First System Area Network, 1996. http://www.tandem.com/INFOCTR/BRFS_WPS/SNTSANWP/SNTSANWP.HTM.
27. Thorsten von Eicken, Anindya Basu, Vineet Buch, and Werner Vogels. U-Net: A User-Level Network Interface for Parallel and Distributed Computing. In *Proc. 15-th Symposium on Operating Systems Principles*, pages 40–53, December 1995.
28. Thomas M. Warschko, Joachim M. Blum, and Walter F. Tichy. The ParaPC / ParaStation Project: Efficient Parallel Computing by Clustering Workstations. Technical Report 13/96, University of Karlsruhe, Dept. of Informatics, 1996.

The HAL Interconnect PCI Card

Jeff Larson

HAL Computer Systems, 1315 Dell Ave., Campbell, CA 95008,
larson@hal.com, (408)341-5648

Abstract. This paper describes HAL's PCI Mercury Interface (PMI) cluster network interface card for its Mercury interconnect. Note: "Mercury" is an internal HAL code name for this interconnect and will not be used on any released product. The PMI card operates in any legitimate PCI 2.1 [4], platform 0-66 MHz, 32-bit or 64-bit address/data widths, and either 3.3v or 5v IO. The PMI requires no additional functionality beyond the PCI specification. The services provided are local to remote chained DMA, messaging, remote memory atomic operations, and barrier.

1 Introduction

The HAL Mercury Interconnect [1] was originally architected to provide short distance communication with the great abundance of bandwidth and the very low latency required for shared memory multicomputing. Since that time, it was determined that the same interconnect could still be economical and effective for applications which have somewhat lesser performance requirements and very high availability requirements. This paper describes a PCI clustering card which implements a familiar message passing architecture and utilizes the HAL Mercury Interconnect.

2 Motivation

The PMI was developed for customers within Fujitsu who are familiar with a clustering network interface similar to that of the AP3000. The platforms include a heterogeneous mainframe database system and a clustered Ultrasparc-based server system. Each includes high-performance 64-bit, 66-MHz PCI bus IO. Care was also taken to get the excellent performance also out of the more common 32-bit, 33-MHz platforms.

3 Mercury Interconnect

Figure 1 shows the picture of a general interconnect, which is also the highest-level view of the Mercury Interconnect as would apply to a PMI card cluster system. A collection of processor/memory nodes with PMI cards are plugged into the interconnect and communicate with one another using the

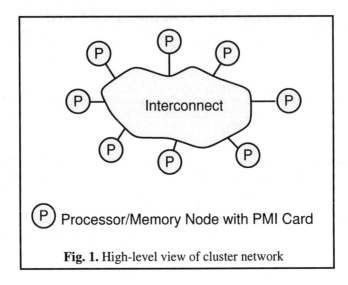

Fig. 1. High-level view of cluster network

network services. The interconnect cloud consists of a collection of six port router boxes which can adjust their operating frequency to accommodate from 2m-10m parallel copper cables. The choice of topology is very flexible. The links within the interconnect have bandwidths that are much higher than that of the PCI bus itself, with current technology amounts to 0.8GBytes/s in each direction for 10m links and 1.6BGytes/s in each direction for 2m links. For design purposes, we always regard the interconnect fabric itself to be "unreliable" and always provide end-to-end reliability services in the processing nodes. In practice, well functioning links as we have implemented them operating at these speeds have proven quite error-free. The routers in the network fabric exchange packets in virtual cut-through as an optimization for shared memory applications, where the maximum packet size would likely be one cache line. The PMI card itself supports up to 64 interconnected nodes, this limitation due to the reliability layer state storage and routing table storage.

4   Services Offered

This section describes the five types of transfers the PMI card offers.

4.1   SEND/RECEIVE

In this type of transfer, the initiating node sends a block of data to the receiving node which determines where to store the data based only on the order of arrival of the send messages. Messages of up to 1MB are supported. This is the type of transfer referred to by the term "messaging." Here are some scenarios where this type of messaging should be used.

Initialization. All other types of transfer require the sending side to be aware of the address to access data on the remote node, which would pose a difficulties in some circumstances.

Queueing. The receiving node stores send messages as they are received which is a natural queue. For instance this could be used for methods requiring mutual exclusion.

Asynchronous Message. In other words a message for which the receiving side was not specifically looking. The receiving side controls where the messages are going and knows how many have been received at all times.

4.2 PUT

Here the initiating node sends the remote node a block of data, the initiating node specifies the PCI addresses of the data buffers on both the remote node and on the local node. Transfers of up to 1MB are supported. The flow of data is exactly the same as in the SEND/RECEIVE, the only difference being that the remote buffer address is supplied by the sending node. Here are some reasons for preferring PUT to SEND/RECEIVE for certain situations.

Less Coordination Required. For the SEND/RECEIVE, the target address has to be set up beforehand on the receiving side. Using a SEND/RECEIVE to implement this type of transfer might involve first receiving the data to a communication buffer, and then copying it again to the proper destination. This impacts processor overhead and message latency.

Long Transfer. Even though SEND/RECEIVE can also be effectively used for long transfers, the implementation assumed that long transfers would primarily use GET or PUT. In particular, care was taken to ensure that possibly critical SEND messages could interleave with possibly very long GET or PUT transfers. For that reason, even 1MB PUT or GET messages can be executed without fear that they will block SEND messages on another channel.

4.3 GET

Here the initiating node asks a remote node to send it a block of data with the initiating node specifying the PCI addresses of the data buffers on both the remote node and on the local node. Transfers of up to 1MB are supported. The reasons for preferring to use GET directly over implementing it with SEND/RECEIVE are the same as for PUT, and the performance savings are probably even greater.

4.4   REMOTE ATOMIC RMW

Or read-modify-write, the initiating node fetches an operand(s) locally and sends it with a RMW request to a remote node. The remote node fetches a memory word, performs an operation with the operand(s) it received and writes back the result if appropriate. The fetched operand is returned to the sending node. The available RMW's are 1)FETCH and ADD, 2) FETCH and AND, 3)FETCH and OR, 4)FETCH and EXCLUSIVE OR, 5)COMPARE and SWAP, and 6)NOOP.

Managing Locks. Probably one of the most important uses of the remote RMW is for locks. Of course a variety of locks can be implemented on top of the SEND/RECEIVE message also and they will be the most efficient in some circumstances, but using the ATOMIC RMW primitives will have lower latency and overhead. One very well-known method for using these functions to implement a lock would involve the COMPARE and SWAP.

Event Indicators. Something happens, so a word in a remote node gets a bit flipped, a number added to it, etc.

4.5   BARRIER

Each PMI card contains a set of barrier registers which can be programmed to wait for any arbitrary subset of all nodes in the system to send barrier requests. Once barrier requests have been received from all expected nodes, barrier responses are returned to each node. This synchronization primitive is useful and efficient in cases where many nodes have a very precisely-balanced workload.

5   Notification

This section explains the notification semantics available for normal transaction completions.

5.1   Background

To understand the following discussion in this section, it is necessary to explain two terms.

Descriptor. A *descriptor* is a 32-byte command. Each of the operations, SEND/RECEIVE, GET, PUT, RMW, and BARRIER are always initiated by executing a descriptor.

Chain. A *chain* is a sequence of descriptors to be executed. In the PMI, all descriptors in a chain are consecutive in a circular memory buffer. Section 10 gives more details.

5.2   Flag Updates

All five transaction types except for the RMW's and BARRIER can be programmed in the descriptor to update a flag in PCI memory remotely, locally, or both on normal completion. The flag update consists of a read-increment-write of a 32-bit data. A flag increment does not stop the progression of the chain. The RMW's and BARRIER can only be programmed to update the flag at the initiating node.

5.3   Interrupts

All five transaction types except for the RMW's and BARRIER can be programmed in the descriptor to interrupt remotely, locally, or both on normal completion. An interrupt on normal completion does not stop the progression of the chain. The RMW's can only be programmed to interrupt the initiating node. On the BARRIER, the only control of whether the remote, or controlling, node get interrupted on barrier completion is via a INTERRUPT MASK register which is accessible over the PCI bus.

6   Error Detection and Retry

Since the router was designed under the assumption that the end nodes offered an end-to-end reliability mechanism, the PMI card includes guaranteed and in-order delivery transport services. Thus soft network failures are automatically corrected and are transparent to software. In the case of hard network failures there are time-outs on the PMI that can be applied to all stages of the progress of any transfer or alternatively the time-outs can be done in software because the progress of a transfer can be killed at any time. The hard error therefore shows up to software as an interrupt and an error status code.

7   Precise Network Error Reporting

It is possible that an error could occur that cannot be corrected by the transport mechanism built into the PMI, for instance it is a hard network failure, the remote node is down, or because of a software error. In that case the PMI card will always indicate the descriptor of the transfer involved in the error in the architected register that points to the chain and no subsequent descriptors in that chain will have been fetched or executed.

8   End-to-End Flow Control - Busy/Retry

In a transfer of a large block of data, the receiving node of the block at times might not have total access to the full bandwidth of the PCI bus for a variety of reasons. Also there may be multiple streams of data arriving at the receiving node simultaneously. In such a case backup of the data packets into the network would cause a loss of network performance that may creep through a large portion of the links by an effect known as tree saturation. The PMI card prevents this by an end-to-end flow control process where the nodes receiving block data transfers reserves some on-card buffer space and sends credit packets to sending nodes before any transfers take place. Another feature that the PMI card implements is BUSY/RETRY from incoming requests for GET's, PUT's, SEND's, and RMW's. If there is no space to accept another request of the given type, the request is rejected and a RETRY packet is returned. The requester then tries again later. There is a aging protocol provided to prevent starvation.

9 Interleaving

It is assumed that very long DMA transfers will occur and that it is important that RMW's and short send messages should not have to wait for long data transfers to conclude. Several mechanisms have been incorporated which work together to prevent this.

9.1 Multiple Simultaneously-Executing Chains and Descriptors

This allows for instance one chain to be reserved for very short and latency critical synchronization primitives (RMW's), a second chain to be reserved for intermediate length SEND/RECEIVEs, and a third chain to be reserved for possibly long GET/PUT DMA transfers.

9.2 Multiple Remote Node Channels

On the remote side of any transfer likewise there are separate DMA register sets for controlling the remote side of GETs, PUTs, RECEIVEs, and RMW's.

9.3 Bypassing Queued Data

Control and header packets are provided with a bypass mechanism to get past queued data in on-card buffers that hold arriving packets. This allow RMW's to bypass the data packets of SEND/RECEIVEs, GETs, and PUTs.

10 Some Important Architected Registers

To illustrate execution of a send or receive chain, this section explains several important per-chain architected registers. See Figure 2.

10.1   DBA - the Descriptor Buffer Base Address

This is a 40-bit address that indicates the base of the descriptor buffer region. There is one such register for each chain. This will indicate the PCI address of the next descriptor to complete in the case where the Offset Processing Address (OPA) is zero.

10.2   OPA - the Offset Processing Address

This is a 32-bit address that indicates the address relative to the base of the descriptor that is executing or if the chain is stopped will be executing. The sum of the OPA and DBA is the next descriptor address.

10.3   OQA - the Offset Quit Address

This is a 32-bit address that indicates the address relative to the base of the descriptor of the first descriptor after the end of the chain. The descriptor pointed to by the sum of OQA and DBA is never executed except for the case of a one descriptor chain.

10.4   DSZ - the Descriptor buffer SiZe

This is a 32-bit number that indicates the size of the descriptor buffer in bytes. This is necessary because the descriptor buffer is a circular queue. This is used for chain address wrapping.

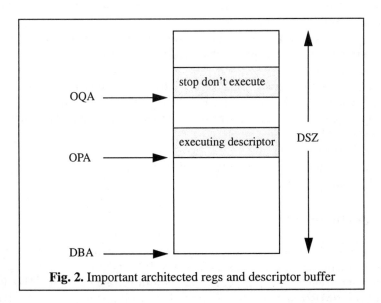

Fig. 2. Important architected regs and descriptor buffer

10.5   CHAIN_START

If a chain is in the stopped state, writing to this register starts it. The descriptor pointed to by OPA will be fetched and executed first and the chain will continue updating the OPA register and fetching and executing new descriptors until the chain completes, *i.e.* OPA=OQA, or an uncorrectable error is encountered.

10.6   CHAIN_INFO

After a chain finished, the CHAIN_INFO register must be read. Reading this register will indicate if the chain completes without error, and if not, which error occurred.

11   Example Operation

To quickly illustrate use of the PMI card, this example shows the required local and remote operations for a single SEND/RECEIVE. This is the most complicated of the transfers that the PMI supports. In the SEND/RECEIVE, the sending node reads a block of data from the local PCI address space, sends the data over the network and the receiving node writes the data to it PCI bus at an address specified by the receiving node.

First, the receiving node creates a 32-byte receive descriptor in local host memory accessible through the host PCI bridge which includes the base address of the receive buffer and controls on what kinds of notifications should occur on completion.

Next, the receiving node sets up four registers on the PMI card that describe the receive descriptor buffer and then writes to a fifth address which starts the receive descriptor chain.

Then the sending node creates a 32-byte send descriptor in local host memory accessible through the host PCI bridge which includes the base address of the send buffer, the size of the transfer, and controls on which notifications should occur on completion.

Finally, the sending node sets up four registers on the PMI card that describe the send descriptor buffer and then writes to a fifth address which starts the send descriptor chain.

12   Performance

The PCI bus which shares address and data lines, achieves highest potential performance in the case of long data bursts. In principle, it might be expected that for long transfers, the expected bandwidth for a 32-bit, 33-MHz PCI bus would be 133MB/s and for the expected bandwidth of a 64-bit, 66-MHz PCI, 533MB/s. The PCI protocol allows for up to 4KB bursts in cases where there is no contention for the bus. When there is contention, then the PCI master may be forced to disconnect early due to the master latency timer.

12.1   The OPB

The Orion PCI Bridge in the INTEL 450 GX chipset is a 33-MHz, 32-bit host to PCI bus bridge for Pentium-Pro motherboards. The OPB is well optimized for long burst reads for PCI "read multiple" transactions. For the length of a long burst read, the OPB injects very few wait cycles once data starts arriving from host memory. On the other hand, as soon as a PCI master which has been doing PCI "read multiple" transactions gives up the PCI bus by raising FRAME#, the OPB discards all further prefetched data. Therefore the penalty for short read bursts is very high, since the next PCI read will have to go all the way to memory even if that read was to an address already prefetched. The result of all this is that in order to get good utilization of the PCI bus with the OPB it is necessary to have long burst reads. Just for this possibility, the PMI card contains a mode bit which when set authorizes the PMI card to attempt burst reads up to 1KByte. With this bit deasserted, the burst reads are limited to 128Bytes before the PMI bus master releases the PCI bus. There is no long burst mode for write line invalidates because it is harder to implement and the OPB forces many fewer wait cycles for write-line/invalidates than for read line multiples.

12.2   The U2P

The Sun Microsystems Ultrasparc to PCI (U2P) chip is a 66-MHz, 64-bit host to PCI bus bridge for the Ultrasparc. The U2P is optimized for maintaining multiple DMA's running simultaneously in an interleaved fashion. The U2P does not automatically drop prefetched cache lines when a burst read is ended early, but rather maintains a single prefetched cache line and snoops the host bus to prevent the data from becoming stale. The U2P also limits burst reads and write line/invalidates to the size of one cache line (64 bytes) before forcing a disconnect. This small block transfer size prevents achieving anywhere near the theoretical 533MB/s for a 66-MHz, 64-bit PCI. There is no way around this, so the PMI card designers determined it was therefore very satisfactory to run the data interface between the two ASICs on the card at a data rate somewhat slower than 533MB/s in one direction (actually 426MB/s) since a long bust at that speed cannot be sustained through the U2P bridge. Should later a bridge be designed which can maintain long full-bandwidth bursts over the PCI, a slight bottleneck may be presented by the PMI.

12.3   Measurements

At the time of the deadline for this paper, software development with working hardware is underway for the PMI card at various Fujitsu laboratories in

Japan. Also testing of the PMI card continues at HAL using both a Pentium Pro 33-MHz, 32-bit PCI motherboard with the Orion chipset and a 64-bit 66-MHz Ultrasparc Server using the U2P bridge. Precise performance measurements are not yet available for the Ultrasparc system, but the general expectation is for an approximate achievable bandwidth of 220MB/s based on existing experience. In the Intel platform, observations show that a SEND/RECEIVE will begin fetching data from host memory and that data will cross the local PCI bus after about 2.4µs. A 1K burst commences with very few wait states on the read side, 125MB/sec, which is 93% efficiency, and writes to the remote side at about 80MB/sec or 60% efficiency. This bottleneck appears on the remote writing side because of the maximum burst size of 64 bytes in our design.

13   Card Design

The PMI card, see figure 3, contains two ASICs, the PCI to Mercury Bridge (PMB) implemented in the LSI Logic 0.25µm, G-10p process, and the Mercury Interface Chip (MIC) which was implemented in the Fujitsu 0.35µm, 5-metal cs60 process. The choice of a two-chip solution was made for modularity. The MIC was designed to be the only chip that interfaces directly into the router network. Since it requires custom IO circuits to interface to the network, it was considered not suitable as a logic macro that could be plugged into just any ASIC vendor's technology. The PMB is an example of a so-called ISM as discussed in [1]. The function of the PMB is to provide the architectural view of the card as is described by this paper. It contains all the architected registers that are accessed after initialization.

13.1   The MIC

The MIC provides the electrical interface into the network and the end-to-end reliability services that were assumed when the router network was architected. The electrical interface and the synchronization methods are similar to those used by the router and is described elsewhere [2],[3]. The end-to-end reliability is described in [1] and is implemented here with the retransmission buffers shown in figure 4.

A copy of each packet is kept in a retransmission buffer at the time that the packet is sent into the network until it is guaranteed that the destination node has received an in-order error-free copy of the packet. This is accomplished by the receiving MIC returning an "ack" packet with the sequence number of the received sequenced packet if it was received in-order and error free. Transmission errors are detected by attaching an EDC to every packet. The buffer size was chosen to be sufficient so that it is never expected that all 12 buffers would be occupied simultaneously even with the latency of a multi-hop (multi-router) network. This mechanism does not present a performance bottleneck.

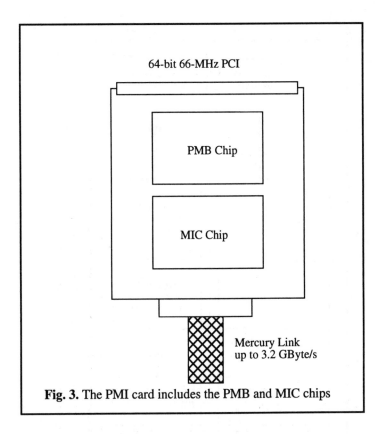

Fig. 3. The PMI card includes the PMB and MIC chips

The Outgoing Partner Information Table (OPIT) and Incoming Partner Information table (IPIT) blocks refer to the sequence number tables which exist for one entry per node per priority level.

The Routing Table has 64 entries, one entry per potential target node. Each entry simply consists of all the output port numbers, 1-6, of all the routers in the path to the target node. The routing table is accessed for every sequenced packet sent and for every "ack" packet sent.

The In-Bound Buffer is divided into two classes. One partition is used for data and the other is used for all other packet types. This has the primary benefit of allowing newly arriving requests, most importantly latency-critical RMW's from being held for a long time behind large blocks of data.

The reliability feature of the MIC greatly simplified the design of the PMB chip. The PMB still required to keep track of certain errors and time-outs, but any network related errors or time-outs could then be reliably detected and determined to be hard fails. The PMB did not have to be concerned with the possibilities of corrupted commands or data.

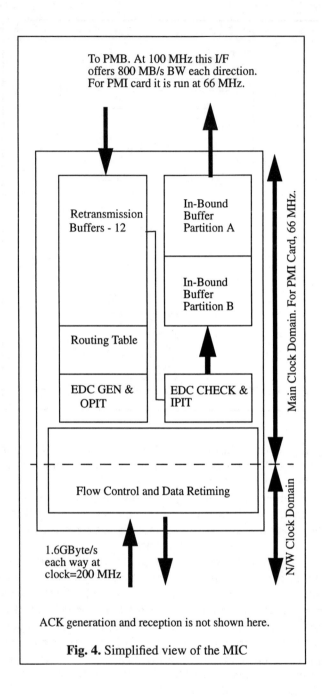

Fig. 4. Simplified view of the MIC

13.2   The PMB

The PMB is the ASIC that interfaces to the PCI bus. It is a very specific design for this particular card and implements the higher level of all the features in sections 3-10. The 0.25u LSI G10 process choice came from the need to meet timing for the 66-MHz, 64-bit PCI bus since experience has shown that timing can be difficult to meet with the older technologies. This ASIC uses all standard rail-to-rail CMOS IO's and the 3.3v 66-MHz PCI buffers are all 5v-tolerant. The PMB features an asynchronous boundary in the PCI interface logic which allows the PCI bus to operate at any frequency from 66 MHz down to 0 MHz.

As shown in figure 5, the PMB serves as a PCI target for accessing architected registers such as the chain control registers as described in section 10. It is also a PCI master when fetching descriptors and reading and writing DMA data, message data, RMW data, and flag data. The PMB contains all the logic for maintaining DMA address counts, forming packet headers, reserving buffer space (DMA Engines & Protocol SM's block), putting the PCI data together with the packet headers and retrying busied requests (Packet Assembly block), and for checking appropriateness of arriving packets, passing data on to the PCI/IF or requests on to the DMA engines block, and for sending back a RETRY packet when there are no resources to handle them immediately (Packet Reception/Retry Generation block).

28

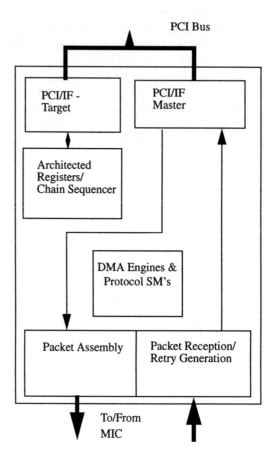

PCI Bus

PCI/IF -
Target

PCI/IF
Master

Architected
Registers/
Chain Sequencer

DMA Engines &
Protocol SM's

Packet Assembly

Packet Reception/
Retry Generation

To/From
MIC

Fig. 5. Simplified diagram of the PMB

Summary

The PMI card motivation, function, performance, and design were presented. It presents a descriptor chain interface to software with three independently executing chains for initiating transactions. End-to-end flow control prevents backup of data packets into the network, and interleaving allows synchronization primitives and short SEND/RECEIVES from being blocked begin long GET or PUT transfers. The latency for short transfers is approximately 3us and long burst reads for high performance can be supported when the platform's host-to-PCI bridge permits it. The modular design of the PMI produced a flexible network interface chip called the MIC which is equally useful for other designs involving the HAL network.

References

1. Weber, W.-D., Gold, S., Helland, P., Shimizu, T., Wicki, T., and Wilcke, W.: The Mercury Interconnect Architecture, A Cost-effective Infrastructure for High-performance Servers. Proceedings of the 24th International Symposium on Computer Architecture (1997)

2. Mu, A., Larson, J., Sastry, R., Wicki, T., and Wilcke, W. A 9.6 GigaByte/s Throughput Plesiochronous Routing Chip. In Digest of Papers of the 41st IEEE Computer Society International Conference (Compcon) (1996) 261-266

3. Mu, A., Chia, B., Kondapalli, S., Koo, C., Larson, J., Nguyen, L., Sastry, R., Satsukawa, Y., Shih, H.-C., Wicki, T., Wu, C., Yu, K., and Zhang, X.: A 285 MHz 6-port Plesiochronous Router Chip with Non-Blocking Cross-Bar Switch. In 1996 Symposium on VLSI Circuits: Digest of Technical Papers (1996) 136-137

4. PCI Special Interest Group: PCI Local Bus Specification, Revision 2.1 (1995)

Implementing Protected Multi-User Communication for Myrinet*

Shailabh Nagar, Dale Seed, and Anand Sivasubramaniam

Department of Computer Science & Engineering
The Pennsylvania State University
University Park, PA 16802.
{*nagar,seed,anand*}@cse.psu.edu

Abstract. A Network of Workstations (NOW) is emerging as a cost-effective solution to high performance computing. However, we need to lower the cost of communicating between the workstations to make this platform viable. With the advent of high-performance networks such as ATM and Myrinet, the physical network is no longer the communication bottleneck. Rather, the major overhead can now be attributed to software. This overhead is a direct result of the cost that a message incurs as it travels through different protection domains. We can alleviate this problem by allowing protected user-level access directly to the network, thereby eliminating the kernel from the critical path. This paper presents a description of the design, implementation and performance of a protected user-level messaging system over Myrinet, called MU-Net, that can handle multiple application processes concurrently. MU-Net has been implemented on the SUN Solaris 2.5 operating system.

1 Introduction

Despite the concerted effort from both industry and academia to design and manufacture multiprocessors, their success in the commercial arena has been limited [7, 9]. Most multiprocessor designs include custom-made components which not only increase the costs, but also the time to market. Recently, there has been a trend to use a Network of Workstations (NOW) as a more cost-effective solution to high performance computing [1]. Rather than relying on custom-made components, NOWs can be constructed from commercial off-the-shelf hardware. This not only decreases the cost, but also increases the availability of high performance computing platforms. Such designs also make it easier to upgrade the hardware with anticipated improvements in workstation and networking technology. Further, the workstations themselves, can be used as general purpose computing engines.

The major limitation of NOWs is the high communication overhead in exchanging messages between nodes. Unlike a multiprocessor that has tightly coupled nodes and a custom low-latency/high bandwidth network, the nodes in

* This research is supported in part by a NSF Career Award MIP-9701475, EPA grant R825195-01-0, and equipment grants from NSF and IBM.

a NOW are loosely connected by a Local Area Network (LAN) with a lower bandwidth. The associated software costs for communication further limit the scalability of the applications executing on the NOW. Therefore, to make this platform more attractive, we need to address three important issues related to communication costs. First, the network connecting the workstations should be fast. Second, the interface to the network should provide an efficient way of transferring data between the memory on the workstation and the network. Finally, the software messaging layers should add minimal overhead to the cost of moving data between two application processes running on two different workstations. Recent research has been addressing these issues. High speed networks such as ATM [4] and Myrinet [2] can potentially deliver point-to-point hardware bandwidths that are comparable to the link bandwidths of the interconnection networks in multiprocessors. To address the second issue, newer network interface designs have been proposed with hardware enhancements to overlap communication with computation and to facilitate direct user-level interaction with the network interface [10]. Finally, low latency software messaging layers have been proposed [11, 6, 3, 8, 5, 12] making use of these network and network interface innovations.

Of all the costs discussed above, the software costs have traditionally been the most dominant for NOW environments. In particular, the involvement of the kernel in the critical send/receive path results in a significant degradation in performance. This is due to the cost of crossing protection boundaries, and multiple levels of copying that must occur between the kernel, user processes, and the network device. A recent research trend has focused on removing the kernel from the critical path of sending and receiving messages to cut down these costs. This has resulted in several user-level messaging platforms such as Cornell's U-Net [10], Myricom's API and GM[2, 5], Illinois' Fast Messages [6], HP's Hamlyn [3], PM [8], and Trapeze [12]. The common goal of these designs is to minimize the end-to-end communication latency of a message by off-loading communication responsibilities from the kernel to both the user and the *smart* network interface. Since the kernel is responsible for providing protection between user processes, alternative communication mechanisms must also enforce this to allow multiple processes to access the network concurrently. If this protection is not provided, then one process may potentially receive or corrupt another process's messages. In NOW environments, which can have multiple application processes executing on each node and sharing the network concurrently, providing protected communication is extremely important.

This paper presents the design, implementation and performance of MU-Net, a user-level messaging platform for Myrinet that allows protected multi-user access to the network. Our design of MU-Net has drawn from ideas of other user-level platforms [10, 6] but there are some key differences. Unlike the original Fast Messages implementation [6], MU-Net allows multiple applications on a node to concurrently use the network in a protected manner. Recently, an implementation of Fast Messages supporting multiple processes on PCs running Windows NT or Linux has been announced, but such a version for SUN Solaris platforms is not yet available. Further, MU-Net provides additional mechanisms for transferring longer messages in cases where the host CPU has other useful work to do, while Fast Messages always employs the host CPU to packetize/reassemble longer messages. Our performance results on a SUN Ultra Enterprise 1 platform running Solaris 2.5 show that despite being able to support multiple application processes, MU-Net performs comparably to Fast Messages 2.0 (the version which supports only one application process per node). Our results also give a detailed breakup of the costs incurred in the various stages of a message as it propagates from the sender to the receiver. The differences between MU-Net and U-Net [10] are in the implementation details specific to the Myrinet platform which will become clearer in the following sections.

The rest of this paper is organized as follows. Section 2 gives a hardware description of the Myrinet platform. The design of MU-Net and a description of its operations is discussed in detail in Section 3 and the performance results are given in Section 4. Finally, we summarize the related work in Section 5 and present concluding remarks in Section 6.

2 Myrinet

Myrinet [2] is a high-speed switch-based network which allows variable length packets. A typical Myrinet network consists of point-to-point links that connect hosts and switches. A network link can deliver 1.28 Gbits/sec full duplex bandwidth. Source routing is used for packets on the Myrinet network. The sender appends a series of routing bytes onto the head of each packet. When a packet arrives at a switch, the leading byte is stripped and used to determine the outgoing port. Myrinet does not impose any restrictions on packet sizes and leaves the choice to the software. Myrinet does not guarantee reliable delivery, however cyclic-redundancy-checking (CRC) hardware is provided in both the network interfaces and switches. This allows for error detection, but reliable delivery is left for higher level software layers to implement. However, the network itself guarantees in-order delivery of messages.

The Myrinet network interface card (which sits on the workstation's I/O bus such as the SBUS on the SPARCstations) consists of a 256KB SRAM and a 37.5 MHz 32-bit custom-built processor called the LANai 4. In addition, there are 3 DMA engines on the card. Two of these engines are responsible for sending(receiving) packets to(from) the external network from(to) SRAM. The third is responsible for moving data between SRAM and host (workstation) memory. All three DMA engines can operate independently. Note that the LANai processor cannot communicate directly with host memory, and therefore must rely on DMA operations for reading and writing host memory. The LANai processor executes a MU-Net Control Program (MCP) that manages and coordinates activities on the interface card and interfaces with programs running on the host CPU. Though it shares the same initials as the Myrinet Control Program supplied by Myricom, it differs significantly in functionality.

3   MU-Net

Our goal is to develop an efficient communication substrate for parallel applications on a Network of Workstations. We have used Myrinet [2] for the network hardware since it has a high raw bandwidth, and puts no restriction on
packet sizes making it convenient to tailor the messaging system to application
characteristics. In developing this substrate, our design draws ideas from the implementation of U-Net [10] on ATM, and Fast Messages [6] on Myrinet. Hence,
the name *MU-Net* standing for Myrinet U-Net. The design goals for MU-net are
summarized below:

- provide a low-latency, high bandwidth user-level messaging layer (to avoid
  costs of crossing protection boundaries),
- support multiple processes running on a workstation to concurrently use
  the network without compromising on protection and without significantly
  degrading communication performance,
- implement optimizations for shorter messages, while lowering the cost of
  packetization/reassembly for larger messages,
- allow alternate send mechanisms that can be used to overlap useful CPU
  computation with communication wherever needed,
- provide in-order delivery with flow control.

The inclusion of these features in the MU-Net design requires detailed development of user level libraries (API), kernel level drivers, and software for
the LANai. We have implemented these components for Solaris 2.5 running on
a range of SPARCstations. The following subsections describe the design and
responsibilities of each of these components.

3.1   User-level Library

As in [10], MU-Net supports the notion of an endpoint that is intended to give
user processes a handle into the network. The endpoint is visible to the user as a
structure which contains state information about pending messages (to be sent
or received) on that endpoint. A user process can only access those endpoints
that it creates. In essence, an endpoint virtualizes the network for each user
process, and uses the traditional virtual memory system to enforce protection
between these processes.

The MU-Net API provides user applications with an interface for creating
an endpoint in the user's address space, destroying an endpoint, sending to and
receiving messages from a destination endpoint. Creation and destruction of
endpoints involve the kernel driver and are expensive. These are done only in
the initialization and termination phases and hence do not impact the latency
of the critical path.

There are two kinds of send operations both of which are nonblocking. The
first is meant for processes which want to minimize latency at the cost of host
CPU cycles. In this kind of send, the host CPU is used to transfer data to the

network interface card instead of the DMA engine, similar to the send mechanism in Fast Messages [6]. However, for long messages, the time spent in the send call (proportional to the size of the message) may become significant especially if the CPU has other work to do. Hence, in our API, we provide a second mechanism called send_DMA(), which uses the DMA for large data transfers to the card. If the length of the data to be transferred is smaller than 128 bytes, send_DMA defaults to the normal send. We expect applications to use this send when they have work that can be overlapped with the operation, and when they can tolerate a slightly higher latency. If the applications cannot proceed with useful computation, and the message to be sent is larger than 128 bytes, then they can use the normal send() mechanism which uses the host CPU to packetize the data and transfer it to the network interface.

There is only one receive call which is used to receive both kinds of messages.

Currently, we are implementing a credit-based flow control strategy for MU-Net similar to Fast Messages [6], that throttles the sender whenever it uses up its credits for a particular receiver. Each endpoint statically partitions its receive buffer area amongst the maximum number of endpoints which could send to it. Flow control is thus implemented fully on the host without taxing the LANai.

3.2 MU-Net Kernel Drivers

MU-Net uses a 2 driver design in the operating system kernel similar to [2]. The MU-Net *myri* driver is used to attach to the Myrinet device, and map the LANai registers and SRAM into kernel memory. The second MU-Net driver, called the *mlanai*, is a *pseudo* driver, and therefore does not actually drive any physical device. Rather, the *mlanai* driver provides ioctls for creating and destroying endpoints. It also maps a communication segment into user space. The details of the communication segment are described later.

3.3 MU-Net MCP

The MU-Net Control Program (MCP) is the program that runs on the LANai processor which is downloaded into the card SRAM by the host during initialization.

The MCP does not directly interact with the host. It detects send requests by polling the SRAM. It multiplexes these send requests and sends them out into the network. Incoming messages are first buffered on the SRAM, demultiplexed and then delivered to the destination endpoint. An examination of an incoming message is required to determine the destination endpoint and a DMA operation is used to perform the delivery.

The maximum number of endpoints supported by the card is statically determined. However, the number of active endpoints is dynamic and communicated to the MCP by the host driver. This ensures that the MCP does not spend time polling for send requests from inactive endpoints.

3.4 Details of MU-Net Operations

The MU-Net operations are described in the same logical order they would most likely occur in a typical user application. The implementation of these operations is also discussed along with other design alternatives.

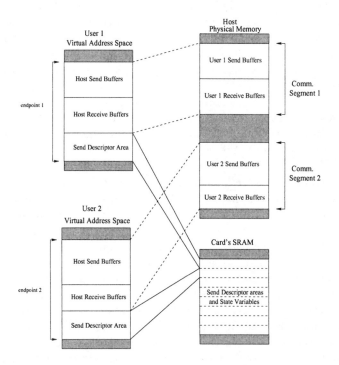

Fig. 1. Mapping of Endpoint into User Address Space

Creating an Endpoint Messages are exchanged between endpoints and not processes. One process could create multiple endpoints though it is not necessary since endpoint communication is connectionless and the same endpoint can be used for sending/receiving from multiple remote nodes. An endpoint consists of three regions, two of which reside on the host memory and the third on the card SRAM. All three areas are mapped into the user processes' address space. The first two regions are the Host Send Buffer and the Host Receive Buffer. The Host Send Buffer is used to store long messages in host memory for a subsequent LANai-initiated DMA to SRAM (send_DMA() operation). The Host Receive Buffer is the target of LANai-initiated DMA's for incoming short and long messages. The third region is the Send Descriptor area located on the SRAM. It is written by the host CPU during a send call. Figure 1 shows two user processes' endpoints and their mappings. The two host buffers together constitute the *communication segment* of the endpoint.

MU-Net allows a user program to dynamically create endpoints. To create an endpoint, the user program calls the user-level MU-Net API and provides the desired sizes of the Host Send Buffer and Host Receive Buffer. The size of the Send Descriptor area cannot be specified by individual user processes. The communication segment needs to be allocated and pinned in physical memory and mapped into the DMA space of the DMA engine located on the card. Since this memory mapping can only be done in kernel mode, the MU-Net API makes an ioctl call to the MU-Net *mlanai* driver to perform these operations.

The communication segment memory is provided by the kernel and is not shared amongst endpoints. The card SRAM, which is a shared resource, is also protected by the selective mapping of only one Send Descriptor area into user space. Moreover, since the MU-Net API library can only use virtual addresses, it can only access those portions of the SRAM mapped in by the driver. Thus, MU-Net uses the operating system's virtual memory system to implement protected user-level communication similar to [10]. The driver, being part of the kernel, is assumed to be secure while the user can potentially use a different library with the same API.

The major design issue relevant to endpoint creation is the partitioning of the communication segment. In MU-Net, the partitioning of the communication segment into Send and Receive areas is done at initialization and cannot be changed in the middle. If the number/size of one type of message (send or receive) is much lesser than the other, the corresponding area is underutilized and may even affect the latency/bandwidth of the other type (when the latter operates at peak buffer capacity). An alternative would be to divide up the entire communication segment into fixed size buffers, which could be dynamically assigned for a send or a receive (by maintaining pointers to these buffers on the host and on the card). This approach, used in [10], has the disadvantage of limiting the size of a single data transfer between the host and the card (in either direction). The fixed size of the buffers would have to be large to avoid multiple data transfers in the average case. However larger sized buffers would also lead to greater internal fragmentation. Hence the rigid partitioning approach was chosen. If the user process has a priori knowledge of traffic patterns, it can choose to have one area larger than the other. With the communication segment being pinned in physical memory, a process needs to exercise restraint in the sizes requested since it can impact overall host memory performance. This restraint can also be enforced by the driver on creation of an endpoint.

Sending a Message From the user's viewpoint, once an endpoint has been created, the process of sending a message is straightforward. The user calls the MU-Net API with a pointer to message data, length of message and destination endpoint.

For a message longer than 128 bytes (henceforth called a long message), the API copies the message data into the Host Send Buffer, creates a Send Descriptor and appends it to the Send Descriptor queue of the endpoint in the SRAM. Within the Descriptor is a pointer to the data in the Host Send Buffer (which is

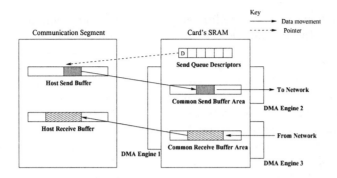

Fig. 2. Anatomy of a MU-Net Operation

part of the DMA space of the card). The MCP polls the Send Descriptor queue to detect messages to be sent. Upon detection of the newly added descriptor, it uses the pointer within it to initiate a DMA of the message data into a Common Send Buffer area in SRAM (Figure 2). The MCP also creates a message header that includes routing information and a 2-byte tag (1 byte for the message type and the other for the destination endpoint number). After the DMA from host completes, the packet (header + data) is DMA'ed from the SRAM onto the network. Figure 3 shows the layout of a MU-Net packet.

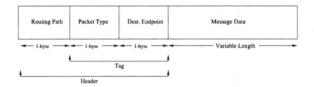

Fig. 3. Structure of a MU-Net Packet

The above send_DMA mechanism works well for situations where the application can tolerate slightly higher latencies because it has other work to do. As observed in [6], it is more expensive to transfer data into the SRAM using DMA than having the host CPU directly write it. So for the normal send mechanism, we have an optimization wherein the descriptor entry itself contains the data (and not a pointer to it). A 128 byte size buffer is part of the Send Descriptor. For messages up to 128 bytes, the API copies the data into the Send Descriptor created. The Host Send Buffer is not accessed. More importantly, the MCP does not have to perform a DMA to get the data from the host and can proceed with the other steps of a message send directly. When the application wants to send messages longer than 128 bytes, the API packetizes the message and places them as separate entries in the descriptor queue. This packetization is transparent to the MCP.

We have found that the performance of the send operation depends heavily on the implementation details. The following are some key issues :

- **Descriptor detection**: Instead of polling head and tail pointers to the descriptor queue (which we have found to be highly inefficient), the MCP can poll a designated location within the next expected descriptor entry to find out if data is ready to be sent. This entry needs to be the last field in the descriptor filled by the host to avoid a race condition.

- **Queue management**: Any queue that is accessed by both the host CPU and the MCP needs to be managed carefully for correctness and efficiency. In MU-Net , there is one producer and one consumer for items in a queue and these are on different sides of the I/O bus. For the Send Descriptor queue, the host CPU is the producer and the MCP the consumer. On the receive side, the situation is reversed (as we shall see later). The host CPU can access the SRAM directly (through memory mapped I/O) but the MCP can only access host memory through DMA operations. DMA is not suitable for frequent accesses to individual variables. So all queue maintenance information is kept on the SRAM in the Send Descriptor Area.

  All queues are circular and both producer and consumer have to wrap around when they reach the end of a queue. Since wrap around occurs relatively infrequently, the cost for checking it need not be incurred on each queue access. Another cost saving measure is to reduce the number of updates required to queue variables by the producer and consumer. Typically the producer increments the tail after putting an item on the queue and the consumer increments the head after consuming an item. Queue full and empty checks require both variables to be read by the producer and consumer respectively. In MU-Net, the user process and the MCP are decoupled as far as possible for purposes of queue maintenance. The user process keeps a local copy of the Send Descriptor head and tail. The portion between the head and tail represent messages queued on the SRAM but not yet sent on the network. Additions to the queue (after a send), result in an update of the local tail alone. Updating the head kept on the SRAM is done by the MCP after it consumes a new message in the queue. The local head is important only when the local tail becomes equal to it (signifying a queue full condition). It is only at that point that the user needs to find out the real value of head (kept on SRAM). As long as both MCP and user maintain FIFO order of the queue, this decoupling improves performance without compromising correctness.

- **Overlap of steps**: The MCP tasks for a send operation need to be carefully examined to maximize overlap of operations without affecting correctness. After initiating a DMA from the host for long messages, the MCP has to wait for it to complete before going on with the next step of the send operation. There is potential for doing useful work here (unrelated to the send) instead of busy waiting which is possible because of the separation of all three DMA engine operations. Trapeze [12] exploits the decoupling of these DMA operations through a mechanism called cut-through delivery.

– **Flow control** : Before starting to compose a message, the API checks to see if the sending endpoint has enough credits for the receiving endpoint. This translates to a guarantee that the receiver has enough buffer space to accommodate the message about to be sent. If the credits are insufficient, the sender checks the received message queue for any credits that might have come in since the last receive was performed. If processing of the piggybacked credit information on newly arrived messages is not enough, the sender busy waits for incoming messages. Running out of credits for sending is not the common case so the impact of the flow control code on minimum latency is limited to the cost of checking for credits before sending. Updating the credit information after a send is not in the critical path and does not impact the latency.

Receiving a Message The MCP detects incoming packets from the network by checking flag bits in a LANai Interrupt Status Register (ISR). The MCP then initiates a DMA from the network into a Common Receive Buffer Area on the SRAM. After this DMA completes, the length of the message and the destination endpoint are read off the message header. A DMA to that endpoint's Host Receive Buffer is initiated. Upon completion of the DMA, the appropriate queue variables are updated for that endpoint. We would like to point out that there is an optimization possible here which we are currently investigating. Instead of DMAing off the net and then examining the header for the length and the endpoint, there is a way to examine just the first bytes of a message and program the host DMA with these parameters in parallel with the DMA of the packet onto the SRAM. Note that the host DMA cannot actually begin before the entire packet is in the SRAM.

The user process calls the MU-Net API to receive a message. The API checks for a pending message by polling the queue state variables. It then copies the message data to the location provided by the the user process and updates the queue state variables to reflect consumption of the message. Some details for the receive operation are discussed below:

– **Short message optimization**: Unlike the send operation, no distinction is made between long and short messages and consequently no optimization is possible for short messages.

In [10], the receive operation is done differently for long and short messages. For long messages, the message data is first DMA'ed to the host. This could require multiple DMA's to be initiated since the host buffer sizes are fixed. After it completes, a *receive descriptor* is DMA'ed to a queue residing in host memory. Besides message length, the receive descriptor contains pointers to the host buffers used as destination for the first DMA. The user detects a message by polling on the receive descriptor. For shorter messages, the data is copied to the receive descriptor buffer and only one DMA is done.

We are not using this strategy because we feel that the LANai processor, which is already quite slow [6], would be taxed more than needed. Also, we are not using the pool of fixed buffers strategy. Instead, we allow the

Host Receive Buffer to accommodate variable sized messages that are placed adjacent to each other in the order received. Hence all messages, short and long, need only one DMA to the host.

- **Message detection**: The only way the MCP can communicate with the host is via the DMA. But, we would like to limit the number of DMA operations to one (for transferring the data to the host memory and to inform the host of the arrival of the message). To ensure correctness, notification should occur only after the whole message data is in host memory. The MCP can determine that this has occurred by checking for completion of the DMA it initiates. The user can determine it by polling for the arrival of the last byte or word of an expected message. Notification is automatic on completion of DMA of the data. The MCP does not need to wait for completion of the DMA it initiates. However, polling for the last word of an expected message has its own difficulties. Instead we use an intelligent probe of the state variables on the SRAM by the host to solve these problems (the details of which are not discussed here due to space limitations).

- **Flow control** : After the received message contents are copied to the application buffer, a part of the Host Receive Buffer is free to receive more messages. This free buffer space is credited to the sender of the message just consumed. The API checks to see if the credits accumulated by the sender has crossed a high water mark. If so, it sends a zero length control message back to the sender containing only the credit information (piggybacked in the usual way). These control message exchanges for flow control are not the common case and have a minimal impact on latency. However the check for accumulated credits and updating the credit information is in the critical path of a message.

Destroying an Endpoint Once a user application no longer needs to access the network, a call to the MU-Net API can be made to *teardown* an endpoint. Destroying an endpoint involves deallocating the associated host memory. We also need to inform the MCP that it need not spend time polling for messages sent using this endpoint. The MU-Net *mlanai* driver must be called to complete this process since these tasks cannot be done at the user level.

4 Performance Results

To evaluate the performance of our MU-Net implementation, we have exercised this software over a couple of SUN Ultra 1 Enterprise servers connected by Myrinet (through an 8-port switch) and present preliminary performance results here. We have used a simple microbenchmark that ping-pongs packets between two SUN Ultra Enterprise 1 Model 170 workstations.

Table 1 shows the roundtrip latencies for messages using this microbenchmark as a function of the message size for MU-Net, Fast Messages (FM 2.0) and Myricom's API for the same hardware platform. The reader should note that

	Message Size (in bytes)							
	8	64	128	256	512	1024	2048	4096
MU-Net	40	50	57	71	104	162	272	495
Fast Messages	47	53	60	80	118	196	334	598
Myricom	211	216	227	243	271	329	447	681

Table 1. Comparison of Roundtrip Latencies (in μs)

the public distribution of FM 2.0 and the Myricom API were actually run on the Ultra Enterprise machines in our laboratory to obtain these results.

For a fair comparison, we run MU-Net using only 1 endpoint though the code for multiple endpoints is in place. The Send_DMA() call is used on the send side which as we mentioned defaults to the normal send (the CPU explicitly copies the entire message to the descriptor on the interface card) when the message size is less than or equal to 128 bytes, and uses the DMA for data transfer to the card (the CPU is free to do useful work) when the message size is larger than 128 bytes.

The results indicate that MU-Net compares favorably with Fast Messages 2.0 for both short and long messages. The Myricom API latencies are considerably higher primarily because the API is a general purpose messaging layer supporting TCP/IP and automatic network remapping. The cost of the additional code is especially noticeable for small messages. For larger messages, the differences between the three layers diminish as data transfer dominates the critical path.

	8 bytes				1024 bytes	4096 bytes
	1 endpt	2 endpts	4 endpts	8 endpts	1 endpt	1 endpt
Detected in send queue	6.5	7.0	7.5	9.0	6.5	13.0
Header sent on network	7.0	7.5	8.0	9.5	12.5	45.0
Data sent on network	8.0	8.0	9.0	10.0	23.5	73.0
Data in SRAM	9.5	10.0	11.5	14.0	47.0	152.0
DMA to host	18.0	18.5	19.0	23.5	70.5	219.5
Message received by host	19.5	20.5	22.5	23.5	81.0	247.0

Table 2. Anatomy of a Message in μs (Effect of message size and multiple endpoints)

Table 2 shows the anatomy of the different operations performed for short and long messages in MU-Net with different number of endpoints (though the remaining endpoints are not exercised, the LANai still has to multiplex/demultiplex messages between these endpoints). The times given in each row are cumulative for the operations that occur from the time the user makes an API send call. The first row gives the time taken by the MCP to detect a message. As expected, this time grows with the number of endpoints being polled by the MCP (even though only one of them is exercised). For messages longer than 128 bytes, there is an additional memory copy within the send call. The cost of this copy, however, shows up only beyond 1K bytes.

The second row gives the time for the MCP to send the header out over the network. The difference with the previous row is insignificant for the small message since it is already on the card SRAM. For the longer messages, the difference is a measure of the cost of a DMA to get the data from host memory.

The third row marks the time for the message to be completely sent out over the network. The difference with the previous row accounts for the cost of network DMA setup and transfer. Again, this is significant only for long messages.

The remaining rows denote operations at the receive end. The fourth row is cumulative until the time the receiver detects the incoming message and DMAs it into the SRAM completely. The reader should note that the receiver LANai is not just waiting for an incoming message, but is also polling its own endpoints for outgoing messages. As a result, an increase in the number of endpoints affects the performance of this operation slightly.

The fifth row shows the time taken for completion of DMA of message data to host memory. Since both short and long messages require a DMA at this step, both show a significant increase from the previous row.

The final row indicates the time when the host has completely received the message in the application. This includes the time to detect the message, copy it to the program specified buffer and update the state variables. The differences with the previous row are almost the same for multiple endpoints since this part of the receive operation is unaffected by the number of active endpoints. For larger messages, the difference with the previous row grows with message size due to the cost of the memory copy within the receive call.

We are currently in the process of evaluating MU-Net with benchmarks to quantify the effect of multiple active endpoints.

5 Related Work

Besides U-Net [10] and FM [6], there are other high-performance messaging layers using Myrinet. Since they run on a variety of workstation platforms and have different objectives, it is difficult to use their performance numbers alone as a means of evaluating their design choices. However, it is instructive to examine their implementation experiences to understand the tradeoffs in design alternatives.

The PM messaging library [8] aims at providing multiple users direct access to the network interface hardware. However, the library is used along with a daemon doing gang scheduling of the user processes. As a result, the network interface is used by only two processes at any time, namely the the daemon process and the user process scheduled by it. Though, they have to deal with the issues of these two processes sharing the Myrinet card, protection is not a serious concern since the daemon process is assumed to be a trusted agent. An interesting idea, called Immediate Sending, to overlap network and host side DMA operations is used by PM to enhance performance. Overlapping (pipelining) DMA operations is also used in Trapeze [12] at both the sender and receiver and is referred to as cut-through delivery.

Hamlyn's [3] design objective is to provide varying levels of protection between user processes. Protection is done more rigorously by comparing keys on each message. As in MU-Net, Hamlyn has two versions of send, one using DMA and the other using a memory copy done by the host. Other notable features of the messaging layer are buffer management by the sender, use of zero copy protocols and provision for out of order delivery.

Myricom also provides a low latency, high bandwidth messaging layer called GM [5] in addition to the API discussed in the preceding sections. GM provides multiple user-level accesses to the network interface simultaneously. It also provides automatic mapping of the Myrinet network and provision for two levels of packet priority. Flow control is an important issue and is made visible to the GM API.

6   Concluding Remarks and Future Work

This paper has summarized our experiences in implementing MU-Net, a user-level messaging platform for Myrinet that allows protected multi-user access to the network. Our design of MU-Net has drawn from ideas of other user-level platforms [10, 6]. It uses the idea of virtualizing the network from U-Net [10] to provide protected multi-user access. However, unlike U-Net, it does not fragment the communication segment into fixed-size buffers, thus being able to avoid multiple DMA transfers for longer messages. The implementation of MU-Net has also benefited from the experiences of [6] in working with the Myrinet hardware. In addition to efficient transfers for short messages as in [6], MU-Net provides a mechanism for transferring longer messages in cases where the host CPU has other work to do.

MU-Net has been implemented on the SUN Solaris 2.5 operating system, and performance results on a Ultra Enterprise 1 platform show that despite being able to support multiple application processes, MU-Net's performance is comparable to other messaging substrates which do not allow protected multi-user access.

References

1. T. Anderson et al. A case for networks of workstations. *IEEE Micro*, pages 54–64, February 1995.
2. N. J. Boden et al. Myrinet: A Gigabit-per-second Local Area Network. *IEEE Micro*, 15(1):29–36, February 1995.
3. G. D. Buzzard, D. Jacobson, M. Mackey, S. Marovich, and J. Wilkes. An Implementation of the Hamlyn Sender-Managed Interface Architecture. In *Proceedings*

of the Second USENIX Symposium on Operating Systems Design and Implementation (OSDI), pages 245–259, October 1996.

4. Martin de Prycker. *Asynchronous Transfer Mode: solution for broadband ISDN*. Ellis Horwood, West Sussex, England, 1992.

5. Myricom Inc. GM Documentation and Software, 1997. http://www.myri.com/GM/index.html.

6. S. Pakin, M. Lauria, and A. Chien. High Performance Messaging on Workstations: Illinois Fast Messages (FM) for Myrinet. In *Proceedings of Supercomputing '95*, December 1995.

7. Kendall Square Research. Technical summary, 1992.

8. H. Tezuka, A. Hori, Y. Ishikawa, and M. Sato. PM: An Operating System Coordinated High Performance Communication Library. In *Lecture Notes in Computer Science*, volume 1225, pages 708–717. Springer-Verlag, April 1997. From Proceedings of High-Performance Computing and Networking '97.

9. Thinking Machines Corporation, Cambridge, Massachusetts. *The Connection Machine CM-5 Technical Summary*, October 1991.

10. T. von Eicken, A. Basu, V. Buch, and W. Vogels. U-Net: A User-Level Network Interface for Parallel and Distributed Computing. In *Proceedings of the 15th ACM Symposium on Operating System Principles*, December 1995.

11. T. von Eicken, D. E. Culler, S. C. Goldstein, and K. E. Schauser. Active Messages: A Mechanism for Integrated Communication and Computation. In *Proceedings of the 19th Annual International Symposium on Computer Architecture*, pages 256–266, May 1992.

12. K. Yocum, J. Chase, A. Gallain, and A. R. Lebeck. Cut-Through Delivery in Trapeze: An Exercise in Low-Latency Messaging. In *Proceedings of IEEE International Symposium on High Performance Distributed Computing*, August 1997.

ECOLE: A Configurable Environment for a Local Optical Network of Workstations

Gordon Brebner and Rob Pooley

Department of Computer Science
University of Edinburgh
James Clerk Maxwell Building
Mayfield Road
Edinburgh EH9 3JZ
Scotland
E-mail: {gordon,rjp}@dcs.ed.ac.uk

Abstract. ECOLE is a project concerned with the implementation of highly efficient parallel computation on a network of generic workstations connected by a very high speed optical LAN. It is founded on research conducted at BT Laboratories, which has resulted in SynchroLan — a multi-gigabit LAN billed as the fastest LAN in the world. A holistic approach to system design is taken, to identify all possible hardware and software improvements that might allow a workstation to harness fully the raw capacity of a multi-gigabit network. Two important features of the work are the inclusion of configurable hardware and the use of active protocols — both of these are to introduce overall flexibility, without compromising efficiency by more than a small amount. The work benefits from the use of advanced techniques for modelling and simulation of experimental architectures. This paper explains how the ECOLE project acts as a very practical focus for several existing lines of advanced systems research being undertaken at the University of Edinburgh.

1 Introduction

The emergence of low cost and high performance workstations and interconnection networks points to the use of network of workstation (NOW) architectures as a compelling alternative to expensive parallel supercomputers. Ideally, NOW architectures would employ totally off-the-shelf workstations and networking. However, the deliberate generality built into these components leads to greatly reduced performance when attempting to compete with supercomputer speeds. To improve the situation, a holistic approach to systems is desirable, reviewing the efficiency of all system components: workstation and networking hardware and software, and also interaction using communication protocols. It is desirable that the resulting systems do not completely sacrifice generality for efficiency, to allow support for a variety of applications with different needs.

The ECOLE (Edinburgh Configurable Optical LAN Environment) project seeks to apply in tandem several currently active areas of advanced systems research at the University of Edinburgh and BT, to provide novel solutions to the problem of implementing efficient, but programmable, NOW architectures based on off-the-shelf workstations interconnected by a very high speed optical local area network. This paper introduces the different research areas, and indicates how their results contribute to the overall aim; future papers will report on system construction and experimentation. The three most central research threads are:

- SynchroLan: an optical LAN demonstrated by BT Laboratories in 1996/97, and rated as the world's fastest;
- Configware: novel solutions to the problem of integrating soft circuitry based on Field-Programmable Gate Arrays (FPGAs) into total systems, particularly with System Level Integration (SLI), also being investigated at Edinburgh University; and
- Active protocols: a flexible and verifiable approach to protocol construction and use, being developed at the Edinburgh University.

and the experimental application of these is much enhanced by research into:

- system modelling using Stochastic Process Algebras; and
- system simulation of high-bandwidth networks and hierarchical architectures.

To complete the picture, the combined research can draw upon the skills of researchers involved in past development of pioneering and parsimonious operating systems for both mainframe computers and workstation computers. There is also ready access to the state-of-the-art supercomputers (e.g., a Cray T3D) of the Edinburgh Parallel Computing Centre (EPCC), allowing comparative benchmarking, as well as providing conventional brute-force computational power for simulation studies.

A technical impetus for the ECOLE project comes just from the raw communications technology. SynchroLan is already able to deliver data rates of 2.5 Gbit/second to workstations, and the technology allows upgrading to at least 40 Gbit/second transfer rates. The problem is that nothing like such rates can currently be delivered to the applications running on workstations. As many other researchers in this area have noted, a main bottleneck lies in the network interface, since current interfaces are not specifically designed for frequent, high bandwidth communication. Apart from this bottleneck, the communications protocols used over the network are another main source of inefficiency. Given good solutions to these two main problems, further gains can be had from holistic improvement of system architectures.

The remainder of the paper is arranged as follows. Section 2 focuses on the network interface, specifically on how the configware research can bring novel benefits. Section 3 focuses on the communication protocols, specifically on how the active protocols research can bring novel benefits. This paper does not include a more detailed description of SynchroLAN, since its operation is not central here; more information can be found in [8, 12, 16, 17]. Section 4 reviews the modelling and simulation technology which will be brought to bear on the problem of designing and experimenting with new system architectures. Finally, there is a brief review of related work, and an outline of the future work programme of the ECOLE project.

2 Configware and the network interface

The overall organisation of the experimental SynchroLAN testbed that will be used for the ECOLE project is shown in Figure 1. Although the testbed in housed

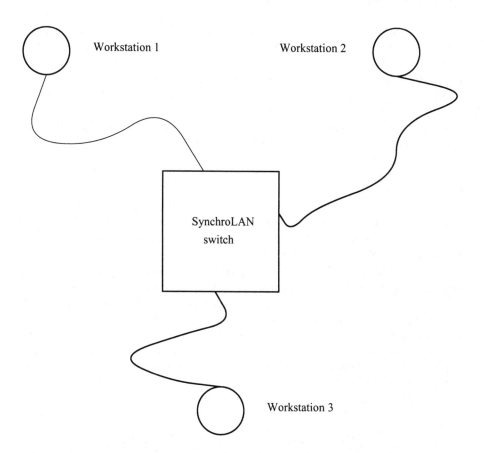

Fig. 1. Experimental testbed with SynchroLAN

in one laboratory, the fibre optic cabling is routed round the entire building, in order to emulate correctly what would happen in a real local area network.

Research at BT Laboratories is currently targeted at designing a single card that contains all of the components needed for the physical optoelectronic interface. The aim of the ECOLE project is to ensure that any extra hardware components needed to support an efficient, but flexible, NOW architecture can also be fitted on this single card, to be consistent with providing a low-cost solution. The card must interface to the system memory bus of the workstation, to provide the fast interaction with the main processor and the main memory that is needed to support application programs. The overall architecture is illustrated in Figure 2.

For ECOLE, low-cost workstations built from PC components will be used, with direct access to the system memory bus being made possible via the Accelerated Graphics Port (AGP) available with the latest Intel 440LX chipset for Pentium II PCs. This allows a point-to-point channel between a graphics controller and the system RAM, which can be exploited by a communications controller in ECOLE. The current generation of AGP interface (AGP 2X) offers a data rate of 533 MB/second, with a rate in excess of 1 GB/second expected in the future from the APG 4X. These rates are acceptable for the ECOLE prototyping work, the project being deemed a success if they can be fully harnessed.

In the short term, there are two approaches to ensuring that the extra hardware can be accommodated on the same card as the optoelectronic interface. The first is to design a custom ASIC once a solution has been selected from the possible design space; for example, this is the line pursued by the Utah Avalanche project [9]. The second is to include one or more Field Programmable Gate Array (FPGA) chips that can be configured with required circuitry. While the second option is more flexible, and allows prototyping, the performance is likely to be slower and the available number of gates will be rather smaller. For ECOLE, a longer-term perspective is being taken, strongly influenced by very active work on System Level Integration (SLI) at Edinburgh University.

With SLI (alternatively known as 'System On Silicon'), a number of major system components are located on a single chip. This is made possible by recent advances in deep submicron fabrication technologies. The complexity of SLI circuitry poses many challenges for the designer, and therefore much research is being carried out into new design methodologies and tools. One initiative is the Virtual Socket Interface (VSI) [24], being developed within a consortium called the VSI Alliance; this is concerned with providing a standard way to integrate 'virtual components' from different sources, on a single chip. There are three major types of virtual component:

- processor cores (microprocessors, DSPs);
- memory devices; and
- configurable logic arrays.

and these can be integrated with more specialised types of component, such as analogue-digital convertors.

Apart from the obvious generic speed benefits of having processors, memories, etc., interfaced at chip level, the advent of SLI is particularly promising for the use of configware — configurable hardware — in this project. At present, configware is severely constrained by the pin interfaces to FPGA chips, or by the bus interfaces to boards containing FPGA chips. This penalises not only the

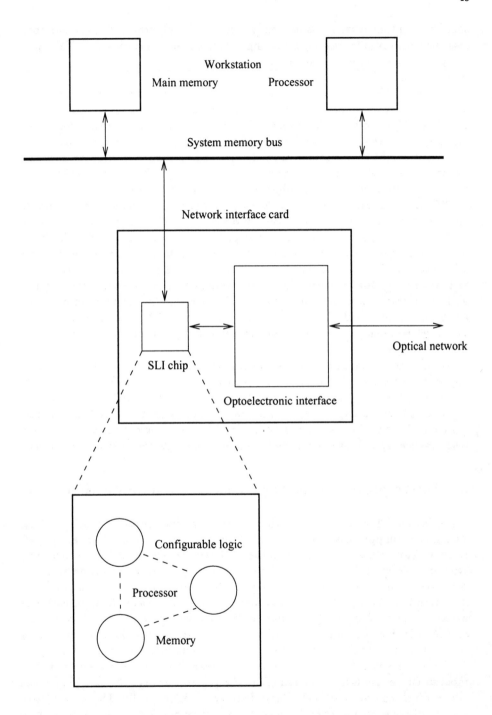

Fig. 2. Overall network interface architecture

speed-ups obtained when using configware as a configurable co-processor but also the time taken to reconfigure configware to change its co-processor function. SLI gives scope for rather more intimate, and fast, configware-processor-memory interactions.

For the ECOLE project, the presence of configware in the network interface is a central feature, in order to add flexible hardware support for communication protocols. This can be useful both for different network environments, for example, different latencies or reliabilities, or for different application requirements. The latter might be variations in model, for example, shared memory, message passing or bit pipe, or in quality requirements. In Section 3, the use of configware for protocol implementation is illustrated by an extended example.

Previous configware research at Edinburgh has focused on how a configurable logic array can best be managed by a processor, resulting in general notions of 'virtual circuitry' — the configware analogue of virtual memory [3, 4]. The fruits of this work gain particularly from SLI, given an integrated processor running a lightweight virtual circuitry operating system. One particular application of virtual circuitry that is currently being investigated results from a convergence with the research described in Section 3. This is where the circuitry implements accelerator components for communication protocols [10]. The general technology developed can be directly applied to particular protocols devised within the ECOLE project.

In summary, configware is not just included as a useful means of prototyping or implementing glue logic — the typical current uses of FPGA technology — although both of these are certainly of use here. It is included to provide support at hardware speeds for dynamically tailoring protocols to their operating environment. The use of SLI in the longer term should deliver satisfactory performance, as well as the means for enabling a single-card network interface.

3 Active protocols and the network communication

There is general agreement that the use of a standard protocol stack, such as TCP/IP, is inappropriate for a NOW architecture because of its relative inefficiency. This is hardly suprising, since TCP/IP was designed for use over any type of networking, of any quality. Just as general-purpose workstation architectures hinder the quest for speed, so do general-purpose communication protocols. As a result, a number of special-purpose protocols have been devised, each one usually associated with a particular NOW architecture. The problem with this approach is that it results in an inflexible environment that does not allow protocol adaptation to deal with different requirements between applications.

To obtain more flexibility of protocols, research on 'active protocols' at Edinburgh University is a key ingredient of the ECOLE project. An active protocol is one which can be constructed and distributed dynamically. The idea is associated with the active network concept [23], which is currently attracting much attention in the networking world. In an active network, packets can contain executable code as well as just processable data, and this code can be executed by intermediate nodes within the network. Active protocols are defined in terms of a few primitive and orthogonal protocol elements, based on the communication principles described in [3]. They can be distributed in an active network using messages that contain executable forms of the protocol description, that is, appropriate packet-handling instructions. As well as practical benefits, the nature of active protocols makes them amenable to rigorous demonstrations that protocols and protocol stacks have the properties required by their users. This is very important in situations where protocols are being devised rapidly, and are not subject to many years scrutiny by standardisation committees.

The use of protocol elements within an active protocol is best illustrated by an example. Consider end-to-end flow control between two communicating parties. This is a feature of many different protocols, with a few standard mechanisms appearing in various different disguises, and often in combination with other protocol features, for example, error correction. The active protocol framework treats flow control as an individual abstract function, and provides mechanisms whereby this function can be combined in a practical implementation with other functions for efficiency reasons. In this example, an abstract solution based on sliding windows will be considered.

The basic idea is that, when information is transmitted, there is an associated sequence number that indicates the place of the information within some (possibly pseudo-infinite) information stream. The receiver controls the flow by informing the transmitter of its current position within the information stream; in general, this is behind the current position of the transmitter. The transmitter is obliged to ensure that the receiver does not fall too far behind. Two possible ways of running the scheme are:

1. the receiver periodically automatically sends back sequence numbers indicating its current position (common in many protocols);
2. the transmitter periodically asks the receiver to send back a sequence number indicating its current position (used in some protocols, for example, the ATM Service Specific Connection Oriented Protocol (SSCOP)).

In both cases, the protocol element at the transmitter sends sequence numbers corresponding to information transmitted. In the first case, the protocol element at the receiver periodically sends back sequence numbers as information is consumed. In the second case, the protocol element at the transmitter periodically sends 'marked' sequence numbers corresponding to information transmitted, and the protocol element at the receiver responds by sending back a sequence number corresponding to information received and consumed. Note how this abstracts away unnecessary detail to give the fundamental protocol operation. It can then be used as a building block for more complex protocols, with the abstract form being useful for verifying that the construction achieves the desired effect. The implementation of this example will be considered further, after the next paragraph.

The active protocol work is being linked with the configware work through the notion of 'circlets' (small circuits, roughly the hardware equivalent of software applets). The virtual circuitry research provides an operating system mechanism for the management and use of a collection of circlets; one application of this is to the case where active protocols are represented by circlet descriptions carried in packets. While the mobility of active protocol circlets is not likely to be useful in a NOW architecture (since it appears more efficient to have a small collection of defined protocols, pre-distributed statically), the capability for defining protocols and then deriving executable circlets is exactly what is required to harness the configware described in Section 2.

Now, continuing the sliding window flow control example, it is possible to sketch an implementation based on circlets. A first point to make is that circlets can be parameterised, to create families of circuits. Here, a natural parameterisation is on the number of bits used for sequence numbers, so a family of circuits reflects a family of protocol elements. The basic circlet layout is shown in Figure 3. It has one register (to the right) used for storing a received sequence

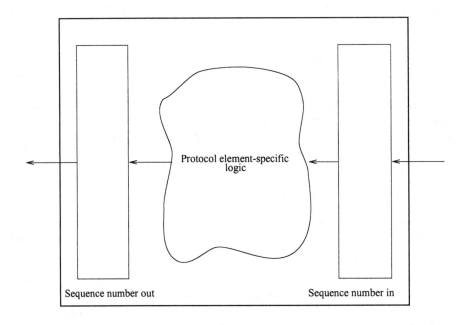

Protocol element-specific logic

Sequence number out

Sequence number in

Fig. 3. Basic circlet layout

number, and another register (to the left) used for storing a transmittable or transmitted sequence number. The height of these registers (and hence of the circlet) is the parameterised feature. The central logic is specialised to give the correct effect, depending on protocol and depending on whether the circlet is being run at the information transmitter or the receiver. The circlet then fits within a surrounding system to implement the context of the protocol element, and this may either involve other circuitry supplying the inputs and using the outputs or some program that delivers the inputs and collects the outputs.

For the transmitter protocol element, the circlet input corresponds to a sequence number sent back by the receiver and the circlet output corresponds to a sequence number sent to the receiver. For the receiver protocol element, the circlet input corresponds to a sequence number sent by the transmitter and the circlet output corresponds to a sequence number sent back to the transmitter. In all cases, the key operation of the central logic is to determine when, and with what value, the output register is updated.

At the transmitter, the essential decision required is that there is information to transmit, and that the values contained in the two registers are not further apart than the current sliding window size.

In the case where the receiver automatically sends back sequence numbers, the central logic at the receiver must update the output register when information has been consumed, possibly tempered by the two registers being further apart by more than some threshold and/or that some time period has elapsed since the consumed information was received. In the case where the transmitter solicits a response, the central logic at the receiver is simplified so that the output register is updated precisely when a marked sequence number arrives. The central logic at the transmitter is more complex, however, since it must decide when to send a marked sequence number, on the basis if the two registers being further apart than some threshold and/or that some time period has elapsed since information was transmitted.

A significant point to note from the above is that only a few different operations occur in the different variants of the central logic:

- sensing new information to send at the transmitter
- sensing new information consumed at the receiver
- comparing the difference of the two register values against a threshold
- running a watchdog timer.

This simplifies the creation of a range of circlets, and fits with the general philosophy of simplicity and flexibility of circuitry. This example has shown how the decomposition of protocols into simple protocol elements facilitates implementation using circlets with desirable properties.

Of course, an important concern is to ensure that introducing the generality of active protocols does not inflict new speed penalties that cancel out the benefits gained from some specialisation of the system architecture and the protocol sets. This should not be the case, since the use of circlets is targeted at various high speed networking operations, fast packet switching for example, that demand very efficient performance.

In summary, active protocols are involved both to provide a convenient framework for design and testing of novel protocols and to provide an implementation route that allows a collection of protocols to be dynamically instantiated on configware.

4 Modelling and simulation of novel architectures

Even with the flexibility in prototyping provided by the configware approach, developing and proving designs by physical prototypes is time consuming and may not deliver sufficient detailed information about bottlenecks, performance and other characteristics of an architecture. It is particularly important to identify serious flaws early in the design process and then to concentrate on only those designs worthy of detailed study.

Edinburgh has considerable expertise in two, complementary, methods for such studies, *stochastic process algebra* and *hierarchical discrete event simulation*. Recent developments in both techniques and tools have greatly increased the power of these techniques, particularly when used in combination, to address this type of design problem [22, 15].

It is a well known property of architectures that many decisions can be made at a high level of abstraction, independently of the detailed working of components. It is, unfortunately, also well known that the detailed working of components may introduce further, equally significant, problems and that these may only become apparent when the full, detailed design is tested. In system testing these are addressed by high level, unit and integration testing respectively. In using performance modelling, a similar strategy is needed. It can be achieved by modelling in a component based manner, using process algebras to provide a hierarchical framework for integration which is fully understood.

4.1 High level modelling

Early modelling of outline designs is greatly facilitated by the use of suitable tools. Edinburgh has considerable experience in developing and using such tools for architectural simulation. By developing models in terms of components, where descriptions can be refined as more details become available, a consistent approach is guaranteed.

Along with the development of outline simulation models, a more formal modelling approach is possible, based on process algebras [20, 21]. This allows equivalent behavioural models, capable of revealing deadlocks and other logical flaws, to be generated from the schematic version of an architecture. This also allows further consistency checking as the design is refined. By enhancing these models with performance information, numerical solutions can also be obtained [11].

4.2 Unit modelling of components

Pre-solution of component models can be used to avoid the complexity of solving a detailed design model. This may then allow these results to be reused within a simpler overall model. The use of such techniques depends on a mixture of understanding of stochastic modelling and behavioural equivalence. Again, work at Edinburgh has shown how such aggregated models can be safely derived, using stochastic process algebra as a framework.

At the level of component modelling, conventional discrete event simulation techniques are generally adequate. It is important, however, to take advantage of well defined experimental techniques, where multiple runs can be used in parallel to explore a design space [14]. The notion of experimental support in a distributed computing environment is a key to effective use of simulation in design.

4.3 Integration modelling of system level designs

Use of a well-understood basis for structuring and unit solving of designs makes the testing of complete systems feasible. Since aspects of component behaviour which are not capable of exerting a global influence on the design will have already been isolated, they can be safely ignored in the complete model. This, combined with the same experimental methodology used in component level simulation, allows a thorough exploration of a complete design, and a good understanding of the results.

Since the ECOLE project is able to exploit state of the art high performance computing, such as the Cray T3D, in the more demanding stages of the work, it will be possible to have considerable confidence in any candidate designs before moving to physical prototyping and testing.

5 Related work, and the future ECOLE work programme

The ECOLE project is one of many that are looking the problem of achieving fast parallel computation using a network of workstations. The adoption of a holistic approach is a central feature, something that is relatively uncommon in other research, one notable exception being the Utah Avalanche project [9]. A major physical difference from Avalanche and other work is that a next-generation general purpose LAN forms the interconnection mechanism, rather than an interconnect such as Myrinet [2]. This is to ensure that workstations can still be used in their more conventional independent manner, as well as just in a NOW architecture.

Another physical aspect of ECOLE is that normal workstations are used, in contrast to more specialised architectures of other work, such as the MIT Alewife [1] or the Stanford FLASH [13] architectures. Indeed, the choice of a PC-based architecture is targeted at the most commonly available workstation — and one that can deliver much-improved performance these days, rather than the HP multiprocessor workstations or Sun SPARCstations used in other work, for example Avalanche, HP Lab's Hamlyn [7] or Illinois Fast Messages [19]. The aim is to add just one extra card, responsible both for physical network interfacing and for tailored hardware/software functions inside the network interface.

A final innovative physical aspect is the inclusion of configurable logic as an integral part of the network interface design, to provide scope for dynamic configurability of hardware. This has not been a feature of other NOW research, due to the relative inflexibility of much current FPGA hardware and to the speed penalties compared with custom ASICs. ECOLE seeks to benefit from emergent improvement in configurable logic technologies that will greatly reduce current performance penalties.

Reduced-weight communication protocols are also important to the holistic approach of the ECOLE project. These have also featured in other NOW research, for example, the DD protocol of the Avalanche project [9] or the PRP protocol of the PARMA project [18]. Gains over more conventional protcols, such as TCP/IP, come from introducing application specificity and from simplied physical channel assumptions, such as error freedom or perfect sequencing. For ECOLE, the framework of active protocols offers a way of experimenting with new stripped-down protocols to find those that fit the application/physical environment efficiently. Moreover, the configurable interface gives a means to avoid the need of selecting a single protocol for all uses.

The work plan of the ECOLE project involves extensive use of modelling and simulation of design alternatives, before any prototyping using PC-based workstations and the SynchoLan optical LAN. The first stage of the holistic approach involves an examination of high-level architectural design alternatives, together with alternative communication protocols. The second stage involves examining major system components. Two particular aspects of this are an investigation of the uses of reconfigurable logic as part of an overall architecture, and an investigation of improved software architectures to support applications. The third stage involves prototyping of chosen designs, by which time it is intended that SLI chip facilities will be available to allow a complete system implementation.

Acknowledgement

The authors thank BT Laboratories, particularly David Cotter, for inspiring this work, and for promising access to experimental optical network prototypes.

References

1. Agarwal A., R. Bianchini, D. Chaiken and K. Johnson, "The MIT Alewife Machine: Architecture and Performance", Proc. 22nd Annual International Symposium on Computer Architecture, June 1995, pp.2–13.
2. Boden N. et al, "Myrinet — A Gigabit-per-second Local Area Network", IEEE MICRO Vol 15 No 10, February 1995, pp.29–36.
3. Brebner G., *Computers in Communication*, London:McGraw-Hill 1997.
4. Brebner G., "A virtual hardware operating system for the Xilinx XC6200", Proc. 6th International Workshop on Field Programmable Logic and Applications, Darmstadt, September 1996, Springer LNCS 1142, pp.327–336.
5. Brebner G., "The Swappable Logic Unit: a Paradigm for Virtual Hardware", Proc. 5th Annual IEEE Symposium on Custom Computing Machines, Napa, April 1997, IEEE Computer Society Press.
6. Brebner G. and S. Haeck, "Active Protocols", in preparation for submission to SIGCOMM'98.

7. Buzzard G. et al, "An Implementation of the Hamlyn Sender-managed Interface Architecture", Proc. 2nd Symposium on Operating System Design and Implementation, October 1996.

8. Cotter D., J. Lucek and D. Marcenac, "Ultra-High-Bit-Rate Networking: From the Transcontinental Backbone to the Desktop", IEEE Communications Magazine, Vol 35 No 4, April 1997, pp.96–102.

9. Davis A., M. Swanson and M. Parker, "Efficient Communication Mechanisms for Cluster Based Parallel Computing", Proc. 1st Internation Workshop on Communication and Architectural Support for Network-Based Parallel Computing, San Antonio, February 1997, Springer LNCS 1199, pp.1–15.

10. Donlin A., "A Dynamically Self-Modifying Processor Architecture and its Application to Active Networking", Internal report, Department of Computer Science, University of Edinburgh, September 1997.

11. Gilmore S. and J. Hillston, "The PEPA Workbench: A Tool to Support a Process Algebra-based Approach to Performance Modelling", Proc. 7th International Conference on Modelling Techniques and Tools for Computer Performance Evaluation, Vienna, May 1994, Springer LNCS 794.

12. Gunning P., J. Lucek, D. Moodie, K. Smith, D. Pitcher, Q.Badat and A. Siddiqui, "40 Gbit/s optical-TDMA LAN over 300m blown fibre", Proc. 23rd European Conference on Optical Communications, Edinburgh, September 1997, IEE Conference Publication 448, IEE London, pp.61–64.

13. Heinrich M. et al, "The Performance Impact of Flexibility in the Stanford FLASH Multiprocessor", Proc. 6th Symposium on Architectural Support for Programming Languages and Operating Systems, October 1994, pp.274–285.

14. Hillston J., A. Opdahl and R. Pooley, "A case study using the IMSE experimentation tool", Proc. 3rd Conference on Advanced Information Systems Engineering, Trondheim, Springer LNCS 498, pp.284–306.

15. Ibbett R., P. Heywood and F. Howell, "HASE: A Flexible Toolset for Computer Architects", Computer Journal, Vol 38 No 10, 1995.

16. Lucek J., D. Cotter, K. Smith and P. Gunning, "Ultrafast Photonic Data Networks" (Invited Paper), IEEE LEOS'96 Annual Meeting, Boston, 18–21 November 1996.

17. Lucek J., P. Gunning, D. Moodie, K. Smith and D. Pitcher, "SynchroLan: A 40 Gbit/s optical-TDMA LAN", Electronics Letters, Vol 33, 1997, pp.887–888.

18. Marenzoni et al, "An Operating system Support to Low-overhead Communications in NOW Clusters", Proc. 1st Internation Workshop on Communication and Architectural Support for Network-Based Parallel Computing, San Antonio, February 1997, Springer LNCS 1199, pp.130–143.

19. Paikin S., M. Lauria and A. Chien, "High Performance Messaging on Workstations: Illinois Fast Messages (FM) for Myrinet", Proc. Supercomputing '95, San Diego, December 1995.

20. Pooley R., *Formalising the Description of Process Based Simulation Models*, Ph.D. Dissertation, University of Edinburgh, 1995.

21. Pooley R., "Integrating Behavioural and Simulation Modelling", Proc. 8th International Conference on Techniques and Tools for Computer Performance Modelling, Heidelberg, September 1995.

22. Pooley R., "Exploiting Functional Properties to Reduce Complexity in Simulating ATM", Proc. Telecommunication, Distribution and Parallelism (TDP '96), La Londe les Maures, France, June 1996, pp 23–34.

23. Tennenhouse D. and D. Wetherall, "Active Networks", Proc. 15th Symposium on Operating System Principles, December 1995.
24. VSI Alliance Architecture Document, VSI Alliance 1997.

The Design of a Parallel Programming System for a Network of Workstations: An Object-Oriented Approach*

Chan Wai Ming and Samuel Chanson and Mounir Hamdi **

Department of Computer Science, The Hong Kong University of Science and Technology, Clear Water Bay, Kowloon, Hong Kong

Abstract. Parallel Computing on a network of workstations (NOW) is receiving a lot of attention from the research community. However, there is still a lack of tools for developing and running parallel applications on a NOW environment. In this paper, we develop and implement an object-oriented parallel programming system that facilitates the implementation of parallel applications on a NOW environment. In our programming system, a conceptual model, named *Synchronous Object Model*, is provided to help programmers write parallel programs. The object model makes use of the inherent parallel nature of an object-oriented model to express parallelism. In addition, an object-oriented framework is included into our programming system that reduces the size of parallel programs through code reuse and design reuse. Our system design further takes advantage of the underlying hardware architecture of the NOW environment to maximize performance by integrating multicast and load balancing support, and this is illustrated through experimental results.

1 Introduction

The computing and the networking technologies has been advancing at a very fast pace. As a result, the aggregated computing power of a network of workstations (NOW) could be more than that of an expensive parallel computing system [5]. This makes NOW an attractive alternative platform for many classes of parallel applications which were limited to expensive parallel machines in the past. However, there is still a lack of tools for developing and running parallel applications on a NOW environment. As a result, relatively few applications exist that can take advantage of the potential of this common and inexpensive readily-available platform.

In this paper, we develop and implement an object-oriented parallel programming system which is very suitable for a NOW environment. In our programming system, a conceptual model, named *Synchronous Object Model*, is provided to help programmers write parallel programs. The object model makes use of the

---

* This research work has been supported by a grant from the Hong Kong Telecom Institute of Information Technology, number HKTIIT93/94.EG01
** Author for Correspondence: Mounir Hamdi, Email: hamdi@cs.ust.hk.

inherent parallel nature of an object-oriented model to express parallelism. With the Synchronous Object Model, programmers can design and write their parallel programs using existing object-oriented techniques without having to think in terms of parallelism in designing the control flow. In addition, an object-oriented framework is provided in our programming system in order to reduce the effort of parallel programming by code reuse and design reuse.

Furthermore, our parallel programming system design takes advantage of the underlying hardware architecture of the NOW environment to maximize performance by integrating multicast and load balancing supports. For load balancing, we have proposed a *Dynamic Decomposition* technique that allows a parallel program to be automatically decomposed by our programming system and allocated to processors for execution. The support of multicast is also a unique feature of our programming system. In an Ethernet environment, data can be sent to multiple hosts efficiently using multicast. To illustrate how to take advantage of that, we implemented a new matrix multiplication algorithm which makes use of multicast support and is compared favorably with conventional algorithms. The experimental results showed that our proposed algorithm outperforms conventional algorithm in terms of efficiency and scalability.

This paper is organized as follows. In section 2, we introduce the design philosophy of our object-oriented programming system. In section 3, we detail a prototype design of our parallel programming system. In section 4, we illustrate how to incorporate efficient load balancing algorithms into our programming system, and in section 5 we show how to take advantage of special architectural features of an Ethernet network to design efficient algorithms. Section 6 concludes the paper.

2 Design of an Object-Oriented Programming System

One of the fundamental problems of parallel programming is that the thinking process of human beings is, by nature, sequential. In particular, it is easy for parallel programmers to make logical errors for handling message passing among the processes of a parallel program. For example, deadlocks are sometimes introduced unintentionally. One way to help programmers avoid or overcome these problems is to provide them with a restricted programming model which could guide them in designing their programs. The shared-memory parallel programming paradigm is an example of a restricted programming model [3]. As a result, writing parallel programs using a shared-memory paradigm is easier than using a message-passing paradigm [3]. Using a shared-memory paradigm, communications among processes are mapped to read/write operations on global data structures which is a familiar concept to most programmers.

Currently the shared-memory programming paradigm cannot be implemented efficiently on a message-passing or distributed memory hardware such as a NOW. This is still a subject of active research [2]. In a shared-memory paradigm, programmers cannot specify the route of data transfers among processors even though it is important to the performance of parallel applications in multiprocessor systems. For the above reasons, the message-passing paradigm has been a more popular programming paradigm for distributed memory hardware.

The design of our programming system was motivated by the desire to make parallel programming possible on an existing object-oriented paradigm [10, 11]. This design approach is different from other design approaches which mainly consisted of adding object-oriented capabilities to the existing parallel programming paradigms [12, 13]. The main advantage of an object-oriented extension on existing programming paradigm is higher re-usability of the code. However, the inherently parallel nature of the object-oriented model is not fully employed in most current systems for solving the fundamental problem that most programmers are not used to thinking in terms of parallelism.

An object-oriented model is inherently parallel and the model fits into a message-passing paradigm. Since new generations of computer science and engineering students learn to design and program in an object-oriented way, the object-oriented model will be familiar to a typical programmer. If programmers write parallel programs based on models familiar to them, writing parallel programs will not be more difficult than writing sequential ones. Therefore, the design of our programming system is guided by the philosophy that programmers will find the inherently parallel object-oriented model easy for use in writing parallel applications.

The characteristics of a NOW must be taken into consideration, besides making parallel programming easier, in designing our programming system. When a parallel program is executed on a dedicated multiprocessor machine, the behavior of processes on each processor is more predictable since the processors are dedicated to the jobs allocated. In a NOW environment, this is not the case. Each workstation can be running a multitasking or multi-users operating system. Hence, the workload of each workstation could vary from time to time as people sign on and off. Static load balancing techniques will not be effective in this dynamic environment. Consequently, parallel programs do not perform well on a NOW environment without load balancing [8]. As a result, we integrated load balancing into our programming system. Programmers would use our programming framework provided by the programming system for writing parallel programs. The programming framework becomes a mediator between the parallel programmer and the underlying run-time system. Programmers are guided to provide the needed information which is then used to make load balancing decisions.

The feasibility and the overhead of the implementation of the proposed programming system is an important issue. In particular, a programming library approach is preferred to extending existing programming languages or designing a new language. Although the library approach would create more restrictions on the design aspects, the complexity involved in the language design and the implementation of compilers may exceed the benefits of creating or extending a programming language. Also, the library approach has the advantage that the design of the programming system would be independent of programming language issues. In other words, the programming system could be implemented using different programming languages for different needs of the users. That is why, in our programming system design, we avoided creating a new programming language. Rather, we relied on using existing object-oriented languages [11].

An overall structure of our proposed programming system is illustrated in figure 1. The programming system consists of the following components.

- A Synchronous Object Model
- An Object-oriented Programming Library Framework
- A Run-time System

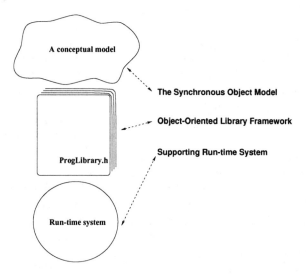

Fig. 1. Overall architecture of our programming system.

The Synchronous Object Model helps programmers in their thinking process for writing parallel programs. The main structure of a parallel program is a *SyncObject*. The SyncObject fits into our object-oriented model without introducing new language constructs for expressing parallelism. Parallelism and synchronizations in a parallel program are expressed through the properties of the SyncObject. The SyncObject is a class which is composed of two main modules:

- Computation Module
- Communication Module

The computation module contains code to be written by the programmer, and the communication module contains two buffers — one for the incoming messages and another for the outgoing messages. In the computation phase, the code written by the programmer inside the computation module is executed by the processor. When the computation module of a SyncObject finishes execution, the instances of the SyncObject proceed to synchronize with one another before the communication phase starts.

In the communication phase, the data in the outgoing buffer are sent out and incoming data are stored in the incoming buffer. The order of sending and receiving is arbitrary. Sending and receiving data can be viewed as taking place at the same time. After that, the execution cycle ends. The cycle starts again when another activation message is received by the object. Figure 2 shows the general structure of the a SyncObject.

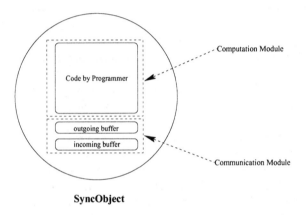

SyncObject

Fig. 2. Structure of SyncObject.

The Synchronous Object Model possesses some useful properties:

- *Compatible with the object-oriented model*
- *Provides a simple structured template*
- *Deadlock free*
- *Encapsulates the synchronization code*
- *Allows different forms of parallelism*

Apart from the Synchronous Object Model, a programming library framework is also provided for the programmer. A parallel program is typically composed of different parts [2]. It is a tedious job for parallel programmers to write a lot of routine code for different parts of the parallel program. Integration of the various components into a parallel program also takes a lot of effort. Since human beings are prone to error, it would be difficult to make sure each part of the parallel program is correct and without problems when the different components are put together. The programming library framework provides an organized parallel program skeleton which guides the programmer to fill in the missing parts that are unique to his/her application. Also, most of the routine code common to many parallel applications are encapsulated in the object-oriented framework for reuse. This in turn reduces the effort of parallel programming. The last component of the programming system is the run-time system. The run-time system provides functionalities which cannot be implemented in the programming library level.

3   ObjectBalance: A Prototype of the Proposed Object-Oriented Parallel Programming System

The previous section describes the general structure of the proposed programming system from a programmer's view point. The details of the underlying structure of the programming system is invisible to the programmers. In order to support the Synchronous Object Model and the programming library framework described above, an implementation design is required. We use a layering design approach to allow more flexibilities in designing the underlying system. Our proposed programming system is portable across different parallel hardware platforms.

In this paper, a NOW is selected as the target platform for the programming system. The prototype, named *ObjectBalance*, of the proposed Object-Oriented Parallel Programming System is implemented on a network of Sparc workstations connected by a 10Mbps Ethernet. In fact, the main goal of the implementation is to verify whether the idea of our programming system, which is based on an object-oriented programming concept, is implementable or not. However, since the focus is not on the performance aspect of the system components, the performance of the ObjectBalance has not been optimized.

ObjectBalance is written using the Objective C language [11]. Programmers are, therefore, required to write their parallel programs using Objective C. Objective C is chosen because of the following reasons. First, the dynamic loading and dynamic binding in the language simplify the implementation of the object control of the system. Second, the language is simple and easy to learn. Finally, the language is supported in the GNU C compiler which is available in many computing platforms.

ObjectBalance was written and tested on Sparc workstations running Sun-OS 4.x. However, it can be easily ported across different Unix platforms with multicast support. In the run-time system, the implementation of the distributed object control is based on a package, named libobjects, obtained from Free Software Foundation. Further, the BALANCE system, developed at our University [1], provides the underlying infrastructure for load balancing in our programming system.

We have implemented a synchronization algorithm, named SyncObject, which is used in our programming system. The main idea of the SyncObject is to have synchronization encapsulated in the SyncObject class for programmers to use without knowing how to implement synchronization code. Different network architectures require different algorithms for performance reasons. Our synchronization algorithm is designed for unreliable broadcasting networks to which the Ethernet belongs. To exploit the architecture of the Ethernet network, we incorporated multicast into our programming system. Since Ethernet is a broadcasting medium, it is more efficient to send data to a set of hosts using multicast instead of sending the data repeatedly to the hosts one by one. In parallel programming, it is common to have the same sets of data sent to multiple hosts. Thus, the support of multicast in our programming system allows efficient data transfers among processors.

The ObjectBalance can be divided into two main parts — the programming interface part and the underlying system. The programming interface part includes the library classes used for writing parallel applications. Moreover, it includes the Synchronous Object Model which guides parallel programmers during their algorithm development. The second part of ObjectBalance is the underlying system which provides the infrastructure for implementing the programming interface part. From the programmers' view point, the underlying system is completely invisible. Programmers only need to learn about the programming interface in order to write parallel programs.

Figure 3 illustrates the structure of the various components in ObjectBalance.

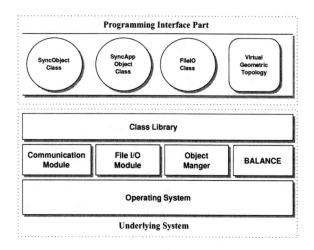

Fig. 3. Architecture of ObjectBalance

The underlying system of ObjectBalance is composed of the following modules:

– Communication Module

- File I/O Module
- Object Manager
- BALANCE
- Classes Library

In ObjectBalance, the data exchanged among instances of SyncObject and the internal control messages of the programming system are transferred by the Communication Module. The implementation of the SyncObject class and the Virtual Geometric Topology are based on the services of this Communication Module. The Communication Module is built from the UDP multicast service. The target network architecture of the ObjectBalance is an Ethernet network which is a broadcasting medium. Multicast is the strength of this type of network architecture. Also, it is frequent to have the same data messages sent to multiple hosts during parallel computations. Multicast is the best way for handling this type of data transfer in terms of performance. Multicast services are provided through UDP in most operating systems. However, UDP is an unreliable protocol. As a result, extra work is required to create a reliable multicast service for our programming system.

The File I/O Module provides service for organizing large data files. The file operations provided in most operating systems are often primitive. The basic operations defined are not adequate for manipulating large structural data files typically used in parallel computations. As a result, the File I/O Module is responsible for more complicated file handling such as efficient I/O when accessing a specific part of a large data file. In fact, the File I/O Module provides the infrastructure for the implementation of the FileIO class in our Programming Library Framework.

The Object Manager is responsible for managing the distributed objects on the workstations. The services provided by this module include object creation and termination on remote workstations, passing signals and methods to the remote objects and recording the output of the remote processes. The SyncAppObject class to be described later is built from the services of this module.

BALANCE [1] is a load balancing system developed at our University. The role of BALANCE in our programming system is to provide load balancing information. BALANCE provides the workload information of each workstation to our programming system. Any parallel program can automatically make use of workload information to distribute the objects to suitable workstations.

The last components of ObjectBalance is the Classes Library which serves as the programming interface to parallel programmers. The purpose of the Classes Library is to make use of the services from the modules described above to create the programming interface part.

4   Load Balancing

In the previous sections, we have shown how to design and implement parallel programming systems that can help programmers write parallel programs and also showed how to make use of the underlying hardware architecture to create an efficient implementation of a programming system. Another important issue in getting good performance is the scheduling of processes of a parallel program to processors. In our case, the problem is how to schedule objects of a parallel program on different workstations. One of the goals of scheduling is to balance the load among the processors. In a parallel program, the elapsed time of a parallel program is measured by the elapsed time of the longest running process of the parallel program. Therefore, a good scheduling decision is to aim at allocating tasks to processors so that they take more or less the same time to finish [7, 8].

Load balancing schemes may be classified into two categories — static and dynamic load balancing. In a static load balancing scheme, scheduling decisions are based on the computational resources required and are decided beforehand. Thus, run-time load information is not taken into consideration. This type of scheduling scheme may work well in dedicated parallel machines. However, it is not suitable when executing parallel programs in a network of workstations.

Workstations are usually shared by many users. Each workstation is responsible for different computational tasks from different users. Since users do not have a global view of the utilization of the workstations in their working sites, jobs are submitted to the workstations according to the users' habit. This creates uneven workload among the workstations. Some workstations may be overloaded while others may be idle. As a result, load balancing systems are needed for networked workstations to maximize the utilization of the workstation. BALANCE [1] is an example of a load balancing system for NOW. The load balancing issues discussed here are a little bit different from those related to parallel programming. Load balancing systems like BALANCE aim at scheduling a set of independent jobs onto the workstations. The goal of the scheduling is to maintain even distribution of the workload among the workstations. The load balancing in parallel programs is to schedule processes of a parallel program onto workstations. The goal is to maintain the elapsed time of the processes more or less the same. Therefore, a parallel programming system with load balancing features on NOW need to achieve the above two different goals. This makes the design of our programming system very complicated [6, 7].

4.1 Encapsulation of Load Balancing Strategies

In most parallel programming systems, programmers are required to handle the load balancing of their parallel programs themselves. However, handling load balancing in a parallel program without any support from a programming system will add a burden to parallel programmers. In ObjectBalance, we provide a way for programmers to use the load balancing strategies encapsulated in a *SyncAppObject* class.

The SyncAppObject class in our programming framework is responsible for the creation of object instances on the workstations. The working procedures of SyncAppObject are designed such that the instance of a SyncAppObject class will establish a connection to BALANCE when the SyncAppObject is created in the program. Then, programmers can use the following method to create remote objects by suppling the class name.

```
- initWithClassName : (const char *) cName;
```

Within the **initWithClassName** class method, a **requestHosts** method defined in SyncAppObject is called to obtain a list of hosts names and then the objects will be created on the hosts in the list. The load balancing strategies and corresponding scheduling code is encapsulated in the **requestHosts** method. Inside the **requestHosts** method, the workload distribution of all workstations are provided by BALANCE. Based on the workload informations, a set of workstation is selected.

Under normal situations, parallel programmers can use a SyncAppObject class or its sub-classes without the need to worry about the **requestHosts** method. This is because each class in the tree classes of SyncAppObject encapsulates a scheduling algorithms within it as shown in Figure 4. Programmers can select the scheduling algorithm suitable for their needs. Then, the programming system is responsible for distributing the objects to workstations according to the scheduling algorithm encapsulated in SyncAppObject.

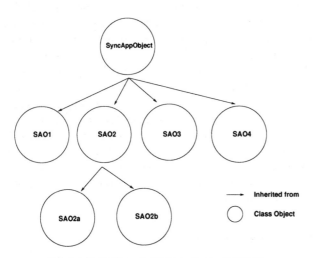

Each class object in the SyncAppObject class tree is with different scheduling algorithm.

Fig. 4. SyncAppObject Class Tree.

Furthermore, our programming system can be enhanced by adding new scheduling algorithms. Scheduling algorithms can be created as a new class by sub-classing the SyncAppObject and then overriding the **requestHosts** method.

Since the necessary code for communicating with the programming system is also inherited in the new class, the scheduling algorithm is implemented without adding code for its integration with the programming system. Therefore, it is much easier to add new scheduling schemes into our programming system. In particular, the programming framework proposed in our system can act as a bridge for combining the efforts of algorithm researchers and parallel programmers.

4.2 Dynamic Decomposition of Parallel Programs

One additional problem of parallel programming on NOW is to determine how many processes a parallel program should contain. In a dedicated parallel computer, the question can be simply solved by using the number of processors available for the parallel program. In a NOW environment, this question is more difficult because computational resources are shared, and hence, the workload of each workstation is dynamically fluctuating. As a result, the best number of workstations needed by a parallel job can only be determined during run-time. If the number of processes of a parallel program is greater than the number of workstations available, some workstations may be assigned more than one process. Uneven distribution of jobs may result. Also, each process of the parallel program incurs an amount of system overhead. Thus, if the processes assigned to the same workstation can be combined to just one process, the overhead due to process management could be reduced. On the other hand, if the number of processes is smaller than the number of workstations available, the computational resources may not be utilized efficiently. The ObjectBalance provides a scheme named *Dynamic Decomposition* as a solution to the above problems. In this scheme, programmers are responsible for informing the system how to decompose their parallel programs, and the programming system would decompose the parallel programs according to the workload distribution during execution time. This scheme provides more flexibility for scheduling decisions.

Dynamic Decomposition is achieved through a *Virtual Geometric Topology*. The Virtual Geometric Topology not only helps programmers in organizing their parallel programs but also provides a method for our system to decompose the task. For example, suppose a program is written as a virtual mesh topology. The mesh is defined as a $m \times n$ grid. A programmer can write his/her parallel program with the variables m and n as the size of the mesh. When the parallel program is executed, the system will select a suitable number of workstations based on the scheduling decision from the SyncAppObject or its subclasses which is selected by the programmer. Then, our system assigns the values of m and n to the parallel program based on the number of workstations available and also assigns the corresponding coordinates of the virtual geometry to the instance objects of the parallel program.

5 Parallel Algorithms for a Network of Workstations

There are many algorithms designed for parallel machines with mesh, ring and hypercube communication topologies [9] but only a few for a NOW environment. This phenomenon is easy to explain. The use of networked workstations as a parallel machine is a recent area of research. Also, high level programming support for using hardware multicast is not included in the operating system in the past. Thus, the advantages of the underlying architectures cannot be fully exploited. Without programming support, the design of algorithms based on the properties of a shared bus network is not useful. As a result, most parallel programs written for a NOW employ the same parallel algorithms designed for other parallel architectures [8]. Consequently, the performance and scalability of these parallel programs are rather poor. Since multicast is included in ObjectBalance, we can design algorithms which make use of the underlying communication hardware and compare their performance with parallel algorithms designed for other parallel hardware systems. In the following sections, matrix multiplication is used as an example for showing the advantages of using multicast in parallel algorithm design for a network of workstations.

5.1 Matrix Multiplication

In order to take advantage of the broadcasting medium (e.g., Ethernet) in a NOW environment, we have designed a new matrix multiplication algorithm. This new algorithm is simple compared with existing matrix multiplication algorithms designed for other parallel architectures [9].

Let A and B be two given matrices, and C be the product of A and B. There are m processors available for computation denoted p_i where $i = 1, \cdots, m$. Matrices A and B are decomposed in strip format and each matrix strip is allocated to different processors. Figure 5 illustrates this decomposition.

Matrices A and B are decomposed into m strips. The strips A_i and B_i, for $i = 1, 2, \cdots, m$, are located on processor p_i. The pseudo code of the parallel multiplication algorithm is listed below:

```
for p = 1 to m;
    if (p == myId)
        send A(p) to all other processor;
        C(p,p) = A(p) * B(p);
    else
        receive A(p) from sender;
        C(p,myId) = A(p) * B(myId);
endfor
```

The parallel algorithm consists of m phases. The value m depends on the number of processors available. Each processor is given an id. In the pth phase, the processor with id equal to p is responsible for sending the matrix strip A_p to the other processors through multicast. Then, each processor (p_i) performs the

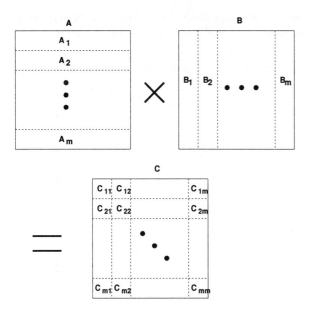

Fig. 5. Decomposition of the matrices.

multiplication on the received matrix strip (A_p) and the stored matrix strip (B_i) and puts the result in C_{pi} which is kept by processor (p_i). After the completion of all the phases, the result of the multiplication (matrix C) is stored in the processors.

Let the size of matrices A and B be $n \times n$, the time complexity of computation of the above parallel algorithm is $O(\frac{n^3}{m})$ and that of communication is $O(n^2)$.

5.2 Experimental Results

Fox's matrix multiplication algorithm is selected for comparison with the new multiplication algorithm. This algorithm is designed for the hypercube and the mesh architectures. The explanation and the analysis of this algorithm can be found in [9]. The time complexity of computation is $O(\frac{n^3}{m})$ and that of communication is $O(\sqrt{m}n^2)$ for this algorithm. Notice, the time spent on communication in our new algorithm does not increase as the data size increases. This is not the case for Fox's algorithm.

An experiment was taken to compare the performance of these two algorithms. Both algorithms were implemented on the ObjectBalance and tested using a set of networked workstations. Each program program multiplies two matrices of size 700×700. The results are shown in figure 6. As can be seen, the scalability of our new algorithm is better than Fox's algorithm. This shows that in order to fully take advantage of a NOW environment, a new thinking has to be put for re-designing parallel algorithms for this computing platform. Otherwise, the computational power of a NOW will not be fully exploited.

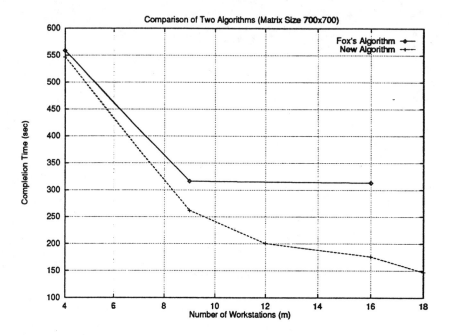

Fig. 6. Computation time of matrix multiplication a NOW.

6 Conclusion

In this paper, we develop and implement an object-oriented parallel programming system that facilitates the implementation of parallel applications on a NOW environment. In our programming system, a conceptual model, named *Synchronous Object Model*, is provided to help programmers write parallel programs. The object model makes use of the inherent parallel nature of an object-oriented model to express parallelism. With the Synchronous Object Model, programmers can design and write their parallel programs using existing object-oriented techniques without having to worry about the application parallelism when designing the control flow. In addition, an object-oriented framework is included into our programming system that reduces the size of parallel programs through code reuse and design reuse. Our system design further takes advantage of the underlying hardware architecture of the NOW environment to maximize performance by integrating multicast and load balancing support. For load balancing, we have proposed a dynamic decomposition technique. The support of multicast is a powerful feature of our programming system especially for broadcast-based networks such as the Ethernet, and its practical advantage is shown through the experimental design of new parallel matrix multiplication algorithms.

References

1. C. C. Hui, S. T. Chanson, P. M. Chui, K. M. La: Balance-a flexible parallel load balancing system for heterogeneous computing systems and networks. Proceedings IEEE INFOCOM'96 (1994) 896-893.
2. D. Skillicorn: Foundations of Parallel Programming. Cambridge University Press (1994).
3. Albert Y. H. Zomaya: Parallel and Distributed Computing Handbook. McGraw-Hill (1996).
4. T. E. Anderson, D. E. Culler, D. Patterson: A case for NOW (Networks of Workstations). IEEE Micro (1995) 54-64.
5. A. S. Tanenbaum, H. E. Bal, S. B. Hassen, M. F. Kaashoek: Object-based approach to programming distributed systems. Concurrency: Practice and Experience (1994) 235-249.
6. T. Casavant and M. Singhal: A Taxonomy of Scheduling in General-Purpose Distributed Computing Systems. IEEE Computer (1994) 31-51.
7. C. C. Hui and S. Chanson: Allocating Task Interaction Graphs to Processors in Heterogeneous Networks. IEEE Transaction on Parallel and Distributed Systems (1997) 908-925.
8. M. Hamdi and C. K. Lee: Dynamic Load-Balancing on Image Processing Applications on Clusters of Workstations. Parallel Computing (Jan. 1997) 1477-1492.
9. V. Kumar, A. Grama, A. Gupta, G. Karypis: Introduction to Parallel Computing. The Benjamin/Cummings Publishing Company Inc. (1994).
10. B. Stroustrup: The C++ Programming Language. Addison-Wesley (1992).
11. N. C. Inc.: NeXTSTEP object-oriented programming and the Objective C language. Addison-Wesley (1993).
12. J. N. C. Arabe: Dome: parallel programming in a distributed computing environment. Proceedings of IPPS'96. The 10th International Parallel Processing Symposium (1996) 218–246.
13. E. A. M. Odijk: The doom system and its applications: Parallel Arch. and Languages Europe (1987).
14. G. C. Fox, S. W. Otto, and A. J. Hey: Matrix Algorithms on a Hypercube: Matrix Multiplication. Parallel Computing (1987) 17-31.

Remote Subpaging Across a Fast Network*

Manjunath Bangalore and Anand Sivasubramaniam

Department of Computer Science & Engineering
The Pennsylvania State University
University Park, PA 16802.
Phone: (814) 865-1406
{*bangalor,anand*}*@cse.psu.edu*

Abstract. While improvements in semiconductor technology have made it possible to accommodate a large physical memory in today's machines, the need for supporting an even larger virtual address space continues unabated. Improvements in disk access times have however lagged improvements in both processor and memory speeds. Recent advances in networking technology has made it possible to go out on the network and access the physical memory on other machines at a cost lower than accessing the local disk. This paper describes a system implemented for such a remote paging environment. This system allows us to use a fine grain (a subpage) data transfer unit for remote memory paging and to employ different algorithms for determining when and how to transfer these units. The novelty of our implementation is that all the policy decisions about the subpage size and the subpaging algorithm are made at the user level, thus letting applications choose their own set of parameters. Performance results indicate that applications can benefit significantly from this flexibility.

1 Introduction

Applications have traditionally demanded a larger address space than available physical memory in machines. The operating system virtual memory management via paging has hidden this limitation from the programmer by transparently transferring pages between physical memory and the swap device. Until recently, the local disk has been the obvious choice for the swap device because any non-local repository has had to use a relatively slow network.

However, recent advances in networking has given us high-bandwidth, switched networks such as ATM [5] and Myrinet [2]. Further, low-latency messaging layers such as Active Messages [6] and Fast Messages [13] can exploit almost the entire promised capabilities of these networks by drastically reducing software costs. As a result, it is now a lot less expensive to go out on the network and access the physical memory of another machine than accessing the local disk. Figure 1 illustrates this point by comparing the transfer times of different data sizes for

---

* This research is supported in part by a NSF Career Award MIP-9701475, EPA grant R825195-01-0, and equipment grants from NSF and IBM.

Myrinet using Fast Messages and a recent disk (a Western Digital Enterprise 9.1
GB Ultra SCSI Harddrive).

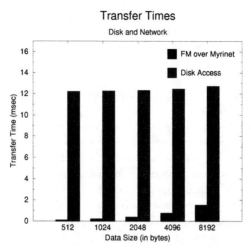

Fig. 1. Comparison of Network and Disk Accesses

A recent study [1] observes that at any particular instant, a large number of
machines on a network are idle. For instance, in a network of 50 workstations,
around 30 were found to be idle at any given time in this study. An application
on a machine could thus benefit from the idle physical memory on the other
machines. Remote paging can help better utilize and manage physical memory
on a global scale across all machines.

To harness and manage the RAM across the machines on the network, there
are three important issues that need to be addressed. First, we need to quantify
the size of the transfer unit (called the subpage) across the network. Second, we
need to implement an access control mechanism that can efficiently handle this
transfer unit. Finally, we need to investigate different algorithms for fetching
subpages from remote memory.

The size of the transfer unit for a paging system depends on the application
memory reference pattern, the size of the physical memory, and the difference
between the access times of memory and the swap device. When we move from
traditional to remote paging, the only difference is the access time for the swap
device. Since paging using network RAM is expected to be more efficient than
using a disk (Figure 1), the transfer unit for remote paging should be smaller
than a traditional page.

Hardware access control is essential to detect accesses to unmapped pages
and writes to read-only pages. The MMU hardware is usually tailored for a
specific page size and is not always controllable in software (and may not allow variable page sizes). Our goal is to provide remote paging mechanisms on
off-the-shelf workstations and networking hardware, so that they can be readily
used in commonplace platforms. Hence, we do not want custom MMU hardware

76

for implementing access control at a finer granularity. In this exercise, we use the Wisconsin Blizzard-E [7] drivers on commodity hardware, to implement access control for subpages on SPARCstation 20 platforms. These drivers modify Solaris' cacheability assumptions about memory and devices, and provide ioctl calls to the user programs to implement fine grain access control. We have chosen this approach over the all-software Shasta [14] approach to avoid incurring any overheads when the accessed memory location is resident locally (which is the more frequent case).

If the hardware determined page size cannot be altered, physical memory allocation has to be still done on the traditional page basis and not on a subpage basis (or else, adjacent virtual pages may not necessarily be physically adjacent). Consequently, we could have situations where one or more subpages within a page are present while the remaining reside on a remote node. It would thus be interesting to study different ways of prefetching these remaining subpages, and compare these schemes to a purely demand based subpaging scheme.

Other studies related to remote paging [12, 3, 10, 11, 4, 9, 17] have considered a spectrum of issues from server loads, to replacement schemes and global memory management issues. It should be noted that our system can be used in conjunction with any of these ideas. The closest study to ours is by Jamrozik et al. [8] where the benefit of subpages to improve performance is shown via trace-driven simulation. They have validated their results with a prototype implementation on the DEC Alpha connected to an ATM network. Fine-grain access in their case is achieved by modifying the PAL code of the memory subsystem. However, their remote paging system is not implemented at the user-level.

This paper presents an implementation of a remote subpaging system addressing some of the above mentioned issues. This system has been implemented on a SPARCstation 20 platform that has a page size of 4K bytes. The user-level Fast Messages [13] layer over Myrinet has been employed for communication. The novelty of this system is that it is customizable to an application's needs in terms of the transfer unit and the remote subpaging algorithms since most of it is implemented as a user-level library. Several applications could thus co-exist on a machine, each with its own choice of subpage size and remote subpaging algorithm.

The design of the remote subpaging system is discussed in Section 2 and the performance results are presented in Section 3. Finally, we present concluding remarks and ongoing research in Section 4.

2 Remote Paging System Design

Towards our overall goal of developing an efficient remote paging system, there are three important issues that need to be answered :

- What is the ideal unit of data transfer *(subpage)* between the workstations on the network? Can we simultaneously support multiple subpage sizes so that each application can choose its own subpage size?

– How do we efficiently implement access control for this transfer unit?

– What are the different remote subpaging algorithms that should be supported? How do these algorithms compare? Can we offer the applications the flexibility to tailor the subpaging algorithms to suit their needs?

To investigate these issues, we have developed a remote subpaging system on SPARCstation 20 platforms connected by Myrinet employing a user-level, low-latency, high-bandwidth messaging layer (Fast Messages [13]). In this paper, we specifically concentrate on issues in implementing the remote paging system at the machine where the application is executing, which we shall call the client, and use a simple server to store and retrieve these pages at the remote machine. There are several research issues in the design of the server but these are beyond the scope of this paper.

There are two basic modules in our implementation of the remote paging system at the client. The first is a *system of loadable device drivers* that executes in the Solaris kernel to provide mechanisms that are needed to implement fine grain access control. The second is a user-level library, linked with the user program, which uses the OS mechanisms to implement different remote subpaging algorithms.

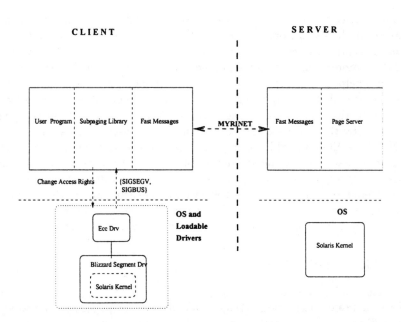

Fig. 2. The Remote Paging System

2.1 The Fine-grain Access Subsystem (Loadable Device Drivers)

Since accesses to remote memory across the network is less expensive than accesses to the local disk (which is the main motivation for this work), the unit of data transfer for remote paging should be smaller (*subpage*) than the normal page. However, not all traditional hardware for virtual memory can be programmed for alternate transfer units. Hence, for finer-grain (smaller than a page) access control, we have to resort to other means. In this exercise, we have used the loadable driver subsystem from the Wisconsin Blizzard-E [7] that provides fine-grain access control for the SPARCstation 20 platform running the Solaris 2.4 operating system. These drivers deliberately force uncorrectable errors in the memory's error correcting code(ECC) and use virtual memory aliases in addition to implement fine-grain access control. They allow a user-level process to set specific parts of a page (subpage) to VALID/INVALID, and a user-level SIGBUS handler is invoked on access violations. Also, a SIGSEGV handler is invoked for accesses to an unmapped page. The fine-grain access subsystem realizes the INVALID state by forcing uncorrectable errors in the memory's error correcting code (ECC) while guaranteeing no loss of reliability. Resetting the ECC bits is done with uncached double word stores using a second uncached mapping on the same pages.

2.2 The Subpaging Library

Our system tries to adhere to the well-known operating system philosophy of separating mechanisms from policy. The kernel component of our system (the loadable drivers) provides only the mechanisms for fine-grain access control. The rest of the remote paging system is implemented as a user-level library. This separation also helps us provide a menu of remote subpaging algorithms and a choice of subpage sizes that each application can choose from based on its expected behavior. Protection violations at page level (first accesses to unmapped pages) are detected by the VM hardware and passed to the user-level handler through the UNIX SIGSEGV signal handling interface and access violations detected by the driver are passed on to the user-level library via the SIGBUS (subpage fault) signals. The library employs the driver to change access rights of subpages when needed. The reader should note that we are not violating any of the traditional memory protection requirements with this design since the user-level library can only manipulate its own pages (and not belonging to anyone else).

2.3 Implementation Details

For a better understanding of our system, let us walk through the sequence of actions in a typical execution. Memory (to be remote paged) is allocated via our user library routine which in turn calls the kernel drivers to initialize the region of memory to an "UNMAPPED" state. An access to any part of this "UNMAPPED" memory by the application would result in a fault (page fault) which is passed on to the user library via a SIGSEGV signal. If space is available for this referenced page in local memory, then a physical page is allocated with a default protection of "INVALID" on the entire page using the kernel driver. The cost of this operation is directly proportional to the page size. The state for the faulted subpage alone is then set to the "VALID" state. Our system restricts subpage sizes to powers of 2.

At this stage, even though the physical page frame has been allocated on the client, the data itself resides on the remote machine. The subpage referred to by the user program access has to be fetched from the server by the SIGSEGV handler before the application can proceed. A subpage request is sent to the server to which the server replies with the necessary subpage. This subpage is then copied to the appropriate part of the allocated physical frame at the client, and control returns to the application program.

When there is no space left in the client physical memory, a victim has to be evicted and sent to the server, and that page is set to "UNMAPPED" at the client. We could use any of the well-known page replacement algorithms to choose the victim. Since our focus here is on subpaging issues, we have chosen a simple FIFO scheme for page replacement, and fancier schemes such as LRU can be substituted without changing the design of the subpaging system. As long as the application keeps referencing the "VALID" subpage in a page, it will not incur further access violations and overheads. The moment it references another ("INVALID") subpage within that page, there is an access violation (note that this is not a page fault since the page has been mapped in), caught by the driver through a memory error (via ECC bits), and passed on to the user-level library by a SIGBUS signal. The user-level SIGBUS handler may have to send a request for the subpage to the server if that subpage has not been already received by the client (which is possible in certain subpaging algorithms to be discussed shortly). The state for that subpage is set to "VALID" using an ioctl call to the kernel driver. When the subpage is received, it is copied to the appropriate part of the physical page. Control then returns to the application which can proceed with accesses to that subpage without overheads.

As we mentioned earlier, the scope of this paper is limited to the client side issues. There are interesting ideas to be explored on the server side which we plan to investigate in the future. Currently, the server side software simply pins the pages that it controls in its physical memory and serves the client requests (*keep-page* and *get-page*) one after another.

2.4 Subpaging Schemes

Once a physical page frame is allocated and mapped in at the client, there are different schemes by which one may fetch the different subpages within that page from the server. In this paper, we examine three such schemes that are described below.

Demand Subpaging: In this scheme, each subpage of a page is fetched one at a time, and only when that subpage is referenced. Each SIGSEGV and SIG-BUS handler invocation has to necessarily fetch the referenced subpage from the server. The advantage of this scheme is that it does not transfer any more sub-pages than needed. The disadvantage is that there is no overlap of data transfer while the CPU is executing the application program. The application has to stall while the request is sent on the network to the server and the server sends back that subpage over the network.

Eager Subpaging: This scheme attempts to overlap data transfer with useful work execution. The SIGSEGV handler works the same way as before on the client side. On the server side however, the server sends the requested subpage in one message. Then, in another message, it automatically takes the remaining subpages of this page and sends them to the client without requiring the client to explicitly ask for them. The SIGBUS handler (at least one subpage request in that page has already been processed) on the client simply polls the network for the requested subpage since the server would automatically send it. It may happen that the user-level library at the client picks up subpages (other than what it is waiting for) and sets those subpages to "VALID". This is possible when the application is referencing multiple pages in a short time span.

The advantage of the Eager scheme is that it could potentially hide data transfer latencies if the gap between the first reference to a page and the first reference to another subpage within that page is sufficiently large. The disadvantage is that the server may be sending more subpages to the client than what is actually needed. Further, even though the SIGBUS handler is waiting for only one subpage it may have to wait longer since the server is sending all the subpages in one shot. It is possible to "stream" the subpages from the server to the client to fix this problem, but we have not explored this improvement in this paper.

Forward Sweep Subpaging: This is a variation of the Eager scheme where the faulted subpage is fetched (on a SIGSEGV), the application continues execution and the server asynchronously sends only the remainder of the page that is ahead/forward (in terms of the address) of the faulted subpage in a single unit. If the application accesses the portion of the page that is behind the faulted subpage, a SIGBUS is incurred. The motivation for this approach draws from a finding in a recent study [8] that in a subpaging system, most of the accesses to a page are in the region that is ahead of the faulted subpage with 70% of them being on the immediately next subpage in the forward direction. This scheme is expected to perform even better than the Eager scheme under such situations since the polling time in a SIGBUS handler is likely to become lower because of the smaller number of subpages being sent.

3   Performance Results

Having, described our remote paging system, we now evaluate the performance of this system. First, we examine the time spent in the different components of the system using microbenchmarks. Next, we evaluate its performance using traces from three of the Spec92 [15] benchmarks with different subpage sizes and subpaging schemes. Finally, we look at how an actual Quicksort application performs with different subpage sizes and subpaging algorithms. We have evaluated this system over two SPARCstation 20s with Hypersparc processors connected by Myrinet through an 8-port switch.

3.1 Microbenchmarks

Subpage Size (in bytes)	Allocate New Page	Set Subpage Valid	Remote Subpage Fetch
2048	1930	150	230
1024	1930	125	167
512	1930	99	119
256	1930	95	111

Table 1. SIGSEGV handling cost in microsecs

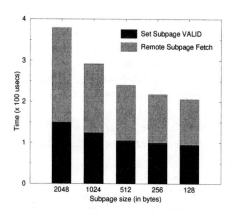

Fig. 3. SIGBUS handling cost

Let us examine where time is spent in handling a typical fault in the remote subpaging system. We have two types of faults namely the SIGSEGV which is incurred on a first-time access to an unmapped page (page fault), and the SIGBUS which is caused on future accesses to a partially resident page (subpage fault). We have measured the time spent in these fault handling routines with a simple microbenchmark. The different operations performed on a SIGSEGV violation are declaring a new page, setting the faulted subpage valid, and fetching the faulted subpage from remote memory. The cost of these operations for different subpage sizes is shown in Table 3.1.

We can see that allocating a new page is a costly operation and takes nearly 2 milliseconds. The cost for setting the subpage valid and the cost for fetching the subpage from remote memory changes linearly with the subpage size. The SIGBUS handler has to set a subpage valid and has to fetch the faulted subpage from remote memory. The cost of these operations is shown in Figure 3.

These operations may seem expensive (even though they are much cheaper than the disk accesses), but we are currently in the process of switching to a fast trap interface on Solaris to transfer signals efficiently (around 5 microsecs) to the user handler.

3.2   Experiments with Traces

In this subsection, we evaluate the performance of the subpaging system by using three traces from the Spec92 benchmarks suite [15] namely gcc, compress, and espresso, which exhibit different memory access patterns. We have used data traces with at least 150,000 references and perform reads and writes depending on the nature of the reference. There is no computation (gap) between these memory references.

In the following discussion, we present results from running these traces on our system with varying subpage sizes and subpaging algorithms. We have also obtained various statistics about the number of SIGSEGV and SIGBUS invocations to explain the behavior of these applications, though they are not given explicitly in this paper. Also, since our focus in this exercise is on the subpaging issues, we use a simple variation of FIFO for page replacement (it is FIFO with higher priority given for partially filled pages). In all the exercises, we have set the amount of physical memory available at the client node to half the virtual memory requirement of the application.

The performance results for the gcc trace with 200,000 references, the compress trace with 200,000 references and the espresso trace with 150,000 references are shown in Figure 4

The advantages of a smaller transfer unit (than a page) for gcc is brought out in the 2K demand and forward sweep subpaging schemes where there is a 13% improvement in performance over the full page size. *Note that the bars for 4096 bytes in these graphs correspond to the results for access control and remote paging at the full page granularity.* From 1K bytes onwards, with decreasing subpage size, the performance suffers due to an increased number of SIGBUS faults. This gets worse with smaller subpage size. While the eager scheme does better, the downside of eagerly transferring the rest of the page in one shot (after the first reference) seems to cause the CPU to stall more than it should. Sending a smaller chunk in the forward scheme helps. The advantages in lowering the number of SIGBUS faults with the forward sweep scheme (compared to the demand based scheme) and not letting the CPU stall too long on a second

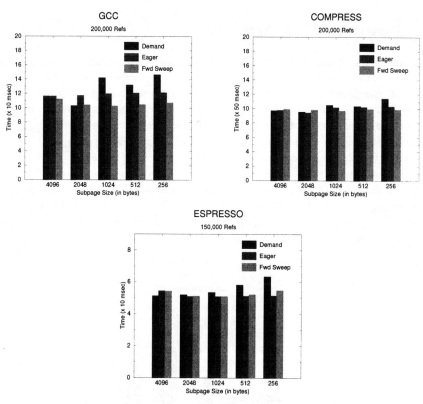

Fig. 4. Performance Results for Traces

subpage reference helps gcc perform the best for this scheme at a subpage size of 1K bytes.

In compress, as one would expect of this application, there is a substantial spatial locality of reference, even at a subpage granularity. Hence, there is not a significant impact from the subpaging algorithm and the subpage size (only a marginal difference) compared to gcc. Still, the eager and forward sweep schemes do slightly better than the demand based scheme since nearly all the subpages within a page are referenced eventually in this application. Here again we find a subpage size of around 1K to give the best performance.

In espresso, the number of page faults (SIGSEGV) itself is fairly low. Once the page is brought in, the references are uniformly distributed spatially and temporally through the page. This makes the eager scheme perform slightly better than the forward sweep scheme. Also, since the number of SIGSEGV violations is low, the higher cost paid by these two schemes in the initial references to a page is not a significant overhead compared to the numerous SIGBUS faults that the demand based scheme experiences.

3.3 Experiments with an Application

One drawback of using traces to examine the behavior of our system as in the previous subsection is that it does not give a realistic picture of what happens in a real execution. Usually, a program does not just make memory references. There is a certain amount of computation performed between these references. While this does not affect the behavior of the demand based subpaging scheme (which does not overlap any communication with possible computation), not modeling this computation is unfair to the other two schemes.

To study the system with an actual application, we have used a Quicksort program to sort 64K integers and we have studied the impact of subpage size and subpaging algorithm on this program. Again, we have set an artificial limit on the available physical memory of the client equal to half the virtual memory size requirements of the program.

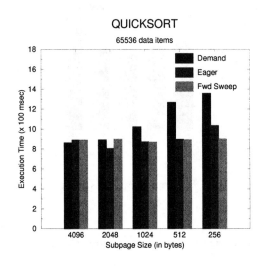

Fig. 5. Total Execution Time for Quicksort

All schemes are seen to perform best (see Figure 5) at subpage sizes of 2K or 1K bytes and the best performance is seen at 2K byte subpage size in the eager scheme. The demand scheme worsens when we go for any transfer unit smaller than a page. This is because the quicksort algorithm eventually accesses every part of a page. Since there is a reasonable amount of computation to be overlapped with fetching the remaining subpages of a page, the other two schemes perform much better. For subpage sizes shorter than 1K bytes, the forward sweep scheme performs better than the eager scheme and the performance is reversed for the larger subpage sizes. The best performance of the lot is for the eager scheme with a subpage size of 2K bytes which is around 11% better than the performance at full page size. While it may appear to the reader that a 11%

saving in execution time is not very significant, we should note that page sizes on machines are likely to get larger (to improve TLB coverage as the physical memory on the machines keeps growing). Hence, transfer units smaller than a page over the network will become even more important with this trend.

4 Concluding Remarks and Future Work

In this paper, we have presented a remote subpaging system that uses recent innovations in networking technology and communication software to provide an alternate and more efficient repository between the physical memory and the disk in the storage hierarchy. We have implemented this system on a SPARCstation 20 platform, connected by Myrinet, using a low-latency user-level messaging layer. The system allows us to use a fine grain (a subpage) data transfer unit for remote memory paging and to employ different algorithms for determining when and how to transfer these units. The novelty of this system is that all the policy decisions about the subpage size and the subpaging algorithm are made at the user level. As our performance results clearly indicate, each application could potentially benefit from a different subpage size and subpaging algorithm. Our system makes this customization possible without interfering with the protection requirements by implementing these policy decisions at the user level.

For most applications, a subpage size of 2K or 1K bytes is seen to give the best performance. In some cases, with these subpage sizes, there was close to a 15% savings in execution time over the full page size on the SPARCstation 20 (4096 bytes). However, the reader should note that page sizes on machines are likely to get larger to improve TLB coverage [16] as the physical memory on the machines keeps growing. This trend is apparent even on the newer SUN UltraSPARC platforms where the page sizes have grown to 8192 bytes. Hence, transfer units smaller than a page over the network will become even more important with this trend.

There are several interesting directions for future work that are currently being investigated as identified below:

– We are trying to use a faster way of processing signals as provided by the loadable device driver under Solaris. This scheme tries to minimize the number of protection boundaries that need to be crossed for every signal. This mechanism can be used for processing SIGBUS faults and would boost the performance of the remote subpaging system.
– We are investigating other subpaging algorithms wherein the different subpages could be streamed to the client one after another without being sent in one big chunk. A variation on the same lines is to get the subpages in the order that they are likely to be accessed.
– Another possibility is to perform subpaging in the kernel space (possibly in the underlying segment drivers that implement fine grain access control) to reduce switching overheads between the kernel and the user space while processing a fault. A comparative study between the performance benefits

of subpaging at kernel-level and the flexibility of subpaging at user-level can be conducted.

- It is interesting to find out what tools the user would need to choose an appropriate subpage size and subpaging algorithm for an application, to benefit from this system.
- The current system is being ported to UltraSPARC architectures running a newer Solaris release.
- There are several interesting research issues to be addressed for the design of the server.

We are expanding our system to provide a custom malloc interface that can manage the dynamic data requirements of applications to use fine grain access control. This would help us run off-the-shelf applications and expand the system evaluation to a larger set of applications.

References

1. R. Arpaci, A. Dusseau, A. Vahdat, T. Anderson, and D. Patterson. The Interaction of Parallel and Sequential Workloads on a Network of Workstations. In *Proceedings of the 1995 ACM Sigmetrics Conference on Measurement and Modeling of Computer Systems*, pages 267–278, May 1995.
2. N. J. Boden, D. Cohen, R. E. Felderman A. E. Kulawik, C. L. Seitz, J. N. Seizovic, and W. Su. Myrinet: A gigabit-per-second local area network. *IEEE Micro*, 15(1):29–36, February 1995.
3. D. Comer and J. Griffioen. A new design for distributed systems: The remote memory model. In *Proceedings of the Summer 1990 USENIX Conference*, pages 127–135, June 1990.
4. M. D. Dahlin, R. Y. Wang, T. E. Anderson, and D. A. Patterson. Co-operative Caching: Using remote client memory to improve file system performance. In *Proceedings of the USENIX Conference on Operating Systems Design and Implementation,*, pages 267–280, November 1994.
5. M. de Prycker. *Asynchronous Transfer Mode: solution for broadband ISDN*. Ellis Horword, West Sussex England, 1992.
6. T. Von Eicken, D. E. Culler, S. C. Goldstein, and K. E. Schauser. Active Messages: A mechanism for integrated communication and computation. In *Proceedings of the 19th International Symposium on Computer Architecture*, pages 256–266, May 1992.
7. Schoinas et. al. Implementing Fine-Grain Distributed Shared Memory On Commodity SMP Workstations. Technical report, University of Wisconsin at Madison, Department of Computer Science, 1996.
8. H. A. Jamrozik et.al. Reducing Network Latency Using subpages in a Global Memory Environment. In *Proceedings of the seventh ACM Conference on Architectural Support for Programming Languages and Operating Systems*, pages 258–267, October 1996.
9. M. J. Feeley, W. E. Morgan, F. H. Pighin, A. R. Karlin, H. M. Levy, and C. A. Thekkath. Implementing global memory management in a Workstation cluster. In *Proceedings of the 15th ACM Symposium on Operating Systems Principles*, pages 201–212, December 1995.

10. E. W. Felten and J. Zahorjan. Issues in the implementation of a remote memory paging system. Technical Report 91-03-09, Department of Computer Science and Engineering, University of Washington, March 1991.

11. M. J. Franklin, M. J. Carey, and M. Livny. Global memory management in client-server DBMS architectures. In *Proceedings of the 18th VLDB Conference*, pages 596–609, August 1992.

12. P. J. Leach, P. H. Levine, B. P. Douros, J. A. Hamilton, D. L. Nelson, and B. L. Stumpf. The architecture of an integrated local network. *IEEE Journal on Selected Areas in Communications*, 1(5):842–857, November 1983.

13. S. Pakin, M. Lauria, and A. Chien. High Performance Messaging on Workstations: Illinois Fast Messages (FM) for Myrinet. In *Supercomputing '95*, 1995.

14. D. J. Scales, K. Gharachorloo, and C. A. Thekkath. Shasta: A Low Overhead, Software-Only Approach for Supporting Fine-Grain Shared Memory. In *Seventh International Conference on Architectural Support for Programming Languages and Operating Systems*, pages 174–185, November 1996.

15. The Spec92 Benchmark Suite, Release 1.1 , 1992.

16. M. Talluri and M. D. Hill. Surpassing the TLB performance of superpages with less operating system support. In *Proceedings of the 6th Int. Conf. on Arch. Support for Programming Languages and Operating Systems*, pages 171–182, October 1994.

17. G. Voelker, H. Jamrozik, M. Vernon, H. Levy, and E. Lazowska. Managing Server Load in Global Memory Systems. In *Proceedings of the 1997 ACM Sigmetrics Conference on Performance Measurement, Modeling, and Evaluation*, pages 127–136, June 1997.

Improved Functional Imaging through Network Based Parallel Processing

F. Munz[1], T. Stephan[2], U. Maier[2], T. Ludwig[2], A. Bode[2]
S. Ziegler[1], S. Nekolla[1], P. Bartenstein[1], and M. Schwaiger[1]

[1] Nuklearmedizinische Klinik und Poliklinik des Klinikums rechts der Isar
[2] Lehrstuhl für Rechnertechnik und Rechnerorganisation
Technische Universität München (TUM)

email: Munz@Informatik.TU-Muenchen.DE

Abstract. This paper deals with currently used algorithms for the reconstruction of functional images which run up to 60 hours or more on a single workstation and deal with hundreds of megabyte of data. A parallel implementation with high efficiency and almost linear speedup of a sophisticated iterative algorithm is given and its applicability to other reconstruction methods is shown. Whereas running this application on a high performance parallel computer is straightforward, there are more issues under production conditions as they are enforced by daily routine in a clinic. We adress the topic of fault tolerant parallelizing and batch queuing of programs which are typically written in a high level language like IDL or MATLAB and show how load balancing can preserve the ownership of workstations in a network of workstations (NOW) which is used for distributed computing during office hours.

keywords: functional imaging, parallel image reconstruction, load balancing, batch queing, network of workstations.

1 Introduction

Medical imaging has become a key technology for modern diagnosis. Techniques such as computer tomography (CT) or magnetic resonance imaging (MRI) yield noninvasively high resolution pictures of internal organs. Newer technologies like positron-emission-tomography (PET) or single-photon-emission- tomography (SPECT) have been developed which enable the direct measurement of function. PET or SPECT images are acquired by measuring the decay of radioisotopes bound to molecules with known properties such as glucose analogues. Reconstruction of PET data is complex and mentioned in the Blue Book edition of 1996 as a "Grand Challenge" for high performance computing. This text deals with the benefits and caveats of parallel algorithms for PET, however, due to the similarity most of it is applicable to SPECT as well.

Most commercially available PET scanners consist of several rings of small detectors. Axial collimation is provided by retractable tungsten septa between the rings. Radioactive decay of the actual tracer distribution $\lambda(x, y, z)$ is characterised by the emission of a positron which annihilates after travelling a short distance, producing two photons, which are propagating in nearly opposite directions. All events are measured in concidence along lines of response (LOR) and are stored dependant of their angle ϕ and distance from the centre of the scanner s in a data structure termed sinogram $p(s, \phi)$, so each sinogram value represents the line integral of tracer distribution with $f = \lambda(x, y, (z = fixed))$:

$$p(s, \phi) = \int f(s \cos \phi - t \sin \phi, s \sin \phi + t \cos \phi) \, dt \qquad (1)$$

$p(s, \phi)$ is the Radon transform of $\lambda(x, y, z)$ and calculating a PET image corresponds to inverting the transform [2, 12]. Figure 1 shows the geometric properties of the PET scanner together with a digital phantom and its Radon transform. A PET scanner can be operated in 3-D mode, then cross plane events are also detected and sensitivity but also scatter fraction is increased.

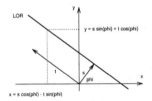
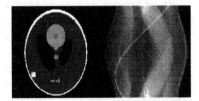

Fig. 1. Coordinate System of Scanner (left) and Digital Phantom with related Sinogram (right)

2 Parallel Image Reconstruction from Projections

Image reconstruction algorithms reflect the statistical understanding of the measurement process. The more comprehensive the theory of PET measurement statistics is understood, the more computationally intense the used algorithms become. Typically more sophisticated algorithms aren't used in clinical routine, not because physicists doubt the improved image quality, but because of the vast computation times on workstations.

2.1 A Taxonomy of Image Reconstruction Algorithms

2-D Algorithms Ignoring the measurement of noise leads to the classical *filtered backprojection* (FBP) algorithm. Reconstruction with FBP is done in two steps: Each projection $p(s, \phi)$ is convolved with a shift invariant kernel to emphasize small structures but reduce frequencies above a certain limit. Typically, a Hamming filter is used for PET reconstruction. Then the filtered projection value $p_F(s, \phi)$ is redistributed uniformly along the straight line (s, ϕ):

$$f_R(x, y) = \int_0^\pi p_F(x \cos \phi + y \sin \phi, \phi) \, d\phi \qquad (2)$$

This approach has several disadvantages: Due to the filtering step FBP yields negative values, particular if the data is noisy, although intensity is known to be non-negative. Also the method causes streak artifacts and high frequency noise is accentuated during the filtering step.

Iterative methods are based on the discrete nature of data and try to improve image quality step by step after starting with an estimate. It is possible to incorporate physical phenomena such as scatter or attenuation directly into the models. It is generally acknowledged that iterative methods yield better images in low count situations.

Shepp and Vardi presented an algorithm to *maximize the likelihood* of the reconstructed data (ML). The aim of this reconstruction algorithm is then to maximize a set of Poisson processes that give rise to the projection data. This algorithm yields images with a small signal to noise ratio without excessive smoothing. The crucial point is to define good stopping criterion, because the likelihood increases with each step unless it reaches the maximum. [7]

Other researchers claim that the data is not Poisson distributed due to a pre-correction done by the PET scanner. Fessler defines a *weighted least squares objective function* to describe the similarity of the forward projected iterated image compared to the measured data. A *penalty function* $\beta R(\lambda)$ is introduced to cope with noise:

$$\Phi(\lambda) = (\hat{y} - P\lambda)^T diag\{\sigma_i^{-2}\}(\hat{y} - P\lambda) + \beta R(\lambda) \qquad (3)$$

$\hat{y}$ is the precorrected sinogram, P the system matrix and λ a vector containing the annihilation rates. This equation is then minimized using conjugate gradient and coordinate descent algorithms. The iterated image doesn't change after some iterations because of the penalize function. The performance of a parallel PWLS algorithm is shown in the following chapters. [1, 2]

3-D Algorithms Operating the scanner in 3-D mode requires special reconstruction algorithms to take advantage of the increased sensitivity, due to the fact that LORs are not restricted to lie within transaxial planes.

The most common approach to reconstruct 3-D data is the *3-D reprojection algorithm* (3DRP) which is an extension of the filtered backprojection algorithm (FBP) to 3-D that estimates data not measured by the scanner.

A *rebinning algorithm* first sorts the 3-D data into ordinary two dimensional sinograms representing transaxial planes. These sinograms can then be reconstructed using e.g. FBP or PWLS. This approach is significantly faster because $O(n^2)$ oblique sinograms are reduced to $O(n)$ ordinary sinograms. Depending on the way cross ring decays are redistributed to ordinary sinograms there are various algorithms termed *single slice rebinning* (SSRB), *multislice rebinning* (MSRB) or Fourier rebinning (FORE).

2.2 Exploiting Data Parallelism

Functional decomposition of these algorithms can't be easily done due to their complex numerical and statistical nature. Some of them consist of complex libraries that change frequently so parallelizing routines inside such a library doesn't seem to be prudent. Building a data parallel program raises the question of granularity, possibilities are LORs, planes or frames[1]. Other partitioning schemes like assigning certain parts of sinograms to individual processors increase the complexity of algorithms. The easiest solution regarding the amount of interprocess communication needed and the complexity of algorithms, is setting granularity of a data parallel implementation to the plane level. This approach works for FBP, iterative algorithms and it can be used for rebinned 3-D data. The rest of this paper deals with an implementation of the PWLS algorithm, as described in the former section, which is a state of the art iterative algorithm.

2.3 Implementation

Data parallelism as described above was exploited. Single planes were assigned to processors in a round robin way. The first implementation was straightforward without queuing, sophisticated load balancing or fault tolerance. The implementation was based on PVM 3.3.7[11]. The time needed to reconstruct one plane was about 2-3 minutes depending on the image size and number of iterations[2] on a single CPU, provided that the workstation was equipped with sufficient memory to prevent the machine from paging. Common setup values for the slave processes are multicasted using pvm_mcast() to all slave processes, e.g. parameters to create the sparse system matrix P.

Memory requirements could be reduced for all involved workstations compared to the serial program. The master process doesn't setup the sparse system matrix, it only holds a stack of sinograms, whereas the slaves need to setup the system matrix but they only allocate memory for a single plane. The main memory chunks for a typical serial reconstruction process (with some 80 MB total) are sinogram data (23 %), the system matrix (76 %), other data and code area (1 %).

2.4 Performance Values

Performance measurements were done on cluster of 30 HP 9000/720 workstations running HP-UX release 9.01, interconnected via 10 MBit/s Ethernet, all machines where in the same IP subnet, every ten workstations were separated by an Ethernet bridge. Measured values in Fig. 2 are averaged over five runs[6].

---

[1] a set of planes acquired at one point of time during a dynamic study

[2] the number of iterations was fixed for all further tests

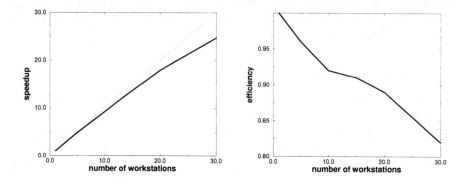

Fig. 2. Speedup and Efficiency on HP Cluster

Further tests were done on a SP/2 multicomputer with 70 RS6000 nodes, also using PVM 3.3.7 because PVMe[3] was too unstable at that time. One reconstruction process was started on each node. As we expected, total execution times of the application were very similar to the NOW, although the IBM high performance switch which connects the RS6000 nodes provides a raw bandwidth of 40 MByte/s and we measured a twelve times higher bandwidth on the SP/2 multicomputer (11 MByte/s) compared to a classical 10 MBit/s Ethernet (0.9 MByte/s) at the PVM application layer. The similar execution times arise from the compute boundness of the parallel algorithm.

3 Distributed Processing in a Clinical Environment

Speedup and efficiency values presesnted in the former sections show that a data parallel implementation is highly suitable for the reconstruction of functional images. Nevertheless there are more issues about using a cluster of workstations instead of a massively parallel computer. These isssues finally decide about the feasibility of parallel applications in clinical routine.

3.1 Batch Queuing

Most current medical software is written in a high level language such as MAT-LAB or IDL. Time critical parts are ported to C or FORTRAN normally and incorporated as dynamic shared objects. Such interpreted languages provide an easy way for scientists to do matrix computations and build a graphical user interface without worrying about the depths of X11. Often portable I/O functions for medical image formats like ECAT 6/7 or ANALYZE are only provided in

---

[3] A special performance tuned version of PVM

such a language. The usage of high level interpreted languages implies some major drawbacks. Besides the fact that they are (orders of magnitudes) slower than C or FORTRAN code, running such a program needs the interpreter of the language and using it is bound to a user license which may not be always available. This prevents the possibility of queuing MATLAB and IDL programs directly, but reimplementing these programs in C or C++ is normally too expensive.

Running the prototype we observed the described speedup but we also blocked all involved computers, thus a new strategy was needed. An interface to DQS was implemented in the program. DQS offers distributed queues using a central qmaster and dqs_execd daemons on every host. IDL is only used to setup the parameters for the reconstruction, to load sinogram data using CAPP[4] routines and to do some precomputations with the data. Once the IDL bound computations are complete, a module implemented in C writes all necessary data to disk, and then creates and submits a batch job to DQS using UNIX system call popen() to communicate with qsub. According to its configuration qmaster attaches the reconstruction process to an appropriate queue at a workstation that doesn't exceed a predefined load threshold. Running the application can now be scheduled to any particular time, e.g. non office hours.

3.2 Load Balancing

As the speedup graph in Fig. 2 shows, load balancing isn't really necessary for performance issues on an empty NOW. However routine clinical computers are used interactively and for batch processing in a more or less arbitrary way during the day and to a lesser extend also during the night and weekends [10]. Using a workstation to reconstruct PET images with PWLS makes their interactive usage very unpleasant because of long response times due to the computation intensive application. We evaluated the benefits of system oriented load balancing and checkpointing but implemented an application oriented adaptive load balancing mechanism because of several reasons[4, 9]:

- A key issue was to gain the users acceptance by releasing used machines as quick as possible. Writing checkpoints and the migration of processes means saving the process context to disk. The required time for this grows linearly with the size of the process context and would need more than one minute in our case[8, 5].
- Saving process context and migrating processes must be done when a load peak occurs, but writing to disk via NFS increases the load even further.
- The time needed to reconstruct one plane is only several minutes and only one plane is assigned to each workstation. Killing the process can be done immediately and reconstructing this plane later will take less time than migrating the process

---

[4] CAPP (Clinical Application Programming Package) is an extension to IDL for medical purposes providing e.g. I/O routines for ECAT data

94

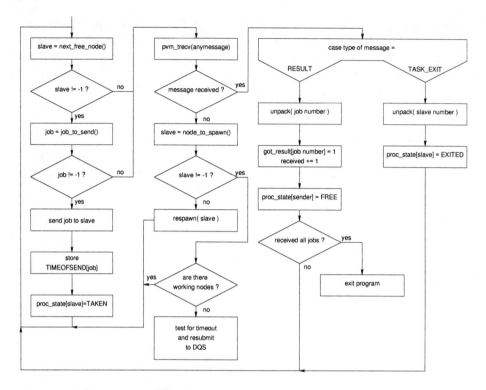

Fig. 3. master process flow chart

After setting up the parallel virtual machine the master process checks for the next free node. It keeps a list with the status of each node (FREE, TAKEN or EXITED). The sinograms are sent in the following order: first all sinograms which were never sent before, then it resends the oldest ones without answer from the remote process, but only if they are older than a heuristic threshold depending on the number of iterations. This is done to avoid resending sinogram data, although a slow node has almost finished the reconstruction or waiting infinitely for a reconstructed image. Figure 3 shows a more detailed flow chart of the master process.

Load monitoring We identified two crucial parameters as useful load indices for our environment of SGI workstations. These parameters are monitored by the loadw process.

– Our major goal was to preserve the "Ownership of Workstations" therefore observing *interactive usage* had to be done with loadw. We neglected mouse and keyboard events of the X server, because the strict security policies don't allow users in a clinical department to have access to other users display. The load monitoring process was optimized for this application and it was a design goal to run `loadw` without root privileges. Therefore, we looked at the idle times of the user terminals. Scanning through `/etc/utmp` gives information about logged in users, user processes marked with `USER_PROCESS` and their open terminals which are found as entries in `/proc`. Modification time of the terminal entries equals the last keyboard event which is compared to the system time.

– To avoid disturbing other programs running on a particular machine without user interaction we looked at *CPU usage* as another load index. Each process has an entry in `/proc` with its process id (PID) and users are only allowed to read entries belonging to their own processes for security reasons. However under IRIX there is a second source of information readable for everyone: `/proc/pinfo`[5]. It provides `loadw` with the name of the program being executed by the process and a `pr_cpu` termed value representing the recent CPU usage - a value which is normally used by the kernel for scheduling. `pr_cpu` is incremented each time the system clock ticks and the process is found to be executing. Every second `pr_cpu` is adjusted by a digital decay filter. This causes 90% of the CPU usage accumulated in a one second interval to be forgotten over a period of time that is dependent on the system load average [3]. Heuristics have shown that `pr_cpu` is smaller than 80 for single process being permanently on the run queue, `pr_cpu` is between 30 and 40 for two processes simultaneously on the run queue and `pr_cpu` is less then ten for system processes which are mostly idle.

`loadw` is operating in two different modes which could be described by an deterministic finite automata with the two states `PET_ALIVE` and `PET_DIED`. In state `PET_ALIVE` it tries to determine whether to stop the reconstruction process because load exceeds the threshold or a keyboard event was registered. Whereas it responds to `SPAWN_REQUEST` from the master process in the `PET_DIED` state, then it acknowledges or denies to restart a reconstruction process depending on the load and time since the last keyboard event.

4 Conclusions

In this paper we presesented a way to implement parallel reconstruction algorithms on a network of workstations. Performance measurements have shown high efficiency and almost linear speedup. Our parallel implementation reduces the vast CPU times and memory requirements, so even very sophisticated algorithms such as PWLS, which provide much better image quality in low count situations, can be used now in daily routine. Figure 4 shows the improved image quality of parallel PWLS over classical FBP in a breast cancer study. The image, which was reconstructed with parallel PWLS, shows less streak artifacts and a better delineation of contours, therefore tumours can be detected easier.

We have shown that parallelizing the program is not sufficient. The successful integration of a parallel program into clinical routine is more complex. We

---

[5] the name may differ on other OS

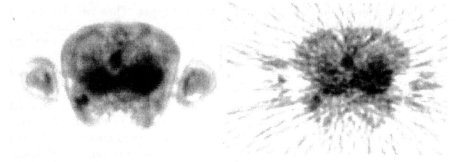

Fig. 4. Image comparison: improved quality with parallel PWLS (left) and classical method FBP (right). Images show F-18 FDG (glucose analogue) distribution in a patient with breast cancer

adressed load balancing and batch queuing to build an application that uses the combined power of all possible workstations in the department whenever they are available without disturbing interactively working users. Our approach, which can be easily adopted by other institutes, hides the concurrency of the program from the user and all the processing is done in the background.

Acknowledgement

We would like to thank Robert Schaller for reading the manuscript, Steffi Becker for reconstructing the images used as an example, Daniel Schad for inspiring discussions and the anonymous reviewers for their valuable comments. This work is part of an ongoing collaboration between the Lehrstuhl für Rechnertechnik und Rechnerorganisation (LRR-TUM) and the Klinik und Poliklinik für Nuklearmedizin rechts der Isar. This Study was partly supported by the Deutsche Forschungsgemeinschaft (SFB 462, Sensomotorik).

References

1. FESSLER, J. A. ASPIRE 3.0 users guide. Tech. rep., University of Michigan, 1995.
2. FESSLER, J. A. Positron Emission Tomography. *IEEE Signal Processing Magazine*, 1 (January 1997), 43–55.
3. LEFFLER, S., MCKUSICK, K., KARELS, M., AND QUARTERMAN, J. *The Design and Implementation of the 4.3 BSD UNIX Operating System*. Addison-Wesley, Mai 1989.
4. MAIER, U., AND STELLNER, G. Distributed Resource Management for Parallel Applications in Networks of Workstations. In *HPCN Europe 1997* (1997), vol. 1225 of *Lecture Notes in Computer Science*, Springer-Verlag, pp. 462–471.
5. MAIER, U., STELLNER, G., AND ZORAJA, I. Batch Queuing and Resource Management for PVM Applications in a Network of Workstations. In *ARCS'97: Architektur von Rechensystemen 1997* (1997), Universität Rostock, pp. 179–188.

6. MUNZ, F. Parallele Rekonstruktion von PET Volumendaten. Diplomarbeit, Institut für Informatik, Technische Universität München, September 1995.

7. SHEPP, L., AND VARDI, Y. Maximum Likelihood Reconstruction for Emission Tomography. *IEEE Transaction on Medical Imaging* (1982).

8. STELLNER, G. *Methoden zur Sicherungspunkterzeugung in parallelen und verteilten Systemen.* Dissertation, Institut für Informatik, Technische Universität München, Juni 1996.

9. STELLNER, G., AND PRUYNE, J. Resource Management and Checkpointing for PVM. In *Proceedings of the 2nd European PVM Users' Group Meeting* (Lyon, Sept. 1995), Editions Hermes, pp. 131–136.

10. STEPHAN, T. Erweiterung eines parallelen Rekonstruktionsprogramms von PET Volumendaten um Komponenten zur Stapelverarbeitung und Lastverwaltung. Diplomarbeit, Institut für Informatik, Technische Universität München, Mai 1997.

11. SUNDERAM, V. S., GEIST, G. A., DONGARRA, J., AND MANCHEK, R. The PVM Concurrent Computing System: Evolution, Experiences, and Trends. *Parallel Computing, Vol. 20 (4)* (1993).

12. TOWNSEND, D. W., AND DEFRISE, M. Image Reconstruction Methods in Positron Tomography. Tech. rep., CERN European Organization for Nuclear Research, 1993.

AutoMap and AutoLink

Tools for Communicating Complex and Dynamic Data-Structures Using MPI

Delphine Stéphanie Goujon[14], Martial Michel[24], Jasper Peeters[3], and Judith Ellen Devaney[4]

[1] Télécom INT [‡], France
[2] RÉSÉDAS [§], France
[3] University of Twente [¶], Netherland
[4] NIST [‖], USA
National Institute of Standards and Technology
Web page : http://www.itl.nist.gov/div895/sasg/
AutoMap & AutoLink Project Leader : Judith Ellen Devaney
AutoMap & AutoLink Project Contact : martial.michel@nist.gov

Abstract. This article describes two software tools, AutoMap and AutoLink, that facilitate the use of data-structures in MPI. AutoMap is a program that parses a file of user-defined data-structures and generates new MPI types out of basic and previously defined MPI data-types. Our software tool automatically handles specialized error checking related to memory mapping. AutoLink is an MPI library that allows the transfer of complex, dynamically linked, and possibly heterogeneous structures through MPI. AutoLink uses files generated by AutoMap to automatically define the needed MPI data-types. We describe each of these tools, and give an example of their use. Finally we discuss the internals of AutoLink design, and focus on the performance rationale behind them.

1 Introduction

Many applications, business and scientific, require intensive and complex processing of data along with computing power. Yet moving these applications to parallel computers has been hindered so far by programming difficulties. The Message Passing Interface standard (MPI) [1] makes development of message passing programs easier through its portability and interface with common high level languages.

[‡] http://www.int-evry.fr/

[§] http://www.loria.fr/equipes/resedas/

[¶] http://www.utwnte.nl/

[‖] Disclaimer: certain commercial products may be identified in order to adequately specify or describe the subject matter of this work. In no case does such identification imply recommendation or endorsement by the National Institute of Standards and Technology, nor does it imply that the products identified are necessarily the best available for the purpose.

However, the MPI standard functions support complex data-types only indirectly. Users may create new MPI data-types out of basic data-types for use with MPI functions, but the process is tedious. Hence it is desirable to have a high level tool that automates the creation of MPI data-types from user-defined data-structures. Likewise, it is useful to simplify the sending and receiving of dynamically linked structures, by having the details handled by a library.

With these tools, compute intensive, data-structure rich application domains are easier to manage in parallel programs. These application domains include speech recognition, data mining, genetic programming, and complex modeling.

The remainder of the paper is organized as follows. In section 2, we present AutoMap, and explain complex and dynamic data-types. We show how to create an MPI data-type from a user defined type, and how AutoMap does it automatically. In section 3, we explain how AutoLink enables sending and receiving dynamically linked data-structures. Performance considerations are discussed in section 4.

2 AutoMap : Generating New MPI Types Out of Data-Structures

2.1 Data-Types

The MPI library can only transfer types that it knows about. The C implementation of MPI knows about the basic types in C. There are basic data-types such as `int`, `char`, `long` and `double` for which an MPI type exists, like `MPI_INT`, `MPI_CHAR`, `MPI_LONG` and `MPI_DOUBLE`. MPI functions can transmit basic C data-types. The MPI standard permits the creation of user defined MPI data-types. But creating an MPI data-type is complicated.

Complex data-types (i.e. struct) can only be sent and received if they are described to the MPI library. AutoMap performs this service for the programmer.

Complex Data-Type. Users may want to use a composition of basic data-types. In C, such a composition may be created using the `struct` operand. A complex data-type is such a user-defined structure, as long as the user doesn't use pointers to other structures or components inside the structure.

So, an example of a complex data-structure may be :

```
struct {
    char     display[50];
    int      maxiter;
    double   xmin, ymin;
    double   xmax, ymax;
    int      width;
    int      height;
} cmdline;
```

Dynamic Data-Type. Dynamic data-types are an extension of complex data-types. Dynamic data-types can handle structures containing pointer fields. Examples of such data-structures [2] are *linked lists, trees,* and *graphs*.

It is possible to send such structures with MPI but the pointer memory references will be invalid on the receiving processor. So the transfer of such data-structures is an operation left entirely to the user, and resolved by the use of the library AutoLink.

2.2 An Example of Complex Data-Type Creation with MPI

Here is an example showing how to create a complex data-type using MPI. Understanding these steps will make the design and use of AutoMap clearer.

Initial C Structure. The C structure used here is the one described in section 2.1. It contains 50 chars, 3 integers (1 and then 2 more), and 4 doubles.

Creation of the MPI Data-Type. The process of creating an MPI data-type involves specifying the layout in memory of the data in the C structure [3]. It is done in six operations :

1. Set up an array defining the number of data of each kind that will be used (in the same order as the structure definition).

   ```
   int           blockcounts[4] = {50,1,4,2};
   ```

   Which corresponds to : 50 char, 1 int, 4 double, 2 int,
2. Set up an array that will contain the type specification for each element contained in the structure. There are four fields in the struct, thus :

   ```
   MPI_Datatype types[4];
   ```

   Even if there are only 3 different data-types, one has to follow the struct type order, meaning char, int, double, int.
   Set the data-type for each element of the data-type to be created :

   ```
   types[0] = MPI_CHAR;
   types[1] = MPI_INT;
   types[2] = MPI_DOUBLE;
   types[3] = MPI_INT;
   ```

3. Set up an internal displacement array containing the memory offset of each field in the struct,

   ```
   MPI_Aint     displs[4];
   ```

   Map onto the displacement array, the MPI data-type on the C structure (by linking it to the very first memory element).

```
MPI_Address(&cmdline.display, &displs[0]);
MPI_Address(&cmdline.maxiter, &displs[1]);
MPI_Address(&cmdline.xmin,    &displs[2]);
MPI_Address(&cmdline.width,   &displs[3]);
```

Adjust the displacement array so that the displacements are offsets from the beginning of the structure.

```
for (i=3; i>=0; i--)
    displs[i] -= displs[0];
```

4. Give a name to the MPI data-type.

```
MPI_Datatype cmdtype;
```

5. Build the new MPI type. Set the container of the MPI data-type .

```
MPI_Type_struct(4, blockcounts, displs, types,
                &cmdtype);
```

6. Validate the type existence to be used with MPI.

```
MPI_Type_commit( &cmdtype );
```

2.3 Developed Software

AutoMap is a source-to-source compiler that automatically translates C structures into MPI data-types. To be more specific, AutoMap works as a lexer and a parser to translate C data-structures into MPI data-structures.

AutoMap was initially designed for sending and receiving complex data-types. Then it was extended to dynamic data-structures [4].

Currently two versions of AutoMap are available : a stand-alone version which operates only on complex data-types and a version coupled with AutoLink which is designed for dynamically linked data-structures.

AutoMap Process. The AutoMap compiler implements a grammar, which reads C structures into an input file and outputs the corresponding MPI data-types. The compiler generator used here is Yacc++ [5].The parsing of the input file is done by generating an Abstract Syntax Tree (AST) that is used in the type recognition process.

In the case of the stand alone version, AutoMap generates only the file containing the MPI data-types from the C structures mpitypes.c. When used with AutoLink, two other files are generated:

- logbook.txt is a log file,
- al_routines.c contains all the functions used internally by AutoLink.

MPI Data-Type Issues. In the case of structures, there are possible interactions between MPI and the compiler [1]. These interactions can affect the way a compiler does padding between one structure and the next.

When sending more than one structure, this can be an issue. There are two possible ways to deal with this. One way is to assume default padding and to create the structure type maps based on it. The other way is to explicitly include the upper bound of the structure with MPI_UB.

It is useful to assume the default case, but have a test that would indicate if things did not match up. The test case could create both data-types, with and without MPI_UB, get their extents, and compare. The current version of AutoMap implements the default, but a future version will provide both options, with a test to ensure correctness if the default is not used.

2.4 Integrated Use of AutoMap

Overview. Whatever version of AutoMap the programmer uses, one will have to run AutoMap on a file that contains its data-structures (struct.h for example). In the stand alone version, the generated file containing the MPI data-types (mpitypes.c) is directly included in the user program (UserProg.c for example). When AutoMap is coupled with the AutoLink library, its output files (mpitypes.c and al_routines.c) are included in the AutoLink source file autolink.c. When writing code, the programmer includes autolink.c.

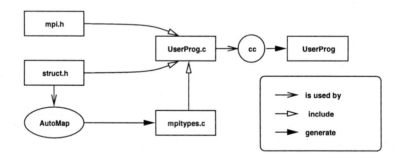

Fig. 1. AutoMap generation of files, Stand Alone version

Figures 1 and 2 illustrate AutoMap in stand alone version and coupled with AutoLink.

Preparing the User-Defined File. The user must modify the source file before running AutoMap. AutoMap recognizes the structures to be converted to MPI types by directives in the C code. In order to read a user's code directly,

---

[1] The authors acknowledge the work of Raja Daoud on this section.

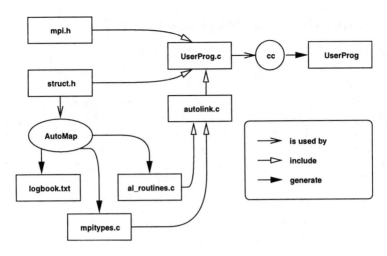

Fig. 2. AutoMap generation of files, AutoLink version

the directives were designed as modified C comments. The modification consists of a '~' just after the usual beginning of a comment "/*". Additionally, this is followed by an `AutoMap_Begin` for the start directive or an `AutoMap_End` for the end directive. Thus a structure is surrounded by :

```
/*~ AutoMap_Begin */
```

```
/*~ AutoMap_End */
```

and the data-type to be 'AutoMap recognized' by :

```
/*~ AutoMap_TpUsed */
```

Here is an example of file **struct.h** defining the data-structure(e.g. a linked list) after modification by the user :

```
/*~ AutoMap_Begin */

#define SIZE 1000

typedef struct LList *LL;
typedef struct LList
{
  float   data[SIZE];
  LL      next;
} LinkedList /*~ AutoMap_TpUsed */;

/*~ AutoMap_End */
```

2.5 Practical Use of AutoMap in the User Code

Stand Alone Version. In the stand alone version, the user will send complex data-types almost in the same way as standard MPI data-types. First, at the beginning of the main program, the user will have to initialize the new MPI data-types by calling the function `Build_MPI_Types()` defined in the generated file `mpitypes.c`. The actual name of each generated MPI data-type is made up of the initial name as written in the `struct.h` file, to which the prefix `AutoMap_` is added. For instance, for the complex data-structure `cmdline` described in section 2.1, the MPI data-type name would be `AutoMap_cmdline`. Then one will use the MPI data-type name in the usual MPI communication function calls. In our example, to send one variable `var` whose type is `cmdline` :

```
MPI_Send(&var,1,AutoMap_cmdline,next_rank,
        MPI_ANY_TAG,MPI_COMM_WORLD);
```

AutoMap Coupled with AutoLink. When AutoMap is coupled with Au-toLink, users will call AutoLink routines to send or receive their dynamic data-structures.

AutoLink's routines consists of two pairs of functions: one for initializ-ing/finalizing AutoLink, one for communicating.

- `AL_Init()` initializes MPI layer, loads the newly created MPI data-types and allocates memory for AutoLink internal structures.
- `AL_Finalize()` finalizes MPI layer and de-allocates memory for AutoLink internal structures.
- `AL_Send()` takes care of the traversing and sending of the dynamic data-structure.
- `AL_Recv()` takes care of the receiving and restoring of the dynamic data-structure.

3 AutoLink : Handling Dynamic Data-Structures

3.1 General Overview of AutoLink

AutoLink is a library that allows the sending and receiving of dynamically linked structures through MPI (a case not handled by 'AutoMap stand alone' version).

In a previous version of AutoLink we had chosen to buffer the whole data-structure before sending or receiving. This was too memory intensive in the case of large dynamic data-structures. On the other hand, sending data without any buffering saves memory but will induce large communication time latency. We choose to send packets of data, which is a good trade-off between memory use and communication time. Additionally, the packet size is configurable.

Furthermore, we manage to overlap communication (sending or receiving of packets) with computation (traversing the data-structure or allocating memory for the data received).

Packet Transmission. From a communication point of view, the general algorithm consists of sending (resp. receiving) the content of the data packet by packet and then the information describing how the data are linked.

- In the sending processor, simultaneously to the traversal of the dynamic data-structure, packets are sent when the packet buffer is full. When the traversal of the data-structure is finished, the information about the links between the data is sent.
- In the receiving processor, as packets arrive, memory space is allocated and the data are copied into memory. When data transmission is over, the data-structure link information is received and the dynamic links restored.

3.2 Storage Structures for Handling the Link Information

Refer to figure 3 for understanding the structures mentioned hereafter.

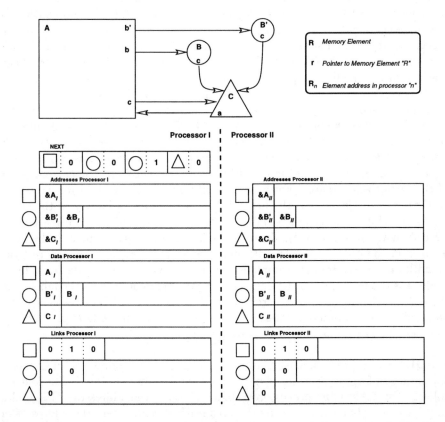

Fig. 3. AutoLink transfer concept. Each shape represents a different type of node. Here there are three types; square, circle, and triangle.

The dynamic pointer structure based on addresses is no longer valid on a remote processor. Therefore a logical representation of the dynamic structure is sent to the remote processor (LINKS array). The logical representation is based on labeling each node of the dynamic structure with a number. Actually there is one labeling per node type. The links between nodes are then represented by labels (integers) instead of pointers. For each node, the label of its children will be stored in the LINKS array.

The role of the traversal function is to construct the array of links sent to the remote processor; on the receiving end, the physical links will be rebuilt from the logical label representation. An iterative breadth-first search is used for traversing the data-structure.

Here are the storage structures used by AutoLink to build the equivalence between the physical and logical representation of the dynamic structure.

NEXT array is useful for the traversing stage. The NEXT array stores the next elements to be visited in the breadth-first search. At each step of the breadth-first search, the children of the current node are stored in NEXT array if they were not marked. In our example (figure 3), in the first step of the breadth-first search, . The children of node A, which are nodes B, B' and C are stored in NEXT. In the second step of the search, node B' is the current node and node C is the child of node B'. Node C won't be stored because it has already been marked during the first step of the search and so forth. Each element of NEXT array is composed of one integer for the data-type (i) and one integer for the label (j). Based on these two indexes, one accesses directly the addresses of a node contained at the position (i, j) in the ADDRESS array. In figure 3, integers representing data-types have been drawn as geometrical shapes. Data-type 0 is represented as a square, data-type 1 as a circle and data-type 2 as a triangle.

Labels are given during the breadth-first search. Let N be the current point of the breadth-first search. For each child of node N, if the child (of data-type i) has not been visited yet, the breadth-first search gives a label j to the child, stores the child data-type and label in NEXT array, and its address in ADDRESS at the position (i, j). There is one labeling per data-type and the label is given in the order of the breadth-first search. For instance, the order of the breadth-first search in our example is : node A, then node B', node B, node C. Node A is the first node of the data-type square, therefore it gets the label 0. In the order of the breadth-first search, node B' is the first node of data-type circle and node B the second one. Thus node B' gets label 0 and node B gets label 1. Node C gets label 0 as first node of data-type triangle.

ADDRESS is a two-dimensional array that stores the address of an element. The address of the jth element of data-type i will be stored in the ith line and j^{th} column. On the sending processor, ADDRESS stores the addresses of the nodes that have already been visited by the breadth-first search, and the addresses of the children of the current node. These addresses are useful for accessing the next node in the next step of the search. On the receiving processor, the ADDRESS array is used to store the address of the newly allocated nodes. These addresses are useful to restore the links.

LINKS is a two-dimensional array that carries the logical representation of the dynamic data-structure. Coupled with ADDRESS, LINKS enables the reconstruction of the data-structure. Each line of LINKS corresponds to one data-type and is decomposed into slots containing as many integers as there are pointers for a given data-type. These slots store the labels given to the children of each node of that data-type.

From AutoMap, AutoLink knows the number of pointers for a given data-type –thus the size of the slot– and their types. For instance, the data-type square contains three pointers : the first two pointers are pointers to data-type circle and the third one points to triangle data-type. Since the nodes of the same data-type are stored together in the same line of LINKS, the reading of a line is completed by a step equal to the size of the slot for this data-type. That way, AutoLink knows the data-type of the element e whose label is currently read. For instance, in figure 3, AutoLink knows that the data-type of the element corresponding to the value read in the second position of the first line of array LINKS is a circle. The value is the label of the element (here the value is 1). Therefore the element that is actually referred to is node B. With the label value, AutoLink knows how to fetch element e. AutoLink reads the address of element e in ADDRESS in the line corresponding to the data-type of element e and in the column given by the label. In our example, it reads the address of node B in the second line, second column of ADDRESS.

TAG or MARK : the library needs a tag (also called mark) to know if an object has already been traversed during the breadth first search. A hash table implements the tag.

3.3 Algorithms

Sending Dynamic Data-Types. Follows a high level algorithm;

```
|Add entry node in NEXT
|Add address of entry node in ADDRESS
|Mark entry node
|While there are elements to visit in NEXT
|  |Reach current node in NEXT
|  |Add node data to PACKET
|  |If PACKET is full, send PACKET
|  |For all children of current node
|  |  |If child does not exist
|  |  |Then Add NO CHILD in LINKS
|  |  |Else |If child has not been marked
|  |  |     |Then |Add child in NEXT
|  |  |     |     |Add address of child in ADDRESS
|  |  |     |     |Mark child node
|  |  |     |     |Add child label in LINKS
```

```
|  |  |      |Else Add child label in LINKS
|  |Go to next in NEXT
|Send last PACKET
|Send LINKS
|Send references of Initial Object
```

Receiving Dynamic Data-Types. High level algorithm for receiving;

```
|While more PACKET to receive
|  |Receive PACKET
|  |For each element in PACKET
|  |  |Create element in memory
|  |  |Add address of created element in ADDRESS
|Receive LINKS
|Receive references of Initial Object
|For each element of LINKS
|  |If value of LINKS is NO CHILD
|  |Then child referred by LINKS refers to no element
|  |Else child refers to correct element in ADDRESS
|Result is Initial Object with recreated links
```

4 Performances Study

There are no performance results yet. Data will be available from the NIST Scientific Applications Support Project Web page (http://www.itl.nist.gov/div895/sasg/). The following explains how the design ideas are optimized.

4.1 Memory Performance

Use of a Link Buffer. Because AutoLink was written in C, the memory overhead generated by AutoLink could be decreased by getting rid of LINKS. Currently, a node is copied into the data buffer with its actual data-type made up of data and pointers. MPI data-types generated by AutoMap out of the actual data-types are used as a parameter in the sending and receiving process, so that in the receiving end the data-type of the structures reallocated correspond to the MPI data-types received.

Since C allows to cast a pointer into an integer, the idea would be to use the space occupied by the pointers in the data for storing the link information as integers. The pointer values would be used as labels. One would force C pointers to be recognized by MPI as MPI_UNSIGNED_LONG. Yet this cast is not allowed in strong typing languages. That's why we have chosen to keep the method as general as possible.

Tag. A tag is simulated by the use of a Hash Table to avoid having the user add one field to their data-structures. A tag included in the user structure would have been memory consuming, since it is used only once.

The pure Hash Table performance is mostly determined by its H-function, and even more by its size, which is configurable.

Use of Packets. The sending process employs packets to utilize memory more efficiently. The size of the packets is configurable.

4.2 Time Performance

Non Recursive Traversal. The Algorithm developed to improve the traversal part is based on an Iterative Breadth First Search Algorithm.

Overlap Communication & Computation. Non blocking communication is used for the sending, so that the traversal of the dynamic data-structure can be carried out while MPI handles the sending of packets.

5 Conclusion

AutoMap and AutoLink are user-friendly tools that make the development of MPI-based applications easier. AutoMap dramatically simplifies the creation of MPI data-types. It simply needs to read the user-defined C data-structure and therefore minimizes the intervention from the user. AutoLink handles the transfer of these data-types in a straightforward way.

AutoMap and AutoLink are flexible and portable tools that can run on any MPI-enabled platform. By removing the bothersome complexity of MPI programming from the user, these tools enable the design of more complex applications.

References

1. Message Passing Interface Forum, http://www.mpi-forum.org/docs/docs.html
2. Aaron M. Tenenbaum, Yedidyah Langsam and Moshe J. Augenstein : Data Structures Using C. Prentice Hall (1990)
3. William Gropp, Ewing Lusk and Anthony Skjellum : Using MPI: Portable Parallel Programming with the Message-Passing Interface. The MIT Press, Cambridge, MA (1994)
4. K. H. J. Vrielink, E. C. Baland and J. E. Devaney : AutoLink: An MPI Library for Sending and Receiving Dynamic Data Structures. International Conference on Parallel Computing, University of Minnesota Supercomputer Institute (October 3-4 1996)
5. Yacc++ and the Language Objects Library Reference Guide. Compiler Resources, Hopkinton, MA (1996)

Analysis of a Programmed Backoff Method for Parallel Processing on Ethernets

Norman Matloff

Department of Computer Science
University of California at Davis
Davis, CA 95616
matloff@cs.ucdavis.edu

Abstract. In many parallel processing applications, task times have relatively little variability. Accordingly, many nodes will complete a task at approximately the same time. If the application is run on an Ethernet, the near-simultaneity of the task completion times implies that when the tasks attempt to communicate with some central task manager, they will bump into each other. This in turn can cause a major slowdown in communication, as the Ethernet hardware generates unnecessarily long backoff times. The work here will analyze a solution to this problem.

1 Introduction

On an Ethernet,[1] if during a transmission one or more nodes produce frames to send and test the line, they then attempt to send as soon as the current transmission ends. If more than one node is involved, the nodes collide, generate a random backoff time, and then try sending again.

Now suppose we have a parallel processing application running on a homogeneous set of workstations connected by an Ethernet, and consider task rendezvous frames sent on it. For example, in a message-passing paradigm, we might have root-finding program [2]. Here, a function is known to have a single root in a given interval, which the program finds (to the desired level of accuracy) in a parallel iterative procedure.[2] In any given iteration, the current interval to be searched is divided into n subintervals, where n is the total number of machines. Each "worker" node inspects its assigned subinterval, and then reports to a "manager" node whether the given function has a sign change in that subinterval. Only one of these subintervals will experience such a change, and it will then become the new interval. The manager will broadcast the values of the endpoints of the new interval to the workers, so that they can divide it

---

[1] The material here will also apply to other carrier sense multiple access/collision detect (CSMA/CD) local area networks, but for simplicity we concentrate here on Ethernets.

[2] We assume here that the evaluation of the function is lengthy enough to make a parallel search worthwhile. For instance, the function may itself be evaluated through a time-consuming numerical solution of a differential equation.

into new subintervals, and so on. Under a shared memory paradigm (in this case distributed shared memory), barrier operations would produce a similar pattern.

A problem which arises here is that in many applications task times (including communication delays) have small degrees of variability [1]. For instance, in the root-finding example above, the function-evaluation times should be fairly uniform. As another example, the mean run time for a Heapsort of r items is $O(r \log r)$, while the standard deviation is only $O(\sqrt{r})$ [5]; the larger the problem, the smaller the standard deviation is relative to the mean.

In applications in which the tasks at several nodes finish approximately simultaneously, the task rendezvous operations will cause collisions on the Ethernet. The random backoffs which result will then slow down the application. In this context the random backoffs produced by the Ethernet hardware are typically much longer than need be. In [4], an approach to solving this problem was proposed, called *programmed backoff*. Suppose n nodes are currently processing tasks, with the task at node k completing at time T_k. At that time, the software running at node k will produce its own backoff, delaying $k\delta$ time before sending its rendezvous frame to the manager node. The goal is that by having the software produce a small, deterministic backoff we can avoid unnecessarily long backoff times produced by the Ethernet hardware.

Under the programmed backoff procedure, collisions are still possible. At that point, the Ethernet hardware will take over anyway. But hopefully this will be a relatively rare event.

In the work here, we present some theoretical models of the effectiveness of programmed backoff. We are particularly interested in the effects of varying the internode backoff spacing δ, for different task distributions.

2 Investigation

2.1 Analytical

Let f denote the probability density function of each T_k. As our first measure of the effectiveness of programmed backoff, let us determine the expected number of first-round collisions. To this end, let 1_{ij} equal 1 if node i and j collide in the first round, 0 otherwise. Then the total number of first-round collisions is

$$N = \sum_{i}^{n} \sum_{j>i}^{n} 1_{ij}$$

Let τ denote the time to transmit a task rendezvous frame. This typically will be much smaller than task times, since the frame will usually contain very little data (such as a 0-1 variable in the root-finding example, indicating whether this node's subinterval produces a sign change for the function). Let U_k denote the actual time at which transmission begins for node k, i.e.

$$U_k = T_k + k\delta$$

and assume the U_k (equivalently, the T_k) to be independent. Then

$$E(N) = \sum_{i}^{n} \sum_{j \neq i}^{n} P(|U_i - U_j| < \tau) \tag{1}$$

where

$$P(|U_i - U_j| < \tau) = \int \int_{|s-t|<\tau} f(s)f(t - \delta(j - i))dsdt \tag{2}$$

Equation (1) suggests that E(N) is $O(n^2)$ in magnitude. This suggests that the benefits of programmed backoff grow rapidly with the system size n, speculation which will be confirmed below.

We can get a lower bound on the quantity in (2) as follows.

Lemma: Suppose X and Y are continuous[3] independent random variables with the same variance γ^2 and with EY = EX + d. Then

$$P(|X - Y| > b) \leq \frac{2\gamma^2 + d^2}{b^2} \tag{3}$$

Proof: First define Z to be X - (Y - d), and thus write $E[(X - Y)^2]$ as $E[(Z - d)^2]$. Then the latter quantity will be equal to $2\gamma^2 + d^2$, since Z will have mean 0 and variance $2\gamma^2$. Then letting g denote the density of X-Y, we have

$$2\gamma^2 + d^2 = E[(X - Y)^2] \geq \int_{|u|>b} u^2 g(u)du \geq b^2 P(|X - Y| > b),$$

yielding the result.

Now taking X and Y to be U_i and U_j, respectively, we have that

$$P(|U_i - U_j| < \tau) \geq 1 - \frac{2\sigma^2 + (j - i)^2 \delta^2}{\tau^2}$$

where σ^2 is the variance associated with the density f.

2.2 Simulation

At this point we turn to simulation. Taking as our criterion the expected time η until all n nodes have successfully transmitted a message, our interest will center on the following questions:

- How much of an improvement can programmed backoff bring over simply letting the Ethernet hardware manage transmission?
- With all other factors fixed, how does the optimal value of δ vary with the system size n?

---

[3] Actually, this condition is could be dropped.

– Let c be a *scale parameter* for a family of density functions for the task times. That is

$$f(t) = \frac{1}{c}h[c(t-q)]$$

for some function h and some constant q. As c increases, we get densities which have similar shapes but are more disperse, and σ will be proportional to c.

It is of interest to investigate how the optimal value of δ varies as c increases.

In the simulations the task time distribution was first taken to be the uniform density U(1-c,1+c). Thus we have a family of distributions centered around a mean of 1.0, with c playing the role of a scale parameter as described above.

Frame transmission time, τ, was assumed to be considerably smaller than 1.0, the mean task time. Specifically, in all the simulations presented here, τ was taken to be 0.1. This is a practical assumption, since otherwise the communication overhead (even without collisions) would be too high for effective speedup due to parallelism. Note also that in many applications of the type we have discussed here, the task rendezvous message is very short. For example, in the root-finding application cited earlier, the message information consists merely of 1 or 0, indicated whether or not a sign change was found in the node's assigned subinterval. (However, the minimum length of an Ethernet frame is 64 bytes [6].) Ethernet hardware backoff was modeled according to the usual binary exponential scheme [6].

Intuitively the quantity (2) will typically be a decreasing function of δ. On the other hand, as δ increases we are adding more delay "at the front end," adding an increasing component to η. Thus we might expect that the graph of η as a function of δ is roughly U-shaped, and this will be seen to be the case.

We begin with a simulation for a small value of c, 0.1, presented in Figure 1 for system sizes 32, 64 and 128. Here we have the near-simulataneity in task time completion which formed the fundamental motivation for our work, so it is not surprising that programmed backoff is shown to be capable of strong speedups in the task rendezvous process, of sizes 292%, 439% and 619% respectively. Note too that the larger the system, the greater the benefit obtainable from programmed backoff.

The optimal value of δ is seen to be relatively constant as a function of n (though showing a slight decreasing trend). The near-constancy makes some sense when viewed in the following context: If the task times were completely constant, the optimal value of δ would be τ; this value would result in a schedule under which the (i+1)st node started transmitting immediately after th i-th.

This reasoning would not apply to the case c = 0.8, shown in Figure 2. Here there is much more variation in task times, and accordingly the speedups in this case, are somewhat more moderate: 158%, 324% and 507%. Yet it is interesting to find that the optimal values of δ are similar to those in the previous case.

As noted above, if the task times were completely constant, the optimal value of δ would be τ. Thus we would expect the optimal δ to be just slightly more than

τ in settings with nearly-constant task times. Preliminary simulations conducted by the author for values of τ smaller than 0.1 (not included here) seem to confirm this. Moreover, typically the user can find the value of τ *a priori*, since it is a known function of Ethernet parameters and the user's message length.

However, even with c = 0.8 the task-time distribution has a fairly small standard deviation, so next we turned to the family of exponential distributions, with the parameter c being the mean of the distribution.[4] Figures 3 and 4 correspond to c = 0.1 and c = 0.8, respectively. The results are similar to those of Figures 1 and 2. However, the results for c = 10.0, shown in Figure 5, are quite different. Here task times have enough variation that programmed backoff simply produces superfluous delay over what is needed to avoid backoffs produced by the Ethernet cards.

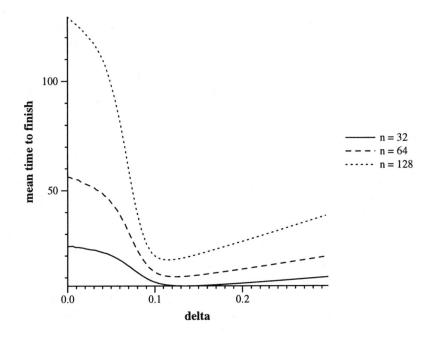

Fig. 1. Results for c = 0.1, uniform distribution

3   Discussion and Conclusions

We have constructed a theoretical model of the effects of small variability in task times in parallel processing on Ethernets. The model suggests that overall task

---

[4] It is thus not a scale parameter in the sense defined earlier, and in fact the mean equals the standard deviation in this distribution.

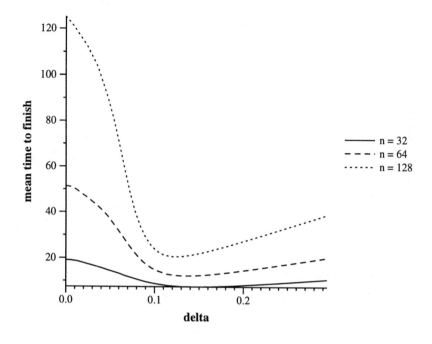

Fig. 2. Results for c = 0.8, uniform distribution

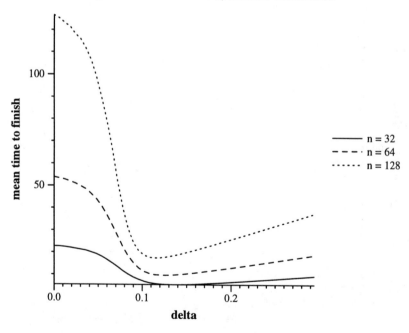

Fig. 3. Results for c = 0.1, exponential distribution

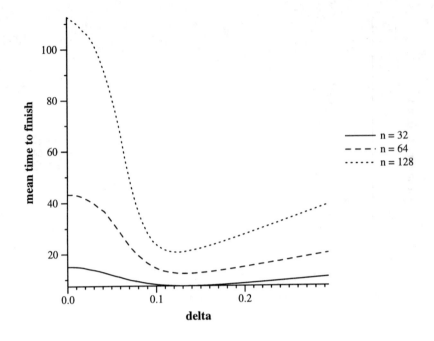

Fig. 4. Results for c = 0.8, exponential distribution

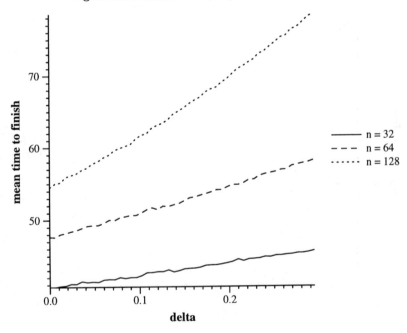

Fig. 5. Results for c = 10.0, exponential distribution

rendezvous time will be on the order $O(n^2)$, and we have derived a lower bound based on the standard deviation of the task times.

As a potential solution to this problem, we have found that programmed backoff can produce very large speedups in cases in which the task time distribution has a small standard deviation. In addition, the optimal value of δ in such cases appears to be rather insensitive to type of distribution, and appears to be typically about 10-20% larger than the transmission time for a task-rendezvous message.

A number of other approaches to the Ethernet backoff problem may be effective. A tree-based barrier [7, p. 247] imposes a partial ordering among the nodes regarding the sequence in which they send barrier messages, thus preventing most collisions. It has recently come to the author's attention that the Genoa Active Message Machine (GAMMA) [3] has now taken this idea a step further, imposing a linear ordering among the nodes. Note, howeer, that these methods are easiest to implement in applications in which there is only one set of nodes which will be involved in barriers, and that set is fixed throughout the program. It may not be possible to implement such "ordered barrier access sequence" methods in full generality.

References

1. Vikram S. Adve and Mary K. Vernon, "The Influence of Random Delays on Parallel Execution Times," *Proceedings of the 1993 ACM Sigmetrics Conference on Measurement and Modeling of Computer Systems*, May 1993, pp. 61-73.
2. S.G. Akl. *"The Design and Analysis of Parallel Algorithms"*, Prentice Hall, Inc, 1989.
3. G. Ciola, G. Ciaccio and L. Mancini. *GAMMA Project: Genoa Active Message MAchine*, Web page http://www.disi.unige.it/project/gamma.
4. Gregory Davies and Norman Matloff. "Network-Specific Performance Enhancements for PVM," *Proceedings of the Fourth IEEE International Symposium on High-Performance Distributed Computing*, August 1995, pp205-210.
5. G. Gonnet. *Handbook of Algorithms and Data Structures*, Addison-Wesley, 1984.
6. Gilbert Held. *Ethernet Networks* (second edition), John Wiley, 1996.
7. G. Wilson. *Practical Parallel Programming*, MIT Press, 1995.

Improving Dynamic Token-Based Distributed Synchronization Performance via Optimistic Broadcasting

Alexander I-Chi Lai and Chin-Laung Lei

Dept. of Electrical Engineering
National Taiwan University
Taipei, Taiwan, R. O. C.
alex@fractal.ee.ntu.edu.tw, lei@cc.ee.ntu.edu.tw

Abstract. In this paper we propose a new dynamic token-based distributed synchronization algorithm that utilizes a new technique called *optimistic broadcasting* (*optcasting*) to improve efficiency. Briefly, an *optcast* message is a reliable unicast one that can also be heard by nodes other than its designated destination. Our algorithm manages pending token requesters by a distributed queue, and *optcasts* a direction towards the current queue end to help new requesters finding the queue end more quickly. Simulated experimental results indicate that our *optcast* algorithm outperforms the already fast Chang-Singhal-Liu (CSL) algorithm by up to 40%, especially for large systems of many processor nodes and under high synchronization loads. In addition, *optcasting* is highly robust and resistant to message loss, retaining at least 63% (86% if *optcasting* is also incorporated into acknowledgment messages) coverage even when the message loss rate approaches 100%.

1   Introduction

Recently, clusters of workstations have attracted more attentions than before. A cluster of PCs/workstations connected by high speed networks possess great computation power and high scalability, facilitating the execution of many parallel as well as conventional distributed applications. However, exploiting such computation potential is challenging because clusters of workstations are intrinsically *asynchronous*. More specifically, processes on such platforms must execute some kind of distributed synchronization algorithm to obtain the privilege (represented by holding a unique token, being granted permission globally, positioning first in a total ordering, etc.) of exclusive accesses to certain resources. Therefore, the efficiency of the distributed synchronization algorithm becomes one of the most important determining factors of the performance of such platforms.

In this paper we present a new technique called *optcasting* (which stands for *optimistic broadcasting*) for optimizing token-based dynamic distributed synchronization algorithms. Unlike reliable broadcasting / multicasting [3, 21] or lossy multicasting [8, 11], an *optcast* message is a reliable unicast message that can also be heard by nodes other than its designated destination. It is *optimistic* in the sense that while acknowledgement from the destination node is required, other receiving nodes need not send back any response. Note that an *optcast* message is capable of delivering information to multiple nodes without causing any extra communication traffic than a regular reliable unicast message. Such a capability is especially useful where listeners can benefit from using the *optcast* information promptly, yet the correctness of the computation results will not be affected without receiving any *optcast* message.

In this paper we develop a new token-based dynamic distributed synchronization algorithm that incorporates *optcasting*. Our algorithm maintains a distributed queue to manage pending token requesters. In addition, each node maintains a guess of the probable token owner. When one node wishes to get the token, it sends the request to the probable owner first. The request will be forwarded elsewhere in the same manner until either it is put at the end of the waiting queue, or the token is found eventually. Clearly, since a more accurate guess of the probable owner means fewer forwarding steps and higher synchronization efficiency, the information related to the token position is a good candidate of *optcasting*. Indeed, our approach *optcasts* a direction towards the current queue end to help new requesters finding the queue end more quickly. Moreover, our algorithm *optcasts* the queue end direction in both the sending and acknowledging phases, further improving the synchronization performance. Our simulation results indicate that this technique is very efficient especially for large systems with many processor nodes and under heavy synchronization conditions, reducing up to 40% of messages of previous dynamic algorithms [1, 6] which have already achieved very good performance. Furthermore, by mathematical analysis we show that *optcasting* is highly robust and resistant to message loss, retaining at least 63% (86% if *optcasting* is also incorporated into acknowledgment messages) coverage even when the message loss rate approaches 100%. This is also supported by simulation results in which the performance gain over earlier algorithms only slightly degrades by 3 to 5 percents even when the probability of message loss is as high as 60%.

The remainder of this paper is organized as follows. In Section 2 we survey related works of distributed synchronization. Section 3 describes the technical details of our *optcast* dynamic synchronization algorithm. Section 4 presents simulated performance results of our *optcast* algorithm. Finally, conclusions and possible future works are summarized in Section 5.

2 Related Works

This section describes several approaches of distributed synchronization. Some excellent overviews on these works can be found in the literature [14, 16, 20].

2.1 Centralized Approach

The most straightforward way to achieve mutual exclusion in a distributed environment is to let one single node handle all synchronization requests. This can be done by assigning one dedicated node as the coordinator to arbitrate synchronization requests from other nodes. Each process that wants to execute in the critical section sends a request to the coordinator. When the node receives a reply from the coordinator, it can proceed and enter the critical section. The coordinating process can be modeled as a simple endless loop dispatching incoming requests.

Obviously this approach guarantees mutual exclusion. Also, no starvation will occur if the scheduling policy within the coordinator is fair (first-come-first-serve, for example). However, the coordinator is a performance bottleneck which results in poor scalability. Moreover, if the coordinator crashes, so does the entire system. Therefore, this approach is not suitable for large distributed systems.

2.2 Causality and Timestamps

Another way to arbitrate contending access requests is ordering them by causality. Just as in the human world, causality is a powerful concept for determining, analyzing, and drawing inferences of a distributed computation. However, there is an important difference: in the human world we use a global and natural time to deduce causality, but distributed computing environments have no global clock. Hence an artificial logical clock scheme must be used instead for timestamping and ordering events in a distributed system.

Scalar Timestamps. The first timestamp approach was proposed by Lamport [9]. In this approach, each processor P_i maintains a non-negative, monotonically increasing scalar T_i as the timestamp. Each P_i updates its own timestamp by executing the following rules:

- Before executing an event, processor P_i updates $T_i=T_i+d$ $(d>0)$ and piggybacks the timestamp onto the outgoing message;
- When a message of timestamp Tm is received, Let $T_i=\max(T_i, Tm)$.

This algorithm requires $3*(n-1)$ messages per request, where n is number of processor nodes. Several improvements of Lamport's algorithm have been proposed to reduce the number of messages, including a $2*(n-1)$ messages per request approach suggested by Ricart and Agrawala [17], an n messages per request one presented by Suzuki and Kasami [18] with the drawback that the sequence numbers contained in the message headers are unbounded, and an $O(\sqrt{n})$ messages algorithm proposed by Maekawa [12].

Vector and Matrix Timestamps. Although scalar timestamping is effective and relatively simple, it is not strictly consistent because the global and local clocks are squashed into one single integer, losing the dependency relations. A solution to this problem is to augment the single scalar into a vector [2, 16]. In this scheme, each processor P_i maintains a non-negative, monotonically increasing integer vector v_i as the timestamp. Each P_i updates its own timestamp by executing the following rules:

- Before executing an event, processor P_i updates $v_i[i]=v_i[i]+d$ ($d>0$) and piggybacks the timestamp vector onto the outgoing message;
- When a message of timestamp vm is received, let $v_i[k]=\max(v_i[k], \ vm[k])$ ($1\leq k\leq$number of processor nodes).

In vector approaches, there exists an isomorphism between the partial ordering of events and their vector timestamps; that is, the timestamp order is guaranteed to be the same as the event order. Thus, it can achieve strict consistency. Such properties make vector timestamping very useful in distributed debugging, implementing causal communication, establishing global breakpoints and checkpoints, etc.. However, the messaging and computation overheads of vector timestamping are likely to be high: The direct implementation requires at least n spaces of messages for n processor nodes. This causes several optimizations and efficient implementations of vector timestamping, including Singnal and Kshemkalyani's differential technique [19], Fowler and Zwaenepoel's dependency technique [4], and Jard-Jourdan's adaptive approach [5].

Note that the same principle of augmenting a scalar into a vector can also be applied to vector timestamping; that is, using matrices instead of vectors. A matrix timestamp contains not only the dependency but also the latest direct dependencies of those dependencies themselves, making it powerful enough for complicated applications such as distributed debugging and garbage collection. The even higher overhead of using matrices can also be alleviated by the same techniques of efficient vector timestamp implementations mentioned before.

2.3 Token-Based Algorithms

In token-based algorithms, a unique mark (the token) is shared among the processes. Mutual exclusion is clearly guaranteed because a process may only enter its critical section if it possesses the token. This principle can be implemented by either broadcasting to other processes when requesting a token (either to a statically or dynamically chosen set of nodes) or by deploying a logical structure on the nodes, which may also be static or dynamic.

Broadcasting Algorithms. These kinds of algorithms do not impose a communication structure on the processes and therefore must send request messages via broadcasting. These algorithms may be static or dynamic. Static algorithms do not record the recent location of the token and hence must broadcast the request to all other processes. On the other hand, dynamic algorithms keep track of the recent locations of the token and therefore request messages may be sent only to possible token owners. If the receiving node does not hold the token, the request is forwarded to the possible owner of the receiving node.

At the first glance, broadcasting should be the most efficient approach because only one message is required to inform all nodes. However, acknowledge responses are indispensable as the network is unreliable. Therefore, both static and dynamic broadcasting algorithms require $O(n)$ messages per synchronization request for an n-node system [20].

Static Logical-Structured Algorithms. To avoid broadcasting overheads, logical-structured algorithms impose some virtual communication topology among processes and make the token traverse through predefined routes. The logical structure can be either static (fixed) or dynamic during run-time. In static approaches, typical candidates of structure include rings [10] and trees [15]. In ring based algorithms, the token circulates on the ring permanently from process to process. This requires $O(n)$ messages per synchronization request for an n-node system. Another family of algorithms, the tree based approaches in which the token travels along the virtual tree edges, are more complicated yet possibly more efficient. For example, Raymond [15] proposed a binary-tree algorithm in which each node keeps a queue to store pending requests and a pointer (served as a guess of possible token owner) to its ascendant or one of its descendants. A request is sent and forwarded through that pointer, until it reaches the token holder or is blocked and put into the queue by another requester. Each node will flip the direction of that pointer when the token walks through. Raymond showed that for an n-node system, the number of message exchanges is $O(\log n)$ in general, whereas under high load only four messages are required per request. Neilsen and Mizuno [13] also presented a modified Raymond's algorithm that allows the token to go to the requester directly rather than travel along the tree edges.

Dynamic Algorithms. Alternatively, some synchronization algorithms may dynamically change their logical communication topology. Such approaches usually deliver higher performance by using aggressive *path compression* techniques to accelerate the token-locating (which is often the most time-consuming) phase of the algorithms. The representative of this category is the one proposed by Chang, Singhal and Liu [1] (abbreviated as CSL algorithm), which is generally the most efficient algorithm among proposed approaches, to our best knowledge. For a system of n nodes, the CSL algorithm generates $O(\log n)$ messages per request, and the actual number of messages are usually far fewer than that upperbound due to its use of path compression.

The key idea of CSL algorithm is described as follows. Each node maintains a guess (called `dir`) of the possible token owner. If a node neither holding nor requesting the token receives a request, it forwards this request to the node indicated by `dir`, and then sets `dir` to point to the new requester (since it will eventually be the one which holds the token). When a node requests the token, it sends a request message to the node indicated by `dir`. It then sets an additional pointer, `next`, to NIL. If a node that holds or is waiting for the token receives a request, and its `next` pointer is NIL, it sets `next` to the number of the node that sent the request. Otherwise, it forwards the request to the node indicated by `dir`, and sets `dir` to the requesting node to compress the path for further requests. Among the nodes that hold the token or are requesting, their `next` pointers form a distributed queue of the pending requesters. If a node is waiting and its `next` pointer is NIL, this node is effectively at the end of the waiting queue. If `next` is not NIL, the end of the waiting queue is at (or beyond) the node pointed to by `dir`. Since the requester will become the one at the queue end, it is appropriate to set the `dir` variable to that requester. When the token holder releases the token, it sends the token to the node pointed to by `next`, if `next` is not NIL. Otherwise, the current token holder keeps the token.

There are other dynamic approaches as well. For instance, Johnson and Newman-Wolfe [6, 7] proposed an algorithm called *List-Lock*. This algorithm also utilizes path compression except that new requesters are inserted amid the waiting queue rather than forwarded to the queue end. The proper positions for insertion are determined by the respective timestamps of the new requesters. The *List-Lock* algorithm delivers almost as good performance as the CSL algorithm, with typically no more than one extra message per request.

3 The *Optcast* Distributed Synchronization Algorithm

In this section we present a dynamic, token-based distributed synchronization algorithm that is inspired by the path compression algorithms mentioned above. We first describe the technical details, then verify the correctness of our algorithm.

3.1 Algorithm Description

The main feature of our algorithm is the utilization of the *optimistic broadcasting*, or *optcasting* technique. As we mentioned before, an *optcast* message is a reliable unicast message that can also be heard by nodes other than its designated destination. Since no acknowledgement will be sent by non-destination nodes, an *optcast* message is capable of delivering information to multiple nodes at exactly the same communication cost of a regular reliable unicast message. On many popular media such as Ethernet, fast Ethernet, and wireless communications, virtually all transmissions can be easily augmented into *optcast* ones. Therefore, the key issue of is to find an appropriate use of *optcasting*. Because pending token requesters are managed by a distributed queue, our algorithm *optcasts* a direction towards the current queue end to help new requesters finding the queue end more quickly.

In our *optcast* algorithm, each node respectively keeps two pointers: a `dir` pointer recording a guess of the possible token owner, and a `next` pointer forming a queue of pending token requesters. Initially, one node is arbitrarily chosen as the token owner, and all nodes set their `next` pointer to NIL and `dir` pointer to the token owner, respectively. In addition, each node maintains a vector timestamp which will be advanced by every incoming and outgoing messages. Note that the timestamp is not for capturing the global causality; the actual usage is described later. Any implementation of vector timestamping mechanism described previously should be sufficient for our use.

The actions of each node in the system can be modeled by a finite state machine as depicted in Fig. 1. Each node is in one of the following states: IDLE, REQUESTING, TOKEN, and TOKENIDLE, which represents the state of idling, requesting the token, using the token, and keeping the token without locking it up, respectively. When an IDLE node requests the token, it enters the REQUESTING state by sending a request message to the node indicated by `dir`, setting its `next` and `dir` pointers to NIL, and waiting until the token has been received. When the token eventually arrives, the REQUESTING node enters the TOKEN state in which it locks up and uses the token for a period of time (to execute a critical section). After finishing its use of the token, the node either enters TOKENIDLE state by just keeping the token if there is no other pending requester, or passes the token immediately to the `next` pending requester, sets the `next` pointer to NIL, and becomes an IDLE node.

When a token request comes, the receiver takes different moves according to its

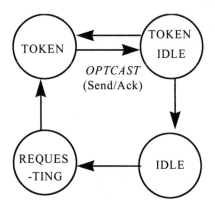

Fig. 1. Finite State Machine of *Optcast* Algorithm

own state. If the receiving node is in TOKENIDLE state (i.e. inactively keeps the token), it makes the requester enter TOKEN state by transferring the token to the requester, and itself becomes an IDLE node. Otherwise, if the receiving node is in REQUESTING state and its `next` pointer is NIL, it hooks the new requester behind itself by setting the `next` pointer to indicate the new requester. In all other cases, the receiving node forwards this request to the node indicated by `dir`. Finally, the receiving node sets its own `dir` to indicate the new requester, just as other path compression algorithms do.

The most important step of our algorithm occurs at the time of token transferring. When the token owner at the waiting queue head has finished its use of the token, it *optcasts* its current `dir` pointer while passing the token to the next requester in the queue. This can be done by appending the `dir` pointer of the old token owner to the token message to be *optcast*. Since an *optcast* message is also a reliable unicast message, the next node in the queue will receive the token, and all other nodes have chances to hear of the *optcast* `dir` of the old token owner. the new token owner also *optcasts* its own `dir` pointer by appending that to the acknowledgment to the previous token owner. When either *optcast* message is heard of, each non-requesting node checks if the timestamp of its own `dir` is older than that of the *optcast* `dir`. If so, the node updates its `dir` to be the same as the *optcast* `dir`. Since a newer timestamp means that the node pointed by the *optcast* `dir` is probably nearer the end of the waiting queue, such an update can help the future requesters to find the queue end more quickly

3.2 Correctness

Theorem 1. The optcast algorithm guarantees mutual exclusion.

Outline of the Proof. Observe that a requesting processor node obtains the token if and only if another processor node (the retired token owner) releases the ownership of the token. Since there is one and only one token in the *optcast* algorithm, mutual exclusion is guaranteed.

Theorem 2. The optcast algorithm is deadlock-free.

Outline of the Proof. A deadlock occurs if and only if the processor nodes are cyclically waiting one another. Also, note that token requests are propagated in the direction pointed by the dir pointers. Hence, a deadlock occurs if and only if there exist some processor nodes whose dir pointers form a cycle; more specifically, a REQUESTING processor node P is deadlocked if and only if there exist 0 or more nodes, say P_x, P_y, etc., such that $P \Rightarrow P_x \Rightarrow P_y \Rightarrow \ldots \Rightarrow P$ where $\Rightarrow$ represents the dir pointer. We show that the *optcasting* step in our algorithm never induces such a waiting cycle. Consider an arbitrary live (not deadlocked) IDLE node P that just receives an *optcast* message indicating a node (say) P_q in the waiting queue, while the current queue end is at node (say) P_t. Observe that for every (except the last one) node in the queue, the dir pointer is indicating another one beyond itself and at most as far as the queue end. Thus we get $P \Rightarrow P_q \Rightarrow \ldots \Rightarrow P_t$ if P updates its dir pointer. Since the dir pointer of node P_t is NIL, we conclude that cyclic waiting will never occur, and the system is deadlock-free as all nodes are initially live.

Remark. In fact, our *optcast* algorithm is still deadlock-free even if the dir pointer of the queue end is not NIL. We make such an arrangement because it can significantly simplify the proof.

4 Performance

In this section we present performance results of our *optcast* algorithm versus previous token-based algorithms. We first describe the methodology of our study, then present the performance results as well as associated analyses and discussions.

4.1 Methodology

To investigate the effectiveness of the *optcasting* technique, we conducted a simulation study for both our *optcast* algorithm and previous non-optcast algorithms. The algorithm we choose as the contrast is the CSL algorithm. the most efficient algorithm among previous approaches under most circumstances. Our simulator models several processor connected by a common network medium with the following assumptions:

- The network medium is not segmented, allowing every node in the system to hear of every transmission on the network without extra communication cost. That is, there is no gateway, switching hub, or any other device to split the network. If two or more nodes initiate transmission at the same time, all of them must rollback and reinitiate transmission later, just as in Ethernet.
- The network is totally reliable and error-free; however, each *node* is subject to lose inbound messages independently. That is, one message may be caught by some nodes while being omitted by others.
- Acknowledgement is necessary for reliable transmissions. That is, each unicast transmission contains two messages (if there is no message loss and retransmission). The purpose of this assumption is to simulate the TCP transmission in TCP/IP-based network environment.
  - The simulator we constructed is configured by the following parameters:
- The number of processor nodes on the network;
- The message transmission delay (mean value 1 clock tick);
- The token lockup time and the idle time between two synchronization periods (explained below); and
- The individual loss rate of a message for each node.

Note that since the degree of overhead of a specific algorithm is difficult to measure, it is improper to assume that different algorithms have the same token lockup and / or idle time. To address this problem, we use a method found in the literature [6] by defining a *load factor* L as $L=n*(C/R)$ where n is the number of processors, C is the token lockup (critical section execution) time, and R is the idle time between two synchronization periods. In this work we fix $C=10$ time ticks and let R be randomly decided (with the average that matches a given load factor). Note that the load factor can be greater than 1, which means that there will be some nodes waiting in the pending queue for the token.

4.2 Results and Analyses

In this study four different levels of load factors are simulated: one light-weight (75%), two medium-weight (100% and 125%), and one heavy-weight (150%), for varying numbers of processors and loss rates. The results are depicted in Fig. 2 to Fig. 5. First we noticed that the CSL algorithm performs just as we expected, yielding near 12 messages for 256 processors in all lossless cases. Since in our simulation one message becomes two because of one acknowledgement (if no retransmission occurs), this result is consistent with earlier results in the literature where the CSL algorithm requires about 5 to 6 messages per request for about several hundreds of processors.

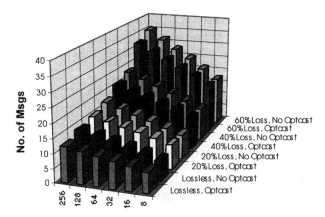

Fig. 2. Simulation Results (Load=75%)

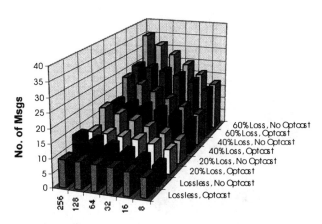

Fig. 3. Simulation Results (Load=100%)

When the load factor is low (Fig. 2), we find that the *optcast* algorithm performs marginally better than the CSL algorithm, reducing up to 10% of messages for large number of processors in the lossless case. Since lower loading factor means a shorter waiting queue (i.e. fewer pending requesters), our *optcast* algorithm only gets little advantage from finding the queue end more quickly. Fortunately, *optcasting* does not increase the number of messages at all, which means that the *optcast* algorithm generates at most as many messages as the CSL algorithm.

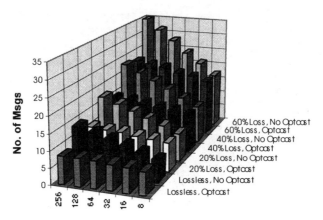

Fig. 4. Simulation Results (Load=125%)

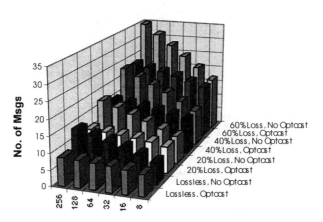

Fig. 5. Simulation Results (Load=150%)

The results are totally different for medium- to heavy-weight load factor scenarios. From Fig. 3 to 5, we find that our *optcast* algorithm yields large performance gains over the CSL algorithm, reducing up to 40% of messages for large numbers of processors in the lossless case. Moreover, we observed that while the CSL algorithm is delivering consistent performance under different load factors, the *optcast* algorithm performs better when the load factor is increasing. Since a higher load factor means a longer waiting queue, it is reasonable that the *optcast* algorithm gets more advantage from finding the queue end more quickly.

We also observed that the *optcast* algorithm is quite resistant to message loss. While both algorithms are generating more messages, the performance improvement of the *optcast* algorithm over the CSL algorithm decreases very little (3 to 5 percents). This phenomenon is very interesting because it is opposite to the common sense, and is worth to be further investigated, which is the subject of the next subsection.

4.3 Robustness of *Optcasting*

Intuitively, the *optcast* algorithm would be very sensitive to message loss because there is no way to tell if an *optcast* message has been ever heard by nodes other than its designated destination. However, our simulation results show that *optcasting* is more robust than it looks. Here we take an analytical approach to explain the reason.

Assume the message loss rate of each node is P. That is, the expected number of transmissions of a message to be delivered reliably is

$$\frac{1}{1 - P} . \tag{1}$$

This is applicable to *optcast* messages since an *optcast* transmission is also a reliable unicast transmission. Thus for a non-destination processor node, the probability of missing all transmissions of an *optcast* message is

$$P^{1/(1-P)} . \tag{2}$$

Since $0 \leq P < 1$, the maximum of $P^{1/(1-P)}$ is e^{-1} which occurs when P approaches 1. That is, any *optcast* message will be received by at lease $1 - e^{-1}$, or about 63% of all processors, even under the worst circumstances where the probability of losing a message approaches 100%. Note that if we assume the nodes are reliable and the network is subject to lose messages, an *optcast* message will be heard by all nodes in a successful transmission, and the *optcast* coverage is clearly 100%, better than the scenario shown above. Moreover, in our algorithm there are *two* occasions to *optcast* newer possible owner information (in both the token forwarding and the acknowledging phases) in one token move, further raising the effective *optcast* coverage to $1 - e^{-2}$, or about 86%. This is the reason why *optcasting* is highly robust and quite resistant to harsh communication environments.

4.4 Discussion

The execution of a distributed synchronization algorithm consists of both communication and computation. While *optcasting* significantly reduces the communication overhead, the speedup of the total critical section executing time is problem-specific as the amount of computation varies from one case to another.

Nevertheless, one can expect that *optcasting* will also significantly improve the execution time in most practical applications because (1) communication bandwidth is far smaller than the data generating rate, making the communication time dominate; (2) programmers tend to shorten critical section executing time, otherwise pending requesters will be blocked too long.

5 Conclusions and Future Works

We have presented a new technique, the *optcasting*, for optimizing dynamic token-based distributed synchronization algorithms. We observe that:

- *Optcasting* is very effective especially for large distributed systems with many processor nodes and high synchronization loads, yielding up to 40% performance improvement over the already fast CSL algorithm. Moreover, *optcasting* is always beneficial because it never induces extra communication overheads.
- *Optcasting* is highly robust and quite resistant to message loss. Even on systems where the message loss rate approaches 100%, the minimal coverage of any *optcast* transmission is about 63%. If *optcast* is also incorporated into acknowledgment messages (like our algorithm does), the minimal *optcast* coverage can be effectively raised to as high as 86%.

In the near future we will investigate the execution latency distribution from simulation with real-world network parameters. Also, we want to apply *optcasting* to other distributed algorithms to exploit possible performance improvements.

References

1. Y.I. Chang et al., An Improved O(log(n)) Mutual Exclusion Algorithm for Distributed Systems, Proceedings of 1990 ICPP, pp. III295-302.
2. C. Fidge, Logical Time in Distributed Computing Systems, Computer, Vol.24 No.8, August 1991, pp. 28-33.
3. Sally Floyd et al., A Reliable Multicast Framework for Light-weight Sessions and Application Level Framing, ACM SIGCOMM 1995, pp. 342-356.
4. J. Fowler et al., Causal Distributed Breakpoints, Proc. Of 1990 ICDCS, 1990, pp. 134-141.
5. C. Jard et al., Dependency Tracking and Filtering in Distributed Computation, Tech. Report No. 851, IRISA, Beaulieu, France.
6. Theodore Johnson, A Performance Comparison of Fast Distributed Synchronization Algorithms, Tech. Report TR94-032, Dept. of CIS, Univ. of Florida, 1994.
7. Theodore Johnson et al., A Comparison of Fast and Low Overhead Distributed Priority Locks, Journal of Parallel and Distributed Computing, Vol. 32 No. 1, January 1996, pp. 74-89.
8. Vinay Kumar, Mbone: Interactive Multimedia on the Internet, Macmillan Publishing, Nov. 1995, ISBN 1-56205-397-3.
9. L. Lamport, Time, Clocks, and the Ordering of Events in a Distributed System, CACM, Vol. 21 No. 7, 1978, pp. 558-564.
10. G. Le Lann, Distributed Systems-Towards a Formal Approach, Proc. IFIP Congress, Toronto, North-Holland Publishing, pp. 155-160.

11. M.R, Macedonia et al., MBone Provides Audio and Video Across the Internet, Computer, Vol. 27 No. 4, April 1994, pp. 30-36.
12. M. Maekawa, A Sqrt(n) Algorithm for Mutual Exclusion in Decentralized Systems, ACM Transactions on Computer Systems, Vol. 3, No. 2, pp. 145-159, May 1985
13. M.L Neilsen et al., A DAG-Based Algorithm for Distributed Mutual Exclusion, Proc. of 1991 ICDCS, pp. 354-360.
14. M. Ramachandran, M. Singhal: On the Synchronization Mechanisms in Distributed Shared Memory Systems, Technical Report OSU-CISRC-10/94-TR54, 1994.
15. K. Raymond, A Tree-Based Algorithm for Distributed Mutual Exclusion, ACM Trans. on Computer Systems, Vol. 7 No. 1, 2989, pp. 61-77.
16. Michel Raynel et al,. Logical Time: Capturing Causality in Distributed Systems, Computer, Feb. 1996, pp. 49-56.
17. G. Ricart et al., An Optimal Algorithm For Mutual Exclusion in Computer Networks, CACM, 24(1), pp. 9-17, Jan. 1981
18. I. Suzuki et al., A Distributed Mutual Exclusion Algorithm, ACM Transaction on Computer Systems, Vol. 3, No. 4, pp. 344-349, 1985
19. M. Singhal et al., An Efficient Implementation of Vector Clocks, Information Processing Letters, Vol. 43, August, 1992, pp. 47-52.
20. M. Singhal: A Taxonomy of Distributed Mutual Exclusion, Journal of Parallel and Distributed Computing, Vol .18, 1993, pp. 94-101.
21. Andrew S. Tananbaum et al., Parallel Programming Using Shared Objects and Broadcasting, Computer, August 1992, pp. 10-20.

Fast Barrier Synchronization on Shared Fast Ethernet

G. Chiola, G. Ciaccio

DISI, Università di Genova
via Dodecaneso 35, 16146 Genova, Italy
E-mail: {chiola,ciaccio}@disi.unige.it

Abstract. Shared LAN is presently the most widespread networking technology, due to its extremely low cost and favourable cost/performance ratio. Clusters of Personal Computers (PCs) leveraging shared 100base-T Ethernet may currently offer the best price/performance in parallel processing. Most numerical parallel algorithms make heavy use of collective communications and especially barrier synchronization. Hence a critical issue on PC clusters is to offer efficient implementations of such primitives even though using low-cost, non-switched LAN technology.

We implemented and studied some simple barrier synchronization protocols atop the Genoa Active Message MAchine (GAMMA), an efficient Active Messages-like communication layer running on a cluster of Pentium PCs connected by a 100base-TX Ethernet repeater hub. In the case of synchronized or quasi-synchronized processes issuing a barrier synchronization, an obvious way to avoid collisions on shared 100base-T Ethernet is to use a barrier protocol which explicitly serializes all the inter-process synchronization communications over the LAN. We propose alternative barrier protocols which avoid Ethernet collisions during the synchronization phase without requiring such a full explicit serialization. One of such protocols definitely outperforms the fully serialized barrier protocol over 100base-T Ethernet as well as the MPI implementations of barrier synchronization on IBM SP2 and Intel Paragon.

1 Introduction

The high cost of massively parallel platforms together with the trend towards high performance and low cost single processor hardware technology have hampered the diffusion of parallel processing techniques in real applications so far. As long as single processors that are much faster and much cheaper than the ones available the year before can be found, no one interested in real applications but with limited budgets is encouraged to move to massively parallel processing technologies involving substantially higher hardware and software costs. In this perspective NOW architectures leveraging inexpensive commodity hardware could offer an important chance for parallel processing techniques to spread, due to their substantially lower cost and to the very trend of single processor hardware technology. The evolution of CPU technology has brought high-end Personal Computers (PCs) to performance levels in the range of workstations at a very competitive cost, so that PCs are already a very cost-effective alternative to workstations as processing nodes in NOW platforms [16]. The only obstacles to be overcome are the lack of efficiency exhibited by the industry standard inter-process communication mechanisms and protocols as well as the complete absence of support to efficient collective communications in industry standard Operating Systems. The latter drawback is a by-product of the evolutional history of LAN communication, which was not originally conceived to support parallel processing of any kind.

The issue of efficiently supporting inter-process communication in NOW platforms has been addressed by a large number of research projects [5, 19, 13, 14, 15, 17, 18] [12, 20, 22, 23]. To the best of our knowledge a comparable effort has not been devoted to the challenge of efficiently supporting collective communication and especially barrier synchronization, despite such cooperation mechanisms being of great importance in parallel processing applications.

A first approach is to port existing collective algorithms atop more efficient low-level communication protocols. The work [4] is a typical representative of such approach in the case of some MPI collective communication primitives. Such primitives were ported on a custom reliable point-to-point low-level communication protocol built just atop the IEEE 802.3 Ethernet protocol and offering efficient broadcast service directly mapped onto the Ethernet hardware broadcast. The implementation is based on "slow" 10 Mbps Ethernet. Absolute communication as well as synchronization performance appears to be not particularly brilliant. However their results are by no means comparable to experiments carried out on Fast Ethernet.

Another approach is to implement more efficient collective algorithms atop existing low-level communication protocols. The work [3] describes the experience of re-implementing some IBM PVMe collective routines on the IBM SP-2 using a simplified version of a complicated broadcast algorithm proved optimal under the "postal" performance model [2]; the obtained performance improvement is significant only for small-size messages. The work [8] reports about an enhancement of the PVM barrier synchronization primitive based on re-implementing it atop broadcast UDP sockets. In this way, performance of PVM barrier is increased by 36% with as many as 32 processors on 10Mbps Ethernet; however the absolute performance remains quite unsatisfactory for real parallel processing purposes (more than 280 milliseconds to synchronize 32 processors).

The two approaches recalled above are mutually complementary in order to achieve best performance with collective communications. Unfortunately much of the efficiency may be lost if the implementation of a collective mechanism does not properly take into account the features and limitations of the underlying communication hardware, which hardly are properly represented in the existing performance models.

In this paper we address the problem of efficiently supporting barrier synchronization in a network of PCs leveraging lowest-cost, shared 100base-T Ethernet LAN technology (so called "Fast Ethernet") and running an efficient point-to-point inter-process messaging system. Although the trend is towards a continuous decrease in the price of switching devices, non-switched Fast Ethernet technology is still substantially cheaper than the switched one, and as such it is very frequently found in today's LANs. Moreover non-switched Fast Ethernet exhibits slightly lower latency time than the switched one, at the expenses of aggregate throughput and scalability. Thus the cost/performance ratio of a shared Fast Ethernet-based NOW may be very appealing for the wide range of parallel applications which make use of short messages and need frequent synchronization among processes.

2 A brief account of Active Messages and GAMMA

Many modern high performance messaging systems have been derived from the Active Message communication paradigm [21]. Active Messages are aimed at reducing the communication overhead by allowing communication to overlap computation. The efficiency of the Active Message paradigm lies in the fact that it eliminates intermediate copies of messages along the communication path, thus remarkably speeding up communications. In a traditional send-receive messaging system, messages delivered to a destination node need to be temporarily buffered waiting for the destination process to invoke a "receive" operation which will consume them. With Active Messages this buffering is no longer needed: as soon as delivered, each message triggers a function of the destination process, known as *receiver handler*, which will consume it immediately. Here "consuming" means integrating the message information into the ongoing computation of the destination process, notifying the reception to the destination process itself, and possibly setting some data structures in order to promptly "consume" the next incoming message as soon as it arrives. A well known commercial application is the Active Message Layer introduced by Thinking Machines Co. in the CM-5 platform [1], yielding user-to-user throughput and latency very close to the limit posed by the hardware devices [11].

The Genoa Active Message MAchine (GAMMA) [5, 6] is a pool of (currently 16) autonomous Pentium PCs networked by a 100base-TX Ethernet repeater hub. Each PC runs the Linux operating system whose kernel is enhanced by an Active Message-like messaging system. GAMMA Active Messages are inspired to Thinking Machines' CMAML library for the CM-5, where each process has a number of *communication ports* and may attach both a receiver handler and a data structure to a single communication port in order to handle all messages incoming through that port. Moving the message from the network to the destination data structure attached to the communication port is efficiently and timely performed by the GAMMA custom network device driver, and need not to be explicitly programmed by the receiver handler.

Differently from the Generic Active Message paradigm [7], in GAMMA the sender process specifies a communication port of the destination process instead of the pointer to a receiver handler, and the receiver handler must not explicitly extract and store the incoming message. The programming paradigm of GAMMA is Single Program Multiple Data (SPMD), although the "port-oriented" approach makes GAMMA suitable for MIMD programming as well, as a common address space among cooperating processes is not required, multi-programming is allowed, and a process may communicate with other processes running different programs.

Most of the GAMMA communication layer is embedded in the Linux kernel, the remaining part being placed in a user-level programming library. All the functionalities of the original Linux kernel were left unmodified. All the communication software of GAMMA has been carefully developed according to a performance-oriented approach. The adoption of the Active Message paradigm allows a true "zero copy" protocol, with no intermediate copies of messages along the whole user-to-user communication path. Differently from many other high performance communication layers running on NOWs, GAMMA yields high performance while still offering a fairly flexible and easy-to-use virtualization of the communication hardware in a multi-user, multitasking UNIX environment.

GAMMA exploits the hardware broadcast features of shared Ethernet, thus providing for native broadcast and multicast communication besides point-to-point one.

The GAMMA messaging system is capable of delivering nearly the whole performance of the raw communication hardware to user applications, substantially outperforming any other known prototype developed on low-cost NOWs. One-way "ping-pong" user-to-user message latency is less than 13 μs, whereas asymptotic bandwidth raises 12.2 MByte/s. Half the asymptotic bandwidthis achieved with messages as short as 200 bytes. In terms of latency GAMMA rivals many much more expensive massively parallel platforms. Obviously GAMMA cannot compete with such platforms in terms of bandwidth as well as scalability. On the other hand no massively parallel computer can compete with GAMMA in terms of performance/price ratio.

3 Two *naive* barrier protocols atop GAMMA

The most straightforward way to implement a barrier synchronization mechanism is to devise a distributed synchronization protocol and to implement it atop a point-to-point inter-process communication layer. If the native inter-process messaging system provides broadcast features, such features may be exploited to increase the synchronization performance. GAMMA provides both point-to-point and broadcast low-latency communication. All the barrier protocols that we have implemented atop GAMMA take great advantage from exploiting the GAMMA broadcast services. All the barrier protocols that we have implemented are based on the exchange of point-to-point as well as broadcast "empty" messages among processes in an SPMD static process group.

Hereafter N will denote the number of members in a GAMMA SPMD process group. Moreover the *master* process in the group (usually labelled by instance number zero) will play a role which is different from all the remaining processes in the group, called *slaves* from now on.

3.1 Concurrent barrier synchronization

In the *concurrent* barrier synchronization protocol each slave issuing a barrier primitive sends an "enter barrier" message to the master, independently of the activity of all the other slaves. Then it waits for an "exit barrier" message from the master. The master issuing the barrier primitive knows that N processes belong to the group and waits for $N-1$ "enter barrier" messages from slaves. The counter for such messages is implemented as a GAMMA semaphore primitive. As soon as the master gets the last of such $N-1$ messages it broadcasts a single "exit barrier" message to all the slaves in the process group, then it terminates the barrier synchronization and resumes normal activity. Each slave eventually receives the "exit barrier" message, then resuming its normal activity as well.

Our concurrent protocol involves sending N small frames over the shared Fast Ethernet channel, thus being theoretically optimal in terms of communications. Indeed it works fine when processes join the barrier synchronization at sufficiently different time instants from one another, that is when they are not already synchronized.

However in the execution of many parallel algorithms with well-balanced load among nodes and frequently issuing barrier synchronizations the opposite occurs. Namely, processes tend to be already synchronized, or at least they happen to join a barrier synchronization during a quite short time interval. In this case the behaviour of the concurrent barrier protocol depends on the underlying LAN hardware: collisions may well occur among many "enter barrier" messages when leveraging shared Fast Ethernet LAN technology. Ethernet contention forces random waitings and frame retransmissions, according to the standard CSMA/CD protocol. As a consequence, the barrier synchronization time becomes unacceptably large even with relatively few processors and very light-loaded channel.

3.2 Serialized barrier synchronization

In the *serialized* barrier synchronization protocol all slaves but the one with highest instance number (namely $N-1$) behave the same, namely: when issuing the barrier primitive the slave with instance number i first waits for an "enter barrier" message from slave $i+1$, then it sends an "enter barrier" message to the process (slave or master) whose instance number is $i-1$. The slave with instance number $N-1$ simply sends an "enter barrier" message to slave $N-2$ right away upon issuing the barrier primitive. After sending its "enter barrier" message, each slave waits for the "exit barrier" message from the master (like in the concurrent barrier protocol). The master issuing the barrier primitive must first wait for a single "enter barrier" message from slave numbered 1, then it broadcasts a single "exit barrier" message to all the slaves in the process group, after which it resumes normal activity. Each slave eventually receives the "exit barrier" message, then resuming its normal activity as well.

Also the serialized barrier protocol is theoretically optimal in terms of communications, exactly as the concurrent protocol is. However, the former is aimed

at avoiding contention over the Fast Ethernet bus in case of already synchronized processes, thus behaving in a totally different way from a practical point
of view when run on our platform of choice. Contention is completely avoided
by imposing a total temporal order among messages during the execution of the
synchronization protocol. Of course the behaviour of the serialized barrier protocol is arguably not optimal in the case of non-synchronized processes as well
as with switched LAN technology.

4 Towards an efficient barrier protocol for shared Fast Ethernet

In between the concurrent and the serialized barrier protocols a number of hybrid protocols may be devised with intermediate degree of serialization among
processes.

The general algorithm for such hybrid protocols works as follows. The set of
slaves in a process group is equally partitioned into K subsets calles *chains*, each
comprising $(N-1)/K$ processes (here we assume that $N-1$ is a multiple of K
for the sake of presentation simplicity). Slaves in each chain behave accordingly
to the serialized protocol. However the chains work independently of (hence
concurrently with) one another during the execution of the barrier protocol.
Each chain has a *leader*, which is the slave with lowest instance number in the
chain. The leader of each chain cooperates with the master in the same way as
the slave with least instance number in the plain serialized protocol. The master
issuing the barrier primitive first waits for an "enter barrier" message from each
of the K chain leaders, then it broadcasts one "exit barrier" message to the
whole process group.

We shall call the above algorithm K-*chains* barrier synchronization protocol.
The K-chains protocol trivially collapses to the plain concurrent protocol when
$K = N - 1$ and to the plain serialized protocol when $K = 1$.

With K ranging between 1 and $N - 1$ one could in principle expect performance profiles intermediate between the profiles of the concurrent and the
serialized protocols. Our original idea was to find out a suitable value for K such
that the obtained barrier protocol worked "fine" with synchronized as well as
non-synchronized processes, by reducing the frequency of collisions without imposing an excessive degree of serialization in the protocol. Clearly we expected
each parallel application requiring its own optimal value for K, depending on
the average degree of synchronization already exhibited by the processes when
they join barrier synchronizations.

However, for some small values of K (say, in the range between two and four)
we could expect better performance than the plain serialized protocol itself (corresponding to setting $K = 1$) even with already synchronized processes. In the
case of $K = 2$ the reason for such expectation is the following. With already
synchronized processes, the two process chains start their activity nearly at the
same time. As a consequence a contention and possibly a collision might occur

138

between the first two "enter barrier" messages arising from the two chains starting their activity. Such contention would force one of the two transmissions to be delayed w.r.t. the other one (in case of Ethernet collision both transmissions are delayed by a random time interval, and one of them will occur after the other with high probability). At this point the activities of the two chains turn out to be slightly de-synchronized w.r.t. each other. This little amount of de-synchronization is maintained along the entire execution of the barrier protocol, thanks to the Ethernet Carrier Sense feature which can now serialize transmissions concurrently performed by the two chains with no possibility of further collisions. Since each chain's activity is a sequence of physical transmissions interleaved to execution of low-level communication software, delaying one chain w.r.t. the other should allow overlapping physical transmission from one chain to software overhead from the other chain and vice-versa. Such "computation-to-communication" overlap cannot occur with the plain serialized protocol by definition, hence a possible advantage of 2-chains protocols over the plain serialized one. The same argumentation might in principle work also with $K > 2$, although in this case the Carrier Sense mechanism is not sufficient to prevent the occurrence of collisions.

5 Performance measurements and comparisons

We have implemented the concurrent as well as the serialized and the K-chains barrier synchronization protocols atop a working prototype of GAMMA equipped with 16 Pentium 133MHz PCs networked by a 100base-TX Ethernet repeater hub. On such system we carried out measurements of barrier synchronization time for each protocol in the case of already synchronized processes.

Time measurements were accomplished by means of the TSC register of the Pentium CPU which is incremented by one every clock tick. By reading the TSC content before and after the execution of the barrier primitive we were able to measure the execution time of that primitive with the accuracy of 1/100 of a microsecond.

Each protocol has been implemented as a function in a user-level C library. For each protocol we have performed 104 trials in a C program loop. Each trial resulted in a single time measurement. The measurement loop of our micro-benchmark looks as follow:

```
#define N_TRIALS 104
#define N_NODES 16

void main(int argc, char **argv) {
    TimeStamp start, end;

    gamma_init(N_NODES,argc,argv);

    for (i=0;i<N_TRIALS;i++) {
```

```
        gamma_sync();
        take_time(start);
        gamma_sync();
        take_time(end);
        record(time_interval(start,end));
    }

    gamma_exit();

    compute_mean();
}
```

The program is launched as a single sequential process on one node of the network. As soon as `gamma_init()` is issued, the process creates a process group, then launches `N_NODES-1` additional copies of the same program on distinct remote nodes via the UNIX `rsh` service, then joins the process group with instance number zero and issues a first (concurrent) barrier synchronization embedded in the `gamma_init()` function. Each copy starts execution from the beginning of the program, and as soon as it reaches the `gamma_init()` statement it joins the process group, issuing the embedded (concurrent) barrier synchronization. As soon as the last process has joint the process group the barrier synchronization succeedes, and execution of each process can continue in the framework of a SPMD process group. `gamma_sync()` is the GAMMA library function for barrier synchronization.

The first two measurements as well as the worst two ones are always discarded. The average execution time of barrier synchronization is then computed as the arithmetic mean among the remaining 100 measurements. From the code fragment above it is apparent that for each trial a preliminary barrier synchronization is issued before the actual barrier measurement. This way we could isolate and measure the overhead of GAMMA barrier synchronization, since processes were always already synchronized.

Figure 1 depicts the execution time curves of concurrent, serialized, 2-chains, 3-chains and 4-chains barrier synchronization protocols implemented atop GAMMA and issued by up to 16 already synchronized processors connected by a shared Fast Ethernet.

The exponential behaviour exhibited by the concurrent barrier protocol is clearly apparent. It is an expected consequence of the great number of collisions arising on the Ethernet bus when slaves try to communicate with the master without coordinating with one another.

The performance profile of the serialized barrier protocol was expected to be a linear function of the number of nodes. Such linear behaviour is clearly apparent and well fitted by the following linear function of the number of nodes N (time is in μs):

$$T(N) = 13.6 \cdot N \tag{1}$$

which simply models the round-trip time among a ring of N nodes on GAMMA assuming a one-way latency time of 13.6 μs (given by the sum of GAMMA

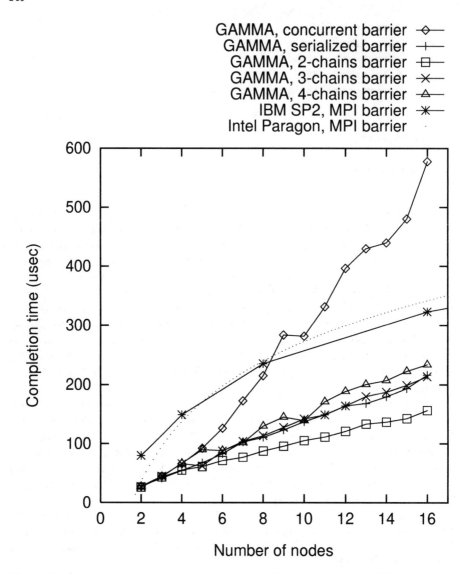

Fig. 1. Execution time of some barrier synchronization protocols on GAMMA compared with MPI barriers on IBM SP2 and Intel Paragon.

latency time plus the 0.9 μs latency of our Fast Ethernet repeater hub).

The performance curve for the 2-chains barrier synchronization protocol in the case of already synchronized processes on a shared Fast Ethernet appears to be linear as well. It nicely fits the following linear equation when $N \geq 3$:

$$T(N) = 20 + 8.5 \cdot N \qquad (2)$$

As expected, the 2-chains barrier protocol not only outperforms the (inefficient) concurrent barrier protocol, but also performs better than the plain serialized protocol. This means that the 2-chains protocol achieves better exploitation of the Fast Ethernet bus without generating collisions, thanks to a greater amount of parallelism compared to the serialized protocol achieved at a very low collision rate (at most one initial collision). Of course the exploited amount of raw Fast Ethernet bandwidth is low, due to the very small size of packets involved in the protocol, but this is not of concern when dealing with inter-process synchronization.

The 3-chains barrier protocol appears to behave the same as the serialized protocol. This means that the contention rate of 3-chains protocol is high enough to compensate the potential performance improvement due to an even greater degree of parallelism. This behaviour can be read as a wrong choice of granularity in exploiting parallelism: The communication overhead (here due to Ethernet contention) becomes too large compared to the potential performance gain when more than two chains are engaged in the barrier protocol. Accordingly, the 4-chains protocol behaves even worse than the 3-chains protocol, denoting an even higher contention rate.

Since the 3-chains protocol performs significantly worse than the 2-chains protocol we can argue that also a tree-based barrier protocol on shared Fast Ethernet would perform worse than 2-chains protocol. Such claim is supported by the consideration that a tree-based protocol has a greater average degree of parallelism compared to the 3-chains protocol already in case of more than eight processors.

A comparison with the performance profile of MPI barrier primitives implemented on IBM SP2 and Intel Paragon is provided. Performance measurements for such two commercial MPPs are quoted from [10]. We argue that the comparison between MPI and GAMMA in the case of barrier synchronization primitive is fair. Indeed the MPI barrier primitive could in principle be implemented as a straightforward mapping onto the GAMMA barrier primitive with very limited additional software overhead. It is quite evident that both the serialized and the 2-chains barrier protocols implemented atop GAMMA perform significantly better than MPI barrier on both MPPs, at least with up to 32 processors. Much of the superiority of GAMMA barrier synchronization over other MPPs is due to the exploitation of the broadcast service offered by the underlying Fast Ethernet LAN. Indeed the logarithmic profile of MPI barrier on both MPPs will eventually win over the linear behaviour of GAMMA barriers, but it is apparent from the execution time curves that the GAMMA 2-chains barrier protocol is able to perform significantly better than the MPI barrier on IBM SP2 and Intel Paragon even with a significant number of processors (at least about 48), not to mention the much better price/performance ratio.

6 Future work

We are currently engaged in designing and implementing a suite of collective communication mechanisms atop GAMMA. The use of hardware broadcast services provided by the Ethernet standard has been of great help in order to achieve the best performance with barrier synchronization. We are working on implementing efficient protocols for other collective communication mechanisms at the very competitive cost/performance ratio offered by shared Fast Ethernet, by exploiting the insight gained with our experience on barrier protocols.

In the short term we plan to implement an MPI programming interface for the GAMMA collective communication suite. Our goal is to address application portability issues by providing a standard programming interface, but without introducing any significant software overhead. With regards to collective communications, the key issue is to re-implement MPI support to process grouping atop GAMMA group mechanisms. MPI offers multi-level hierarchical process grouping and support for some predefined process topologies. The current version of GAMMA supports only basic and static process grouping. One way to support MPI atop GAMMA is to extend GAMMA itself with some of the advanced MPI grouping facilities. However the most immediate and cost-effective solution for achieving an efficient MPI implementation on a network of PCs appears to be a modification of a public domain MPI implementation such as, e.g., Argonne's MPICH socket-based library [9]. We could map only the basic process grouping services directly onto GAMMA while keeping all the remaining grouping services on the (inefficient) socket implementation. Such approach would allow us to efficiently support a large number of MPI applications which are based on very elementary SPMD process grouping mechanisms, with no loss of generality and completeness in the MPI interface.

References

1. Connection Machine CM-5 Technical Summary. Technical report, Thinking Machines Corporation, Cambridge, Massachusetts, 1992.
2. A. Bar-Noy and S. Knipis. Designing Broadcasting Algorithms in the Postal Model for Message-Passing Systems. In *Proc. of the 4th ACM Symp. on Parallel Algorithms and Architectures (SPAA '92)*, June 1992.
3. M. Bernaschi and G. Iannello. Efficient Collective Communication Operations in PVMe. In *2nd EuroPVM Users' Group Meeting*, Lyon, France, September 1995.
4. J. Bruck, D. Dolev, C. Ho, M. Rosu, and R. Strong. Efficient Message Passing Interface (MPI) for Parallel Computing on Clusters of Workstations. *Journal of Parallel and Distributed Computing*, 40(1):19–34, January 1997.
5. G. Chiola and G. Ciaccio. Implementing a Low Cost, Low Latency Parallel Platform. *Parallel Computing*, (22):1703–1717, 1997.
6. G. Ciaccio. Optimal Communication Performance on Fast Ethernet with GAMMA. In *Proc. International Workshop on Personal Computer based Networks Of Workstations (PC-NOW'98), to appear (LNCS)*, Orlando, Florida, April 1998. Springer.
7. D. Culler, K. Keeton, L.T. Liu, A. Mainwaring, R. Martin, S. Rodriguez, K. Wright, and C. Yoshikawa. Generic Active Message Interface Specification. Technical Report white paper of the NOW Team, Computer Science Dept., U. California at Berkeley, 1994.

8. G. Davies and N. Matloff. Network-Specific Performance Enhancements for PVM. In *Proc. of the Fourth IEEE Int'l Symp. on High Performance Distributed Computing (HPDC-4)*, 1995.

9. W. Gropp and E. Lusk. User's Guide for MPICH, a Portable Implementation of MPI. Technical Report MCS-TM-ANL-96/6, Argonne National Lab., University of Chicago, 1996.

10. K. Hwang, C. Wang, and C-L. Wang. Evaluating MPI Collective Communication on the SP2, T3D, and Paragon Multicomputers. In *Proc. of the 3th IEEE Symp. on High-Performance Computer Architecture (HPCA-3)*, February 1997.

11. L.T. Liu and D.E. Culler. Measurement of Active Message Performance on the CM-5. Technical Report CSD-94-807, Computer Science Dept., University of California at Berkeley, May 1994.

12. P. Marenzoni, G. Rimassa, M. Vignali, M. Bertozzi, G. Conte, and P. Rossi. An Operating System Support to Low-Overhead Communications in NOW Clusters. In *Proc. of the 1st International Workshop on Communication and Architectural Support for Network-Based Parallel Computing (CANPC'97), LNCS 1199*, pages 130–143, February 1997.

13. R. P. Martin. HPAM: An Active Message layer for a Network of HP Workstations. In *Proc. of Hot Interconnect II*, August 1994.

14. S. Pakin, V. Karamcheti, and A. Chien. Fast Messages (FM): Efficient, Portable Communication for Workstation Clusters and Massively-Parallel Processors. *IEEE Concurrency*, 1997 (to appear).

15. S. Rodrigues, T. Anderson, and D. Culler. High-performance Local-area Communication Using Fast Sockets. In *Proc. USENIX'97*, 1997.

16. T. Sterling. The Scientific Workstation of the Future May Be a Pile of PCs. *Comm. of ACM*, 39(9):11–12, September 1996.

17. T. Sterling, D.J. Becker, D. Savarese, J.E. Dorband, U.A. Ranawake, and C.V. Packer. BEOWULF: A Parallel Workstation for Scientific Computation. In *Proc. 24th Int. Conf. on Parallel Processing*, Oconomowoc, Wisconsin, August 1995.

18. M. R. Swanson and L. B. Stoller. Low Latency Workstation Cluster Communications Using Sender-Based Protocols. Technical Report UUCS-96-001, Dept. of Computer Science, University of Utah, January 1996.

19. T. von Eicken, V. Avula, A. Basu, and V. Buch. Low-latency Communication Over ATM Networks Using Active Messages. *IEEE Micro*, 15(1):46–64, February 1995.

20. T. von Eicken, A. Basu, V. Buch, and W. Vogels. U-Net: A User-Level Network Interface for Parallel and Distributed Computing. In *Proc. of the 15th ACM Symp. on Operating Systems Principles (SOSP'95)*, Copper Mountain, Colorado, December 1995. ACM Press.

21. T. von Eicken, D.E. Culler, S.C. Goldstein, and K.E. Schauser. Active Messages: A Mechanism for Integrated Communication and Computation. In *Proc. of the 19th Annual Int'l Symp. on Computer Architecture (ISCA'92)*, Gold Coast, Australia, May 1992. ACM Press.

22. T. M. Warschko, W. F. Tichy, and C. H. Herter. Efficient Parallel Computing on Workstation Clusters. Technical report, http://wwwipd.ira.uka.de / warschko /parapc /sc95.html, Karlsruhe, Germany, 1995.

23. M. Welsh, A. Basu, and T. von Eicken. Low-latency Communication over Fast Ethernet. In *Proc. Euro-Par'96*, Lyon, France, August 1996.

Parallel Routing Table Computation for Scalable IP Routers

Xipeng Xiao *and* Lionel M. Ni

Department of Computer Science
3115 Engineering Building
Michigan State University
East Lansing, MI 48824-1226
{xiaoxipe, ni}@cps.msu.edu

Abstract: The exponential growth of Internet traffic requires that routers be scalable. A generic scalable IP router is typically composed of a number of routing nodes (RNs) interconnected by a scalable switching fabric. A critical issue in the design of scalable IP routers is to provide a global and consistent routing table in such distributed-memory architectures. A parallel routing table computation approach is proposed in this paper. By dividing an OSPF area into a number of disjoint Within-Area-Routing-Regions (WARRs), the computation required to calculate the routing table can be divided into multiple independent portions and done by different RNs in parallel. Compared to conventional approaches, this approach can have a speedup between n and n^2 for within-area link state updates and n for outside-area link state updates, where n is the number of RNs in the router. This parallel routing table computation approach requires no modification of OSPF.

1. Introduction

The Internet traffic has been doubling every 9 months. This trend has lasted for a long time and will continue for many years. Such growth far outpaces the progress in the speed and capacity of semiconductors. In order for the Internet to survive, routers must be scalable. In other words, users must be able to add more processing power and internal bandwidth to the router and improve the performance proportionally.

Many scalable router architectures have been proposed recently. Among the most popular are the *Massively Parallel Router* (MPR) of Pluris Inc. and the *GRF IP Switch* of Ascend Inc. A MPR consists of a large number of processing nodes. Each processing node is a single-board computer. These processing nodes are interconnected by a *Self-Healing Butterfly Switch*. Each processing node has its own routing table. They share the routing load of the router. A GRF IP Switch is composed of multiple *IP Forwarding Media Cards* interconnected by a crossbar switch. Each media card has its own processor, network interfaces and routing table. All media cards perform IP routing independently. More scalable router architectures can be found in [9][10]. Despite the superficial differences, the architectures of these scalable routers are very similar. A high-speed (crossbar) switch interconnects multiple *Routing Nodes* (RNs). Each RN has its own processor, network interfaces and memory. It provides one or more ports of the router. All the RNs route packets independently. If a packet must go through the port of another RN, that RN will not route the packet, it simply forwards the packet through the link layer. A generic scalable router architecture is depicted in Fig. 1. The scalability comes from the ease to add more processing power and internal bandwidth to the router. Doubling the number of RNs and switches will double the throughput of the router.

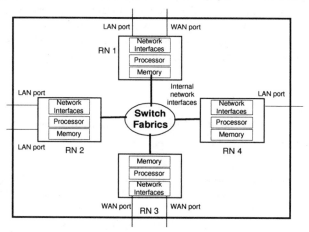

Fig. 1. Generic Router Architecture

How to compute and maintain the routing table in such router architecture is an important and challenging issue. Currently the most popular routing protocols are *Open Shortest Path First* (OSPF) and *Border Gateway Protocol* (BGP). OSPF has many good features including fast convergence and light traffic overhead. But whenever the topology of the network changes, the router has to re-compute part or the entire of its routing table. The Internet consists of more than 20 millions hosts and more than 1 million named-domains [7]. It was reported that there are more than 40 "*route flaps*" per second in the Internet backbone [7]. They put a heavy computation load on the routers. Besides normal route updates that reflect network topology changes, it was reported that "99 percent of routing information is pathological and may not reflect real network topology changes" [5]. Although a single pathological route update only requires some minimal CPU cycles and memory buffers, "sufficiently high rate of pathological updates (300 updates per second) are enough to crash a widely deployed, high-end model of Internet router" [5]. "Internet routing has become less predictable in major ways" [6]. Many reports on the increased instability of Internet routing can be found in [7]. Therefore, it is imperative to make the routing table computation faster and more robust.

Both OSPF and BGP run as a monolithic process. This is because they were designed at a time when most of the routers only have a single processor. In scalable routers, there are multiple RNs. We can significantly improve the routing information processing speed by having different RNs process different routing information in parallel. In this paper, we proposed a parallel routing table computation algorithm for

OSPF on the generic scalable router architecture. We will show that by introducing the concept of *Within-Area-Routing-Region*, we can significantly reduce the amount of the computation needed to process the routing information. Moreover, the computation is done by different RNs in parallel. We restrict the discussion to OSPF in this paper for description simplicity. The idea can be easily applied to other protocols like BGP and RIP.

The organization of the rest of this paper is as follows. We present an overview of the current routing table computation approaches for scalable routers in Section 2. A parallel routing table computation algorithm for OSPF on generic scalable router architecture is described in Section 3. The correctness and efficiency of the algorithm are also illustrated in this section. In Section 4, we discuss design issues of our parallel routing table computation approach. Finally, we summarize the paper in Section 5.

2. An Overview of Routing Table Computation Approaches for Scalable Routers

All the scalable router architectures emerged only recently. To the best of the authors' knowledge, there is no prior parallel routing table computation algorithm for any scalable router architectures. Some parallel processing ideas are expressed in the Zebra Project in Japan [8]. The key idea is to implement the popular routing daemon *gated* with multiple processes, not a traditional way of a single process. Thus, if a router has multiple RNs, these RNs can do the work simultaneously. It is known that the speedup of such *control parallelism* will not be large, because all kinds of data/control dependencies will limit the amount of work that can be parallelized. Besides, this approach doesn't provide the desirable scalability: even if you can increase the number of RNs in the router, the program simply doesn't have that such parallelism to keep them busy. Adding more RNs thus will not improve the performance proportionally.

All RNs in the generic scalable router architecture has its own memory. Such architecture is more scalable than the shared-memory architecture because the adding of a RN will not affect other RNs in any way. In such architecture, there are a number of ways to compute the routing table.

The simplest way is to designate one RN as the *Routing Server* (RS). When other RNs receive any routing information (i.e. *Link State Advertisements*, LSAs), they simply forward the routing information to the routing server. The routing server will compute the routing table on behalf of all RNs. After the routing table is computed, the routing server broadcasts it to other RNs. Other RNs store the routing table and use it to route packets.

The most attracting property of this approach is its simplicity. We don't have to change the routing table computation algorithm (named *Shortest Path First*, SPF) of OSPF at all. Another advantage is that only the routing server will do the routing table computation. Other RNs can concentrate on forwarding. This can improve their forwarding efficiency. The disadvantages of this approach are (1) the load of the routing server is significantly heavier than other RNs. This may hinder the router's scalability. (2) A single point failure at the routing server will bring down the router. This routing table computation approach is in fact the same as the routing table computation approach for conventional single-RN routers. Currently this approach is used in most commercial scalable routers including Pluris MPR, Ascend GRF IP Switches, and Cisco 12000 Routers.

Another straightforward approach to compute the routing table is to let each RN in the router compute its own routing table autonomously. In this approach, each RN regards itself and other RNs as independent routers connected by a *non-broadcast multiple access* network (NBMA). Each RN forms adjacency with all other RNs in the router. These RNs run their own OSPF protocols. They forward routing information to their neighbors as required by OSPF. Since these RNs get the same routing information, they will eventually come up with identical routing tables.

The advantage of this approach is its simplicity. We don't need to do any work at all. Even the forwarding of routing information to other RNs are done by OSPF. However, from a router point of view, it does n times as much work as a conventional router, where n is the number of RNs in the router. It also requires n times as much memory to store the routing table.

Some parallel processing ideas are embedded in this approach. The reason these RNs do identical and redundant work is because they all receive identical routing information. More specifically, all the RNs have complete (and thus identical) topology information of the network. When the topology of the network changes, all RNs will do re-computation and come up with identical results. This naturally leads us to do the following things: divide the topology information of the network among RNs, let each RN compute part of the routing table on the basis of its own topology information. We then combine the routing tables of all RNs to get the global routing table of the router.

This is the basic idea of our parallel routing table computation algorithm. Obviously, if the networks and routers that are reachable from one RN are unreachable from other RNs (Fig. 2a), then this approach works beautifully. Each RN keeps topology information of its own *routing region*, which consists of all the networks and routers that are reachable from that RN. A RN only receives routing information from its own routing region. It doesn't forward this routing information to any other RNs. Each RN autonomously computes the routing table for all the destinations in its routing region. We then combine all RNs' routing tables to get the complete routing table of the router. None of the work done by one RN is redundant,

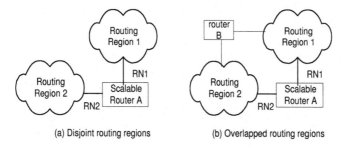

(a) Disjoint routing regions   (b) Overlapped routing regions

Fig. 2. Routing Regions of A Scalable Router

because all RNs have different topology information. This approach is naturally parallel. If the computation work is balanced among the n RNs in the router, we can achieve a speedup of n.

However, if the routing regions of two RNs overlapped (Fig. 2b), both RNs will receive identical routing information due to the flooding propagation of the link state advertisements. Therefore these two RNs will do identical work if they all compute the routing table. In order to avoid redundant work, we naturally want to stop one RN from computing the routing table and let it copy the routing table of the other RN. The problem with this approach is that there are many service providers in the Internet. For the same destination, different providers will provide different routes. Therefore, it is very likely that different ports (i.e. RNs) of a router will lead to common destinations somewhere in the Internet. In other words, the routing regions of different RNs will overlap somewhere in the Internet In this case, only a single RN will compute the routing table. The attempted "parallel" routing table computation approach is thus reduced to the routing server approach. This may be the part of the explanation why Cisco, Pluris and Ascend all adopt the routing server approach.

Now the point is clear. In order to compute the routing table in parallel, we must find out a way to divide the computation work among RNs. We cannot divide the computation according to the routing regions of RNs, because these routing regions are likely to overlap. In the next section, we will show that by introducing a concept called *Within-Area-Routing-Region* (WARR), this problem can be solved elegantly.

3. A Parallel Routing Table Computation Algorithm for the OSPF

The key observation in leading us to solving the problem is that, although it is likely that the routing regions of two RNs will overlap somewhere in the Internet, they are not likely to overlap within the *Area* where the router is deployed. Area is a concept defined in OSPF as "a group of networks (whose IP addresses fall in a user specified IP address range), together with the routers having interfaces to any one of these networks". An *Autonomous System* (AS) with four areas is shown in Fig. 3.[1] Define the *Within-Area-Routing-Region* (WARR) of a RN as all the routers and networks within the area that are reachable from the RN without going through other RNs in the router. In Fig. 3, for router RT1, the WARR of RN1 consists of networks n2, n3, n4 and routers RT2, RT3, RT4; the WARR of RN2 consists solely of network n1. For router RT6, WARR1 (of RN1) consists of router RT4, RT5 and RT7; WARR2 (of RN2) consists of RT3; WARR3 (of RN3) consists of RT10. Now our objective is to find out a scheme to divide the routing table computation work among different RNs according to their WARRs, instead of their routing regions (which will extend outside the area), so that different RNs can compute the routing table in parallel. In this section, we describe such an algorithm and illustrate its correctness and surprisingly high efficiency.

---

[1] This figure is not coined by the authors. It is quoted from the RFC for OSPF (RFC 1583)

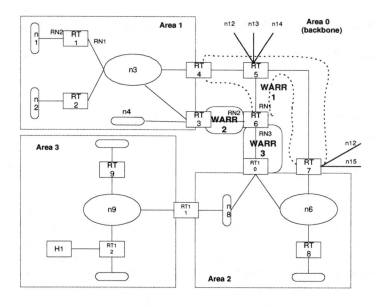

Fig. 3. An autonomous system with 4 areas

3.1 Description of the Algorithm

One important observation on the definition of WARR is that, the WARRs of two RNs are either disjoint or completely overlapped. It will never happen that two RNs have different WARRs, but these two WARRs are overlapped partly. This is because if two WARRs overlap, then all the networks and routers in one WARR are reachable from the other. By the definition of WARR, they form a single WARR (i.e., the two RNs have the same WARR). Mathematically speaking, WARR is defined on *reachability*. Since reachability is an *equivalent relation*, different WARRs must be disjoint. For example, the WARRs of RN1 and RN2 of router RT6 are disjoint now. But if we add a new link between routers RT3 and RT4, both RNs will have an identical WARR that consists of routers RT3, RT4, RT5 and RT7. Besides, disjoint WARRs can lead to common destinations outside the area. For example in router RT6, the WARR of RN1 and WARR of RN 2 can both lead to network n3.

If the WARRs of multiple RNs are the same, whatever link state advertisements received by one RN will also be received the other RNs, due to the flooding propagation of the link state advertisements in OSPF. Therefore, all these RNs will have identical topology information of the WARR. If they computed the routing table, they would come up with identical results. Therefore, these RNs can just elect one RN to compute the routing table. This RN is called the *Designated Routing Node* (DRN) of that WARR. Others are called non-DRNs. The non-DRNs will stop running the OSPF protocol and just copy the routing table computed by the DRN. If a RN doesn't share its WARR with other RNs, it is the DRN for that WARR by default.

Given the definition of WARR, our parallel routing table computation algorithm can be summarized below:

1. Every RN runs its own OSPF protocol as if it was a conventional router. If multiple RNs have overlapping WARRs, a single RN will be elected as the DRN for that WARR.
2. Every DRN computes its part of the routing table
3. Every DRN broadcasts the changed entries of its routing table to all other RNs.
4. Every RN selectively installs the received routing table entries into its own routing table

We have already explained why the RNs should elect a DRN if they share the same WARR. After the election, different DRNs have different and disjoint topology information of the area. Each DRN will compute its part of the routing table using only its own topology information stored in its *Link State Database* (LSDB). Before going into detail, let's illustrate the idea of the algorithm with the following example. In Fig. 3, RN2 of RT6 will compute routes to networks in Area 1 by examining the *link state advertisements* (LSAs) from router RT3. The LSAs from RT3 describe the shortest paths from RT3 to all the routers and networks in Area 1. By adding the cost from itself to RT3, RN2 can compute the shortest paths from itself to all networks in Area 1. RN2 will not compute the routes to networks in Area 2 and Area 3, because it never receives any LSAs for Area 2 and Area 3 from anybody. RN2 doesn't even know the existence of Area 2 and Area 3 from the routing table computation perspective. Similarly RN3 will calculate routes to destinations in Area 2 and Area 3 by examining the LSAs from RT10, but not to destinations in Area 1. RN1 will compute routes to Area 1 by examining the LSAs from RT4, and routes to Area 2 and Area 3 by examining LSAs from RT7. After a RN finishes computing its routing table, it broadcasts the changed routing table entries to other RNs. Each RN then merges its own routing table with those received from other RNs. If multiple RNs have paths to a destination, the shortest one will be selected as the route to that destination for the router. Other paths are discarded. For example, assuming that the cost of every link in Fig. 3 is 1, RN1 has the shortest path to n3 with cost 3, RN2 has the shortest path to n3 with cost 2. After merging their routing tables, RN1 and RN3 will adopt the shortest path provided by RN2 as their routes to n3. They will send packets destined to network n3 through the port of RN2. From now on, RN2 will be in charge of the route to n3. If RN2 finds out that the cost of the route to n3 has changed, no matter whether the cost has increased or decreased, it will broadcast the changed route to RN1 and RN3. In contrast, if RN1 or RN3 finds out that the cost of the route to n3 has changed, it will broadcast the change only if the new cost is lower than the cost of the route provided by RN2. Please note that although both RN1 and RN2 compute routes to a network n3, none of their work is redundant. This is because RN1 computes the shortest path to n3 via RT4. RN2 compute shortest path to n3 via RT3. If router RT6 was a conventional router or a scalable router with a routing server, it has to compute and compare the shortest path to n3 via RT3 and the shortest path to n3 via RT4 and then take the shorter one anyway. Therefore, the work done by the routing server is the same as the total work done by RN1 and RN2 with our approach. The reason why RN1 and RN2 can compute their own shortest paths to n3 independently is because the WARRs of RN 1 and RN2 are disjoint. Any paths from RN1 to n3 will never go through WARR2 of RN2. So RN1 can compute its shortest path to n3 without counseling RN2, and vice versa. We have a very efficient scheme for each RN to send its changed routing table entries to other RNs. The overhead of sending such entries will not be a concern.

Now we are ready to explain the working mechanism of our algorithm. The following procedure details the operations of a RN upon receiving any link state advertisements.

2.1 For a non-DRN, it simply forwards the link state advertisement to its DRN;

2.2 For a DRN, it proceeds like a normal router. It may update its link state database, re-compute part of or the entire of its routing table.
- If any of the routes are changed:
  - If this DRN currently provides the shortest path to that destination,
    - If the cost of the path changes, no matter if it becomes higher or lower, or the DRN now has more or fewer equal-cost paths to that destination, replace the current routing table entry and broadcast the new entry.
  - If this RN does not currently provides the shortest path to that destination.
    - If the cost is lower than the original route, replace the current entry and broadcast it.
    - If the cost is equal, add it as an equal-cost path and broadcast it.
    - If the cost is higher than the original route, just append this path to the current routing table entry but not broadcasts it. This is to temporarily store this path for later comparison.

After a DRN computes its routing table, it will broadcast the changed entries other RNs in the router. When a RN computes its routing table for the first time, all the routing table entries are considered changed and broadcast to other RNs. The transmission of changed routing table entries should take precedence over other traffic to be forwarded by the router.

When a RN receives any changed routing table entries from another RN, it performs the following operations:

3.1 Examines its own routing table to see if an entry for the destination has already existed.

3.2 If there is no such an entry,
- The received entry is added to the routing table.

3.3 Otherwise,
- If the receiving RN is a non-DRN, it installs the received entry to its routing table
- If the cost of the received entry is lower, then it replaces the current entry with the received one.
- If the cost of the received entry is higher and the receiving RN is a DRN, the RN will examine the received entry.
  - If the path specified by this entry is an *intra-area path*, then the entry is installed in the receiving RN's routing table.
  - If the path is an *inter-area path* or *external path*
    - If there is no temporary entry (computed and stored in step 2.2) for this destination, start a re-computation to see if it has a shorter path to the destination.

- If there is no path to the destination, or if the cost of the temporary path is higher than the received entry's cost, replace the current routing table entry with the received entry.
- If the temporary path's cost is lower, the received entry is discarded. The temporary entry will be broadcast to all other DRNs in the router.

Since the WARRs of different DRNs are disjoint, only one DRN will have the path to a destination within the area. Therefore, upon receiving any changed intra-area path, there is no need to do any re-computation. However, if the cost of an inter-area route or external route increases, the re-computation is necessary for the receiving DRN, because the originating DRN only computes the shortest route via its own WARR. Although originally it may have the shortest path to the destination, after the cost become higher, other DRNs may have a shorter path. For example, if the link between RT3 and n3 breaks, RN2 of router RT6 will announce to RN1 and RN3 that n3 is unreachable (infinite cost). In this case, RN 1 and RN3 must compute their own shortest paths to n3. RN1 will produce one with cost 3. This route will be broadcast to RN2 and RN3. Here RN1 and RN3's work in computing the shortest path to n3 is done in parallel.

Obviously, every RN in the router will have identical routing table in this way.

The correctness and efficiency of the algorithm are illustrated in Section 3.2.

3.2   Correctness and Efficiency of the Algorithm

For two arbitrary WARRs, they can either lead to common destinations outside the area or not. For a topology change, it can either happen within the area or outside the area. This leads to four possible combinations. In this section, we will demonstrate the correctness by showing that, in all cases, the shortest paths produced by our algorithm are the same as those produced by a conventional router with the SPF algorithm. We will demonstrate the efficiency by showing that, in all cases, our approach will do less work and do it in parallel.

Case 1: Within-area Changes without Common Outside-area Destinations

Considering router RT1 in Fig. 3, its two RNs have disjoint WARRs. RN1's WARR consists of n2, n3, n4, RT2, RT3 and RT4. RN2's WARR consists of n3. Now assume that the link RT1-n1 changes. Since this is a within-area change, for the SPF algorithm, RT1 will have to re-compute routes to all destinations including network n1, n6 and n9 [4]. Using our algorithm, since the WARRs of RN1 and RN2 are disjoint, RN1 and RN2 will compute their own routing tables independently, using the topology information of WARR1 and WARR2, respectively. When link RT1-n1 changes, only RN2 will receive such link state advertisement and re-compute its routing table. This includes only a single route to n1. Even though RN2 doesn't have the topology information of WARR1, it can still compute shortest path to n1. This is because the shortest route will not go through WARR1 anyway. Otherwise WARR1 and WARR 2 would be overlapped. After the computation, RN2 will broadcast the new route to n1 (with the changed cost) to RN1. Since this is an intra-area route, RN1 simply replace its original route to n1 with the newly received entry (Step 3.3 in the algorithm). RN1 need not do any computation at all. We clearly see that a large amount of computation is saved. The speedup here can be far greater than 2, even though there are only two RNs in the router. Similarly, if something within WARR1 changes, RN2 need not do any computation. Our approach works even better if something within WARR1 changes at about the same time as something else changes within WARR2. For a conventional router, it will have to compute the whole routing table twice, in a serial fashion. With our approach, RN1 and RN2 only compute their own parts of the routing table. Each of them does less work than a conventional router does with a single change. And they do their work simultaneously. For a router with n RNs, if n changes happen simultaneously at n different WARRs, and the loads of the n RNs are balanced (This happens when the routing regions of these n RNs are about the same size), it takes each RN $1/n$ time unit to compute the routing table with our approach, while it takes a conventional router n time unit. Here a time unit is the time it takes for a conventional router to re-compute its whole routing table. Therefore our approach achieves a speedup of n^2 over a conventional router.

Case 2: Outside-area Changes without Common Outside-area Destinations

Considering router RT1, if the link between RT4 and RT5 breaks, RN1 will receive the link state advertisements reflecting this change. RN1 will re-compute routes to all the destinations (router RT5 and RT7) affected by this change. RN1 then broadcasts the new routes for RT5 and RT7 to RN2. We clearly see that RN1 doesn't need any information in order to compute the shortest paths to RT5 and RT7, thus our approach will correctly produce the shortest paths in this case. Since the cost of the routes to RT5 and RT7 increases, RN2 will try to compute its own routes (Step 3.3 in the algorithm). Since RN1 doesn't have any link state advertisements about RT5 and RT7, RN2 will end up doing nothing. Please note that if RN2 does have to examine some link state advertisements, a conventional router will have to do that either. Even in that case, if multiple changes happen at about the same time in the routing regions of different RNs – from the introduction we know that this will be the common case – all the RNs will be kept busy. The speedup is n compared to a conventional router.

Case 3: Within-area Changes with Common Outside-area Destinations

Now let's consider router RT6. The WARRs of RN1 and RN2 can both lead to network n3 (and other networks) in Area 1. Assume that the link between RT3 and RT6 breaks. RN 2 of RT6 will re-compute its routing table and finds out that network n3 is unreachable, because RN 2 only has the topology information of WARR 2. Before link RT3-RT6 breaks, RN 2 provides the shortest route to n3, so even the cost of the new route is higher than the previous one, RN 2 still broadcasts the it to RN 1 and RN 3 (Step 2.2). RN 1 and RN 3 will notice that the cost of the received route is higher than the cost of the route in their own routing table. Therefore, RN1 and RN 3 will try to compute a shorter route to network n3. RN1 will come up with such a route with cost 3. So RN 1 broadcasts this route to RN2 and RN3. RN2 and RN 3 then install this route into their routing tables.

If RT6 was a conventional router, when link RT3-RT6 breaks, it will re-compute routes to all the networks, within or outside the area. With our approach, only RN2 will re-compute its whole routing table, RN1 and RN3 only re-compute routes for destinations with increased cost. They will not re-compute the external routes and the inter-area routes to Area 2 and Area 3. Besides, RN 1 and RN 3 do their work in parallel. Therefore a large amount of work is saved. The speedup can be more than 3 for RT6. In general, if multiple changes happen at about the same time in n different WARRs, all the RNs will be kept busy. Each of them will do less work than a conventional router with a single within-area change. Therefore, the speedup is between n and n^2.

If link RT3-RT6 changes in a way that its cost becomes lower. Then RN1 and RN3 will not be triggered to do any computation at all. Much less work is done by our router than a conventional router. The speedup can be far higher than 3 for RT6.

Case 4: Outside-area Changes with Common Outside-area Destinations

Let's consider router RT6 and assume that link n3-RT3 breaks. RN1 and RN2 will receive the link state advertisements from RT4 and RT3, respectively. Both RN1 and RN 2 will re-compute the shortest paths to those destinations affected by the change. RN1 will find out that via its WARR1, the shortest route to n3 has cost 3. RN2 will find out that n3 is now unreachable via WARR2. Since RN2 previously holds the shortest route to n3, it will announce the new route to RN1 and RN3. Let's assume that RN1 has found out a route of cost 3 before it receives the new route of infinite cost from RN 2. Since the newly computed route's cost is higher than cost of the current route in its routing table, and since RN 1 doesn't provide the current route, RN 1 will not broadcast this newly computed route. It will store the route temporarily instead (Step 2.2). When RN1 receives the new route of infinite cost from RN2, it realizes that the cost of received route is higher than the cost of the temporarily stored route. RN1 will discard the received route, replace the current route in its routing table with the temporarily stored route, and broadcast it to RN2 and RN3. If RN1 comes up with the route of cost 3 after receiving the route of infinite cost from RN2, it simply replaces the received route with the newly computed one and broadcasts it to other RNs. In both cases, RN2 and RN3 will install the route provided by RN1 into their routing tables.

The total amount of computation done by RN1 and RN2 is the same as the work done by a conventional router. But the work is done in parallel. If multiple changes happen at about the same time – from the introduction we know this is the common case – the speedup is n for a router with n RNs.

In summary, different WARRs either lead to common destinations outside the area or not. A link state change either happens within the area or outside the area. We have showed that our algorithm can correctly compute the shortest paths in all cases. Therefore we conclude that the algorithm is correct. If a link state change happens within the area where the router locates, our router has a best case speedup higher than n, where n is the number of RNs in the router. If a link state change happens outside the area, the best case speedup is n. Realizing that the best case speedup comes when multiple changes happen at about the same time at different places, as is the common case in today's Internet, we conclude that the average case speedup will be close to the best case speedup.

4. Other Design Issues

In this section we address a series of important issues related to this parallel routing table computation approach.

4.1 WARR Discovery, Merging and Splitting

WARR is the cornerstone of our parallel routing table computation approach. Each RN dynamically discovers its WARR as follows. At the router startup, every RN regards itself as an autonomous router. It runs its own OSPF protocol and computes routes to all the reachable destinations. If the RN comes up with a route to another RN (also regarded as an autonomous router before this moment) in the same router, then the RN knows that its WARR overlaps with the other RN's. At this moment, if the discovering RN finds that its ID (e.g. IP address) is smaller than the other RN's, then it sends a message to tell the other RN to stop running OSPF. Otherwise, it simply stops running OSPF itself.

A link state change may cause two different WARRs to merge or cause a WARR to split into two different WARRs. For example, if a link is added between routers RT3 and RT4, then the WARRs of RN1 and RN2 merge into a single WARR. RN1 and RN2 will soon discover this merge when they discover a route to each other. This merge can be easily handled. RN1 and RN2 will elect a DRN for the new WARR to compute the routing table. The DRN will mark the ports of the non-DRNs as its own ports. For example, if RN1 is elected, it will mark the port of RN2 as its own. Logically this has the effect of inheriting the topology information of WARR2 because RN1 will start considering router RT3 as its neighbor. Thus the link state advertisements about WARR2 will be used by RN1 to compute its routing table [4]. RN2 will stop running OSPF and just forwards the link state advertisements it receives to RN1. RN2 also receives the computed routing table from RN1.

Let's assume that after adding link RT3-RT4, RN1 becomes the DRN of this WARR. Then link RT3-RT4 breaks and the WARR splits into two separate WARRs. At this moment, RN1 still has the complete topology of the two WARRs. So even if no action is taken, RN1 can still compute all the routes correctly, provided that RN 2 forwards the link state advertisements it receives to RN1. RN1 acts like a routing server in this case. But since now the WARRs of RN1 and RN2 are disjoint, we can achieve better performance by letting RN1 and RN2 do the work in parallel. One approach to do this is as follows. When link RT3-RT4 breaks, RN1 will find out that RN2 is now unreachable via route outside the router. In addition to broadcasting the changed routing table entries to other RNs, RN1 will also send its link state database to RN 2 and notify RN 2 that it becomes a DRN. Physically, both RN1 and RN2 have complete topology information of WARR1 and WARR2 at this moment. But this will not cause RN1 or RN2 to do any redundant work because RN1 will unmark the port belong to RN2 (That port was marked previously when the WARR1 and WARR2 merged). This has the effect of discarding the topology information of WARR2 for RN1, because RN1 will not consider router RT3 as its neighbor anymore. Those link state advertisements about WARR2 will never be used by RN1 again [4]. Besides, RN1 and RN2 don't forward link state advertisements to each other. RN1 will eventually flush the link state advertisements about WARR2 because they are refreshed. As is similar for RN2.

4.2 Overhead of Broadcasting the Changed Routing Table Entries

The sending and receiving of changed routing table entries consumes CPU cycles as well as internal bandwidth of the router. If the number of messages or the size of the messages is large, the communication overhead can significantly affect the router performance. Large number of messages is especially harmful because the RNs will be frequently interrupted to receive messages.

Broadcast over a switch is usually done by sending the messages one by one to all the receivers. If all the n RNs in a router have some changed routing table entries, every router will receive (n-1) messages. This is not acceptable. We design an efficient broadcasting scheme for our router. The basic idea is to assign a sending order to all the DRNs. A DRN only sends the changed entries to the next DRN in this order, and the last DRN in this order will send the changes to the first one. More importantly, when the i-th DRN sends the changed entries to the $(i+1)$-th DRN, it packs the changed entries originated all other DRNs except the $(i+1)$-th one, and sends all these changes in one message to the $(i+1)$-th DRN. Since the i-th DRN does not send changed entries originated from the $(i+1)$-th DRN back to it, no changed entries will circulate among the RNs forever. Every changed entry of a RN will be received by other RNs exactly once. We call this broadcasting scheme the *Circular Accumulative Broadcast* (CAB). Since every RN only receives the changed routing table entries from its left neighbor in the sending order, the number of messages is reduced $(n-1)$ times. This scheme is essential in preserving the speedup we gained from parallel routing table computation.

The size of the messages is determined by the number of changed routing table entries. In general, the number of changed entries will not be large because in a large network, it is very unlikely that a single link state change will considerably alter the topology of the network. Although a single link state advertisement may cause a RN to re-compute its whole routing table (say, a within-area change), after the computation, most of the entries will still be the same as the old ones because the topology of the network doesn't change much. In a small network, the number of routing table entries is small. The number of changed entries will not be large either.

4.3 Routing Table Inconsistency among Different RNs

During a very short period of time, i.e. after one DRN finishes calculating a new route and before other PEs receives this changed route, the routing tables of different RNs are different. But this will not cause any serious problems. Imaging that instead of having a router with n RNs, we have n routers. During a short period of time, the routing tables of these n routers can be different too. The behavior of our router is no worse than the interaction of these n routers.

4.4 Load Balancing among DRNs

In the extreme case that all the RNs have the same WARR, only the DRN will compute the routing table. In this case, our parallel routing table computation approach is reduced to the routing server approach. But within an area, the path between two nodes (networks or routers) is usually unique. Therefore, it is unlikely that two different RNs will have the same WARR. In fact, we cannot find any two RNs with the same WARR in Fig. 3.

However, even if all the RNs have different WARRs, the loads of different RNs can still be unbalanced. For example in router RT6, RN 1 will do more work than RN2 and RN3. This is because all the external routes to network n12, n13, n14 and n15 are computed by RN1. In general the number of external routes are far more than the number of intra-area and inter-area routes. In order to handle this problem, we can use a more powerful processor for RN1. Besides, if there is any non-DRN in the router, we may off-load some work from the RN1 to the non-DRN. This can be done by keep another copy of RN1's link state database at the non-DRN. When RN1 receives a link state advertisement and it is busy, it simply forwards the link state advertisement to the non-DRN and let the non-DRN do the computation and broadcasting on RN1's behalf.

The above situation will happen mainly in an autonomous system with only one or two links to the Internet backbone. For a router in the backbone, it is more likely that each interface of the router has to handle a large number of routes, the loads of different RNs tend to be balanced. But in a non-backbone AS, most of the routers will use the default route to route packets to external destinations. The strongly unbalanced load case will be rare too.

4.5 Fault Tolerance of the Router

In a conventional router or a scalable router with a routing server, a single point failure will cause the whole router to fail. In a router with our parallel routing table computation approach, since all the RNs compute and maintain their routing tables independently, a single RN failure will not cause the whole router to fail, only the routes provided the failed RN are affected. Therefore such a router is more robust.

5. Summary and Future Work

In this paper we proposed a parallel routing table computation approach for generic scalable router architecture. By dividing an OSPF area into disjoint WARRs, we divide the computation work needed to calculate the routing table into independent portions and assign them different RNs. Each RN dynamically discovers its own WARR, keeps topology information of its own WARR, and computes routes via its own WARR independently. Each RN also broadcasts the changed routing table entries to other RNs and receives the changes from other RNs. Each RN merges other RNs' routing table with its own to get the global routing table of the router. The Circular-accumulative-broadcast scheme is used for the RNs to broadcast their changed routing table entries. It reduces the number of broadcast messages *(n-1)* times for a router with n RNs. Compared to conventional approaches, our parallel routing table computation approach can have a speedup between n and n^2 for within-area link state updates and n for outside-area link state updates in the best case. Because it is very likely that multiple link state changes will happen at about the same time at different places, multiple RNs will be kept busy at any moment. Therefore the average-case speedup will be close to the best-case speedup. This parallel routing table computation approach requires no modifications of OSPF itself.

We are now extending this parallel routing table computation approach to other routing protocols like RIP, BGP and IS-IS. There are many interesting works that can be done, like off-loading some work from a busy DRN to the non-DRNs (if any), storing a single routing table distributed at all RNs instead of replicating the whole routing table at different RNs, and so many more. Since scalable routers are the trend of future router implementation, we believe parallel routing table computation will become an interesting new research field.

References

1. Vibhavasu Vuppala and Lionel M. Ni, "Design of A Scalable IP Router", Proceedings of the 1997 IEEE Hot Interconnect, Aug. 1997.
2. Pluris Inc, "Pluris Massively Parallel Routing", White Paper, http://www.pluris.com
3. Ascend Inc., "GRF IP Switch", http://www.ascend.com
4. J. Moy, "OSPF Version 2", RFC 1583, Mar. 1994
5. C. Labovitz, G.R. Malan and F. Jahanian, "Internet Routing Instability", CSE-TR-332-97, Dept. of EECS, University of Michigan
6. V. Paxson, "End-to-End Routing Behavior in the Internet." ACM SIGCOMM '96, Aug. 1996
7. Internet Performance Measurement and Analysis Project (IPMA), http://www.merit.edu/ipma
8. K. Ishiguro, Zebra Project, ftp://ftp.zebra.org/pub/zebra
9. http://www-eecs.mit.edu/
10. http://www.cisco.com/

A Tool for the Analysis of Reconfiguration and Routing Algorithms in Irregular Networks

Rafael Casado[1], Blanca Caminero[1], Pedro Cuenca[1], Francisco Quiles[1], Antonio Garrido[1], and José Duato[2]

[1] E. Univ. Politécnica, Universidad de Castilla - La Mancha, Albacete, Spain
{ rcasado, bcaminero, pcuenca, paco, antonio }@info-ab.uclm.es
[2] Facultad de Informática, Universidad Politécnica, Valencia, Spain
jduato@gap.upv.es

Abstract. High performance interconnection networking is one of the most active research fields in the area of communications. Their quick development has been increased by the interest in using multiple workstations in parallel processing. These local networks use ideas that are already successfully applied in parallel computer interconnection networks. However, their more flexible and dynamic environment exposes new problems, such as topology configuration and message routing, which are difficult to solve with the current methods used in regular networks. Therefore, it is advisable to apply tools that help the researcher to develop and verify the behavior of new algorithms for these new networks.

Nowadays, the RAAP group (Redes y Arquitecturas de Altas Prestaciones, High Performance Networks and Architectures) of the University of Castilla-La Mancha is working in this way. In this paper, we present a software tool developed by the RAAP group with the aim of helping in the research. It does not try to simulate the communications within the network (where a long computation process would not be able to guarantee none of its properties) but to analyze its behavior, through the channel dependency graph. The result is an agile and practical tool that provides conclusions in a quick and reliable way.

1 Introduction

The technological convergence between local area networks and massively parallel multicomputers has caused the development of new high performance local networks, (Autonet [1], Myrinet [2] and ServerNet [3]). These networks are being used with excellent results in different applications, from the interactive ones to the distributed and parallel ones.

High performance local area networks are structurally composed by point-to-point links between hosts and switches. The physical placement of the terminals depends on the users' needs. Under these conditions, the resulting topology is likely not to be regular. This situation does not occur in a conventional LAN, because the topology is irrelevant, as far as routing is concerned, when using a diffusion technique. The lack of regularity is one of the most important aspects to keep into account when transferring routing techniques, previously used in multicomputers, to local area environments. The routing algorithm is usually implemented in tables placed in the nodes.

Another important point is that, the topology of a multicomputer is pre-established by the architecture and it never changes, except in case of failure, i.e., it is a static environment. On the other hand, local area networks are dynamic environments, because the connection and disconnection of the nodes may occur frequently. Therefore, the development of reconfiguration algorithms is needed in order to update the information used to route user's packets in each node, when the topology changes.

Each network node can be involved in two reconfiguration situations. First, when the node is incorporated into the network, it receives its topology information. Then, we can reconfigure it as many times as necessary according to the modifications made on the initial structure.

Obviously, when we develop new routing algorithms, we have to guarantee that they are deadlock-free, unless we use recovery strategies. In order to achieve it, we must verify the nonexistence of cycles in the channel dependency graph [4]. This can be a simple task when dealing with regular networks, although it depends on the complexity of the routing algorithm used, or rather, on their level of adaptivity, i.e., the amount of possible tracks offered for the messages to advance. Anyway, the regularity facilitates this task greatly. This is because the routing algorithm is simple and the same (or slightly different) for all the nodes and mainly because starting from the analysis of small networks, which can be easily handled, we can extend it to bigger ones.

Unfortunately, in an irregular topology the process is not so simple, because we cannot solve the problem for a portion of a network and generalize the result to the whole network. The situation becomes still more complicated when we consider different routing functions (one for each configuration change) coexisting inside the network at a given time. Then, it would be necessary to guarantee that the interaction among routing functions does not produce deadlocks in the traffic of user's packets. This hard task can involve errors if it is manually performed, becoming complicated even for reduced size networks.

Several theories have been proposed for deadlock avoidance: wait channels [5], message flow model [5][6], channel wait graph [7], etc. Among them, the proposal from Dally and Seitz [8] is one of the most used. These authors establish a necessary and sufficient condition to guarantee deadlock freedom in *wormhole* routing (WH), *virtual cut-through* routing (VCT) or *store-and-forward* routing (SAF), based on the concept of *channel dependence* [4]. When a packet uses a channel, and it requests the use of another one, a dependence of the second channel takes place on the first one. In WH, these channels may not be serial. On the other hand, in VCT and SAF, the dependences only take place between adjacent channels. To guarantee deadlock avoidance, cyclic dependence chains should not exist among channels supplied by the routing function. Channels and their dependences are modeled in a graph. If nodes represent channels and an edge from node i to node j represents that channel i depends on channel j, then the condition means that the graph has no cycles.

One of the first approaches to the efficient reconfiguration in irregular networks appears in [1] for the Autonet network. A distributed reconfiguration algorithm is triggered when a significant change in the topology occurs, spreading it to the whole network, and updating the routing tables in the nodes. This algorithm does not solve the problem of deadlocks, but rather it avoids it. The reason is that user's packet traffic is stopped to avoid their blocking. When the process finishes, its circulation is reactivated. This kind of method is grouped under the definition of *static* reconfiguration techniques. It is important to point out that when static reconfiguration occurs, the network performance gets degraded.

On the other hand, there exists a great number of distributed applications that need certain quality of service (QOS) [9] to be guaranteed to their users. Video on demand [10] could be a good example. When an application with these characteristics is executed on a switched local network, it might be affected by topology changes. During reconfiguration process, the bandwidth available decreases and latency increases. Thus, as we are not allowed to stop the flow of information generated by the application, we will not be able to guarantee the requested QOS either.

Another option could be to carry out the network reconfiguration without stopping user's packets. It means that certain nodes would route messages according to old tables while other nodes would be already using the new ones, because they have already assimilated the change, i.e., more than one routing algorithm may be working simultaneously in the network.

1.1 Dynamic Reconfiguration

The application of an asynchronous total reconfiguration technique (where each node is reconfigured completely) is not enough. Fig. 1 shows an example of a network in which any reconfiguration sequence guarantees deadlock freedom. Interconnection network and routing table are shown by a directed graph that implicitly represents the *up/down* algorithm.

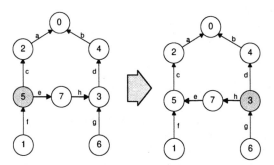

Fig. 1. Interconnection network

Fig. 2 shows dependence graphs corresponding to the initial and final topologies. The *combined graph* [11] is also shown. We can observe several dependencies arising during the transition, caused by the interaction of different routing functions.

As an alternative to this situation, we propose a progressive partial reconfiguration technique (PPR) of the network. We want to obtain the final topology from the initial one, by replacing routing tables systematically.

Performing the reconfiguration process while user's packets are travelling through the network implies modifying the system architecture. It could be done by adding specific circuitry to the usual switch in order to carry out the configuration changes in parallel with message distribution. As it is shown in Fig. 3, the switch is divided into two parts. One of them controls the switch by applying the routing function associated to the initial topology. In the other one, simultaneously with message flow, the new routing function associated with the final topology is generated. When it is possible, the switch control is passed over from the first circuit to the second one.

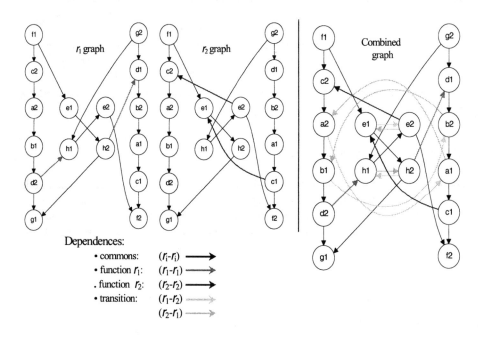

Fig. 2. Channel dependence graphs

A multiplexer could divert configuration messages from/to the configuration system. Then, they will be able to reach their destination avoiding user messages, which are retained in buffers because of flow control.

When we establish an order relationship among subsets of routing tables, we can observe how the possibilities grow exponentially. This problem does not have a straightforward solution, because the amount of manipulated data is huge and the possibility of making errors is very high.

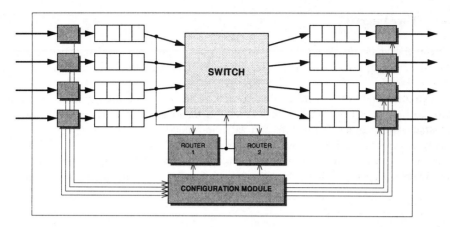

Fig. 3. Switch architecture

There is not a general reconfiguration theory in current literature. Therefore, we have decided to implement a helping tool for researchers to develop new PPR algorithms. The main purpose of this tool is to detect possible deadlocks that can occur when we apply a specific routing function on an arbitrary and variable topology network.

1.2 Desirable Features for the Tool

We are dealing with an analysis tool instead of a simulation one, because it produces correct results in a short time. To obtain the same conclusions by simulation, it would be necessary to make the network operate during a certain time (which will be considerably longer than the previous one) and check if deadlocks appear. As simulation time increases, there is a bigger probability of obtaining a reliable result. However, we will never be able to assure that a network is free of deadlocks, since an exhaustive simulation of all possibilities is impossible.

On the contrary, it would be desirable to define an initial network state and a routing function. We should also be able to modify this situation quickly. It would be interesting for us to consult the information we consider more suitable. Especially, information related to physical connection of the network, logical connection of the routing function, reachable destinations, dependence graphs or deadlock cycles presence. In general, we try to observe the evolution of the system when a reconfiguration occurs.

2   The Interconnection Network Analyzer V.2.1

The program is written in standard C++ and it can be run under MS-DOS, although it could be also run under Unix/Linux without great modifications. In the following section, we will describe the main functions of the tool.

2.1 User Interface

The analyzed system is modeled by using a reduced programming language designed just for this purpose. This language is similar to standard C and its grammar is shown in Fig. 4.

Non-terminal symbols are written in capital letters, and terminal symbols (reserved words) in lowercase. Complete denotational semantic, that includes concrete syntax, abstract syntax, semantic algebras and valuation functions, were reported in [12]. The analyzer accepts text files (programs) as its parameters.

The screen is the standard output, and is configured to 120 character per line. If we introduce a second parameter, then the information is written in a file with that name.

```
Language grammar

I                    = Identifiers
STRING               = Chains of characters

PROGRAM ::=          net { node NODES; link LINKS; };
                     DEFROUTING COMMANDS

NODES ::=            I  |  I, NODES
                     I(on) | I(on) NODES
LINKS ::=            I=I<=>I  |  I=I<=>I LINKS
DEFROUTING ::=       φ  |  routing { ROUTING };
ROUTING ::=          table I: TABLE
                     |  table I: TABLE ROUTING
TABLE ::=            use IDES;  |  use IDES; TABLE
                     |  to IDES use IDES;
                     |  to IDES use IDES; TABLE
COMMANDS ::=         φ  |  COMMAND; COMMANDS
COMMAND ::=          set node IDES=STATUS
                     |  set table I={TABLE}
                     |  wait CHANNELS
                     |  show SEES  |  cls  |  pause
STATUS ::=           on | off
CHANNELS ::=         I(I)  |  I(I), CHANNELS
SEES ::=             SEE  |  SEE, SEES
SEE ::=              "STRING"
                     |  net  |  routing
                     |  dependences
IDES ::=             I  |  I, IDES
```

Fig. 4. Language grammar

2.2 Definition of the Initial Configuration

Network definition. The interconnection network is defined by enumerating every node and bi-directional link (by indicating the nodes located at both ends). The compiler automatically decomposes a bi-directional link into two opposite unidirectional channels. Fig. 5 shows a topology example and a program that describes it.

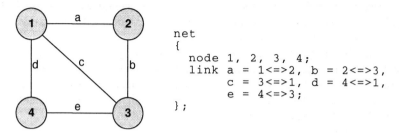

```
net
{
    node 1, 2, 3, 4;
    link a = 1<=>2, b = 2<=>3,
         c = 3<=>1, d = 4<=>1,
         e = 4<=>3;
};
```

Fig. 5. Interconnection network

The analyzer verifies the physical connectivity within the network, that is, it determines if a message would be able to reach every destination node. This checkup is a preprocessing function oriented to detect errors in input data. The network should be totally connected before the analyzer evaluates the routing function.

Routing definition. The routing function considers the current and destination nodes, and provides a set of output channels. Input channels are not considered. Therefore, the mathematical expression is the following:

$$F: \underset{\text{(current)}}{\text{Node}} \times \underset{\text{(destination)}}{\text{Node}} \rightarrow \underset{\text{(output)}}{\mathcal{P}(\text{Links})}$$

This notation is powerful enough for a wide range of (complete or partially) adaptive algorithms. Nevertheless, a more general notation has been specified in order to be included in future versions of the analyzer. This specification is mainly influenced by last generation routing algorithms, designed to be applied in irregular topologies [13].

As a descriptive example, Fig. 6 shows a routing function and the corresponding code. In order to simplify, the network has not been included.

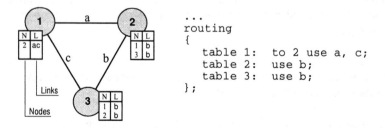

```
...
routing
{
    table 1:  to 2 use a, c;
    table 2:  use b;
    table 3:  use b;
};
```

Fig. 6. Routing function

The analyzer determines the topologic knowledge of the network: in a connected node distribution, each node keeps the portion of the routing function that concerns itself, using a table structure. The information about the rest of the network is placed in this table. Nevertheless, a node may not have stored information about any of the other nodes. In this case, it's said that a node does not know the existence of another. The analyzer informs the user about that situation and continues its analysis. This undesirable situation has special importance during an irregular LAN reconfiguration, which occurs when a switch is connected.

Then, the compiler determines the logical connectivity of the routing function. Each node has associated a routing table. All tables should be built in a coherent way; so, packet delivery can be guaranteed. Fig. 6 shows a connected network and a non-connected routing function. It can be observed that the *node 1* is not reachable from the others. In the following text, we show the result given by the analyzer when it processes this input:

Example: Results obtained by the compiler

```
Interconnection network analyzer
Version 2.1  (September 97)

Syntax........... OK
Topology......... OK

Warning:   (R) Node '2' doesn't reach node '1'.
Warning:   (R) Node '3' doesn't reach node '1'.
Error:     (R) Unconnected function.

Interrupted analysis.
```

2.3   Successive Reconfigurations

Analyzer's version 2.1 shows dynamic evolutions of the network by using a single program. Let us examine some interesting characteristics related to reconfigurations.

Node State Assignments. In order to introduce dynamic alterations in the topology, we should enable or disable some network nodes, using the *set node* command. This operation can be made in an individual or collective way. When a node appears (or disappears) all connected links do the same. The disappearance of a node causes a new network checkup.

Routing Table Assignments. We can change the routing table associated to the active nodes by using the *set table* command. Each table reassignment triggers a connectivity function checkup and a search of possible deadlocks.

Zombie Dependences. Some dependences, which might disappear when a change in routing tables occurs, do not do it immediately. We call these dependences *zombies*, and they stay because of the flow control effect on user's packets. They will not disappear until buffers are released.

Zombie dependences are controlled by using the *wait* command. It indicates explicitly when the reconfiguration should wait for the channel liberation.

2.4 Visualization Primitives

The user can specify the data he wants to see. As a result, we get the information we consider interesting, avoiding the confused treatment of many data.

The output screen is formatted to 120 columns, which leads to a reduction in the size of the printed characters, and therefore to a increase in the amount of information per page.

A brief description of the visualization primitives is now presented.

Show net. Using this command, we can show the node state (on/off) within the network. The analyzer generates a listing containing all the node labels. If the node is active, the label is shown enclosed in brackets.

Show routing. This command allows checking the routing function integrity. As routing tables are defined by *to...use* command sequences, a destination node may appear in several of these instructions. Therefore, routing information is spread all over the program. This command is doubly useful because it presents a compact information in the screen.

Show dependences. The analyzer provides the channels dependence graph associated to the routing function by using this command. The information is shown by textual enumeration of all dependences. Common dependences are shown with an arrow '->'. For zombie dependences, the arrow will be crossed out '+>'.

Other commands. Finally, the analyzer also incorporates instructions to stop the listing in the screen (*pause*) and to clear it up (*cls*).

2.5 Deadlock Detection

Deadlock detection is carried out according to Dally and Seitz theorem [8]. In order to achieve it, the analyzer examines the channel dependences graph searching cycles. When a cycle is detected, the implied channels are indicated in order. The program stops after the first deadlock has been found. If there are no deadlocks, it will finish successfully.

3 A Program Example

Next, a complete example of the application of the tool in deadlock analysis is shown. First, we will see a deadlock free situation and then, we will see how slight modifications in the routing function may change this circumstance.

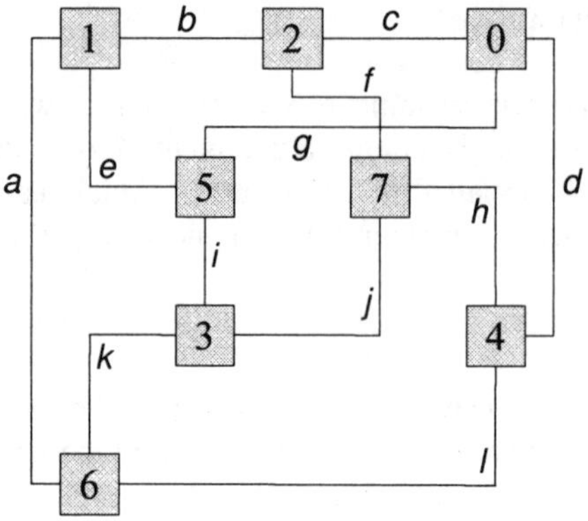

Fig. 7. Network topology

	Source node							
	0	**1**	**2**	**3**	**4**	**5**	**6**	**7**
Destination node	**1** c1 g1	**0** b1 e1	**0** c2	**0** i1	**0** d2	**0** g2	**0** l2	**0** f2 h2
	2 c1	**2** b1	**1** b2	**1** i1	**1** d2	**1** e2	**1** a2	**1** f2
	3 g1	**3** e1	**3** c2	**2** i1	**2** d2	**2** g2	**2** a2	**2** f2
	4 d1	**4** b1 e1	**4** c2	**4** i1	**3** d2	**3** i2	**3** k2	**3** j2
	5 g1	**5** e1	**5** c2	**5** i1	**5** d2	**4** g2	**4** l2	**4** h2
	6 d1	**6** a1	**6** b2	**6** k1	**6** l1	**6** e2 i2	**5** a2 k2	**5** j2
	7 c1 d1	**7** b1	**7** f1	**7** j1	**7** h1	**7** i2	**7** k2 l2	**6** h2 j2

Fig. 8. Routing function

Fig. 7 shows a topologic node distribution. Network connections are shown in Fig. 8. The routing function is expressed by source/destination table. Starting from this initial situation, we can write the code for the input program:

Input program

```
// Initial configuration
net
{
   node 0(on), 1(on), 2(on),
        3(on), 4(on), 5(on),
        6(on), 7(on);

   link
        a=1<=>6,  b=1<=>2,
        c=0<=>2,  d=0<=>4,
        e=1<=>5,  f=2<=>7,
        g=0<=>5,  h=4<=>7,
        i=3<=>5,  j=3<=>7,
        k=3<=>6,  l=4<=>6;
};
```

```
routing                                    to 1,2 use a;
{                                          to 3   use k;
    table 0:                               to 5   use k,a;
        to 1   use c,g;                    to 7   use k,l;
        to 2   use c;                  table 7:
        to 3,5 use g;                      to 0   use f,h;
        to 4,6 use d;                      to 1,2 use f;
        to 7   use c,d;                    to 3,5 use j;
    table 1:                               to 4   use h;
        to 0,4 use b,e;                    to 6   use h,j;
        to 2,7 use b;                  };
        to 3,5 use e;
        to 6   use a;              show "Initial configuration \n";
    table 2:                       show dependences;
        to 0,3,4,5 use c;          pause;
        to 1,6     use b;
        to 7       use f;          // Reconfiguration: Node 1 to 4
    table 3:                       cls;
        to 0,1,2,4,5 use i;        show "Performing a change...\n";
        to 6         use k;        set table 1 =
        to 7         use j;        {
    table 4:                           to 0   use b,e;
        to 0,1,2,3,5 use d;            to 2,7 use b;
        to 6         use l;            to 3,5 use e;
        to 7         use h;            to 4   use a,b,e;
    table 5:                           to 6   use a;
        to 0,2,4 use g;            };
        to 1     use e;            show "... Change performed \n";
        to 3,7   use i;
        to 6     use e,i;          show "\nReconfiguration\n";
    table 6:                       show dependences;
        to 0,4 use l;
```

Following, we can see the output report given by the analyzer:

Output report

```
Interconnection network analyzer
Version 2.1   (September 97)

Syntax..... OK
Topology... OK
Tables..... OK

Initial Configuration
Channel dependencies:
=========================================
            b->f   b->c
            c->f   c->b
            d->h   d->l
            e->g   e->i
            g->e   g->i
            i->e   i->g
            a->b   a->e
            b->a
            c->d   c->g
            d->c   d->g
            e->a
            f->b   f->c
            g->c   g->d
            h->l   h->d
```

```
            i->j   i->k
            j->i   j->k
            k->i   k->j
            l->h   l->d
============================================

Performing a change...
Dependencies cycle:
a->l->d->c->b->a
Warning: (R) Routing function no deadlock-free.
... Change performed

Reconfiguration
Channel dependencies:
============================================
            a->l
            b->f   b->c
            c->f   c->b
            d->h   d->l
            e->g   e->i
            g->e   g->i
            i->e   i->g
            a->b   a->e
            b->a
            c->d   c->g
            d->c   d->g
            e->a
            f->b   f->c
            g->c   g->d
            h->l   h->d
            i->j   i->k
            j->i   j->k
            k->i   k->j
            l->h   l->d
============================================
```

End of the analysis.

When the program is run, the analyzer returns a textual description of the channel dependence graph associated to the initial situation. Fig. 9 shows this graph with an appropriate disposition of the links, broken down in channels. Indeed, it is easy to verify that the function does not contain cycles.

Then, a small modification is introduced in the routing function: we add the shortest path to reach node *4* from node *1*. That is, going through link *a*. After making the change, the analyzer detects a dependence cycle. The program shows a new channel dependence graph and finishes. The cycle can be observed in Fig. 10.

This example could be a typical intermediate step in any reconfiguration process. If the network were blocked, it would be permanently.

4   Conclusions

The RAAP group focuses in high performance local area networks (HP-LANs). This field offers a wide range of issues that should be studied. Two of them are the problems of network reconfiguration and packet routing. The dynamic nature of these networks as well as their irregularity make this task to be hard and laborious if it is tackled using manual methods. This paper has outlined this problem and has presented a software tool for the analysis of this kind of networks. When a reconfiguration algorithm evolves within a network, this tool verifies its deadlock absence, applying Dally and Seitz theorem. This is just a first step to reach the final aim of the research, which is the production of efficient reconfiguration and routing algorithms suitable for high performance networks.

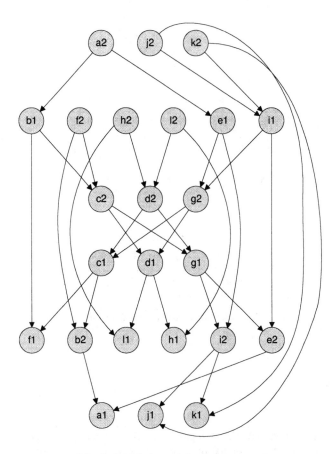

Fig. 9. Initial channel dependence graph

5 Acknowledgements

This work was supported in part by the Spanish CICYT project TIC97-0897-C04-02, Caja Castilla-La Mancha and a FPU grant from the Spanish Ministry of Education.

172

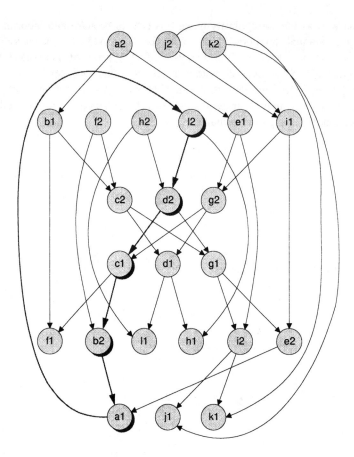

Fig. 10. Graph after reconfiguration

References

1. Schroeder, M.D. et al.: Autonet: A high-speed, self-configuring local area network using point-to-point links. IEEE Journal on Selected Areas in Communications, Vol. 9. n⁰ 8. October 1991.

2. Boden, N. et al.: Myrinet: A gigabit per second LAN. IEEE Micro. February 1995.

3. Horst, R.W.: Tnet: A reliable system area network. IEEE Micro. February 1995.

4. Duato, J., Yalamanchili, S., Ni, L.: Interconnection networks: An engineering approach. IEEE Computer Society. ISBN 0-8186-7800-3. August 1997.

5. Lin, X., McKinley, P.K., Ni, L.: The message flow model for routing in wormhole-routed networks. Proc. of the 1993 Int. Conference on Parallel Processing. August 1993.

6. Lin, X., McKinley, P.K., Ni, L.: The message flow model for routing in wormhole-routed networks. IEEE Trans. on Parallel and Distributed Systems, Vol. 6, n⁰ 7. July 1995.

7. Schwiebert, L., Jayasimba, D.N.: A necessary and sufficient condition for deadlock-free wormhole routing. Journal of Parallel and Distributed Computing, Vol. 32, n⁰ 1. January 1996.

8. Dally, W.J., Seitz, C.L.: Deadlock-free message routing in multiprocessor interconnection networks. IEEE Transactions on Computers, Vol. C-36, n⁰ 5. May 1987.

9. Knightly, E. W., Zhang, H.: D-BIND: An accurate traffic model for providing QoS guarantees to VBR traffic. IEEE Trans. on Networking, Vol. 5, n⁰ 2. April 1995.

10. Bhaskaran, V., Konstantinides, K.: Image and video compression standards. Algorithms and architectures. 1995.

11. Casado, R., Caminero, M. B., Cuenca, P., Quiles, F. J., Garrido, A.: Una herramienta para el análisis de algoritmos de configuración y encaminamiento en redes irregulares. Proc. of the VIII Jornadas nacionales de Paralelismo. Spain. September 1997.

12. http://fierabras.info-ab.uclm.es/raap/raap.html

13. Silla, F., Malumbres, M. P., Robles, A., López, P., Duato, J.: Efficient Adaptive Routing in Networks of Workstations with Irregular Topology. Workshop on Communications and Architectural Support for Network-based Parallel Computing. 1997.

Real-Time Traffic Management on Optical Networks Using Dynamic Control of Cycle Duration

Cheng-Chi Yu   Sourav Bhattacharya*

Computer Science and Engineering Department, Arizona State University,
Tempe, AZ 85287-5406,{cyu, sourav}@asu.edu

Abstract. This paper proposes a new approach to real-time traffic management over a multihop optical network. Unlike the current preemption-based real-time traffic scheduling approaches (where, the QoS of the preempted traffic may suffer significantly), the proposed approach is based on dynamic creation of logical channels to support new arriving real-time messages. The logical channels are mapped to the TWDM (time-wave division multiplexed) transmission schedule of the optical media. Since, the new logical channels can support the fresh arrival of real-time messages, it may no longer be necessary to preempt an existing message. This feature offers significant QoS benefits to the existing traffic. The price paid for creation of the logical channel(s) is via an *extension* of the cycle time in the TWDM transmission schedule. Such extension of the cycle time imparts a uniform degree of slowdown to all the existing channels, and enforces excellent load balancing. A state machine model for dynamic control (i.e., extension, and/or shrinking) of the TWDM transmission schedule is proposed. Performance is measured using simulation.

1 Introduction

The rapid growth of information technology and its applications require high bandwidth transmission across communication networks. The vast bandwidth, high reliability, and easy extentions to distant nodes of optical networks provide attractive features to satisfy such needs. Real-time is a critical need for many computing and communication applications. Timing deadlines are also key components of the quality-of-service (QoS) requirements. WDM (wavelength division multiplexing) provides an efficient method of using the optical fiber spectrum through multiplexing signals on different frequencies of the optical fiber. On the other hand, TDM (time-division multiplexing) allows to accommodate multiple data streams (each of slower bandwidth) into one faster bandwidth wavelength. Combination of WDM and TDM leads to TWDM (time-wave-division multiplexed) media access control for the optical fibers. TWDM media access control has many benefits including high bandwidth utilization, proper coupling between electrical media data rates and optical media data rates, and firmware control

---

* Also affiliated to the Honeywell Technology Center, Phoenix, Arizona.

of the optical media resource to best fit the bandwidth resource to the traffic needs. An discussion on TWDM embedded optical networks may be found in [8], which proposes a combined model of WDM and TDM for long haul transmissions. The growing usage of optical networks and the need for real-time traffic evolve the research direction of real-time optical network. The WDM, TDM or TWDM Transmission Schedules (mentioned as TS later) [1] require to accommodate real-time traffic management algorithms, which is the focus of our paper.

Previous Research: Extensive research has been done in the areas of WDM optical networks. WDM based logical topology construction algorithms have been proposed by [1][5][7]. Wavelength assignment and reuse approaches are proposed in [1][7]. However, these results do not address real-time traffic scheduling issues using dynamic management of wavelengths. [2] proposes an approach to derive the optimum transmission schedule in a TWDM embedded optical network. It is a static scheduling policy, which allocates (time, wavelength) slots node pairs, and can minimize the average traffic delay. However, the individual needs of hard real-time messages remain an open question. Dynamic aspects of TWDM protocol has been proposed in [3], which uses a control wavelength to maneuver the optical network for packet switched traffic. [4] proposes a multihop optical network architecture with a fixed TDM-WDM assignment scheme, where a TDM frame is employed to implement the TS. The notion of deadline, and real-time traffic support remain an open question. 'Delay' concepts in optical network has, however, been addressed from a complimentary point of view - namely, the tuning latencies of tunable transceivers. [10] proposes the design of optimum TDM schedule for broadcast WDM networks, to construct TSs of length constrained by the lower bound of tuning latencies. Real-time TWDM network issues have been discussed in [11], which proposes a distributed adaptive protocol for deadline critical services on an optical network. The protocol uses a single token circulating through a control wavelength for communicating status information between each node and controlling access to each of wavelength. The dynamic control of TS a way that the deadline needs of multiple priority class traffic are traded against each other (i.e., preemption scheduling) described in [12]. Also, the design extensions for multihop networks are addressed. Finally, and most critically, analytical techniques to compute the number of slots required for each real-time message at each optical passive star is contributed in [12]. However, the dynamic control of cycle duration of TS employed to efficiently promote the bandwidth utilization is a key, and unique contribution in this paper. Real-time traffic management for other networks, e.g., ATM, FDDI, wireless etc., have been extensively studied. Real-time ATM network is an widely addressed research topic [6]. Pre-dominantly, these techniques deploy a static admission control periphery across the network, usually implemented with a queue and scheduling policy. The static scheduler allows to prioritize higher priority traffic over lower ones, as well as selective inclusion of periodic real-time messages in a

---

[1] A transmission schedule indicates or governs the time, wavelength allocation policies underlying to the WDM, TDM, or TWDM media access policy. It is, therefore, the basic operation of an optical MAC (media access control).

way to guarantee their deadline satisfiabilities. For multihop networks, such analysis can include derivation of the routing path, and hop by hop decomposition of the admission control criteria [9].

Contribution: Real-time traffic (or, task) scheduling has been traditionally addressed using preemptive scheduling policies. Preemptive scheduling approaches preempt a lower priority message, and enable a higher priority message to transmit, and this is an inevitable policy to let a higher priority user share a common resource with a lower priority user. Although, preemption based task scheduling has been extensively studied, the same for optical networks has received limited attention. The authors have recently addressed the design and implementation aspects of real-time TWDM TS [12]. A priority-based preemptive scheduling approach, alike in the current research, may be adequate to manage limited bandwidth resource in heavy traffic. However, preemption in essence implies temporarily disable one user from availing the shared resource, and allow the other user. This approach is inevitable, i.e., cannot be avoided, but has some severe drawbacks. Most important disadvantage is that the user who gets preempted has a drastic change in its service level, e.g., it may go to a complete lack of QoS situation from an acceptable QoS level. Also, the preemption approach penalizes only those users who get preempted. It does not distribute the effect of "system load" *uniformly* to all the users.

We propose a fundamentally different paradigm of real-time traffic management. The idea is to avail the fast reconfigurability and dynamic control capability of the firmware media (e.g., optical, or wireless), so that new logical resources can be created dynamically to meet the needs of the real-time messages, instead of having to preempt existing messages. Creation of the new logical resources is done by extending the cycle time of the TWDM transmission schedule, however, this can impart a uniform slowdown to all the existing channels. We advocate that this 'uniform' slowdown of all (i.e., global) channels is a preferred approach than selective channel preemption. Thus, using our approach, hot-spots can be easily eliminated, and we can achieve what might be termed as a "load balancing utopia", wherein the local hot-spot traffic load gets uniformly distributed by every segment of the global networks' resource. When the TWDM cycle time is extended, care must be taken to ensure that none of the existing traffic may miss their respective deadlines, due to such, albeit uniform, slowdown. If so, additional time slots must be allocated to upgrade the minimum laxity messages. This step requires an analytical approach to compute the minimum number of slots (per cycle length) required for each deadline-bound message, which is another contribution of this paper. Extension of the TWDM cycle time can aid in high-traffic load situations, but once extended, and particularly when the network traffic reduces to normal or low load values, the cycle time must also be reduced, as otherwise the network utilization can become low, and individual channels can become unnecessarily slow. We propose a garbage collection algorithm, which can periodically detect unused TWDM (time, wavelength) slots, and the *shrink* algorithm can coalesce the TWDM TS to a shorter cycle time format, by eliminating such 'holes' in the extended TS.

The objective is two fold: *first*, with incoming real-time messages, i.e., fresh arrivals, create new logical channel resources to support the real-time messages, instead of preempting existing traffic. The process of mapping the logical channels to physical media would allow the "load of the logical channel" to get distributed evenly to all the existing resources, instead of badly affecting few users/resources, and not affecting other users/resources at all. This approach can work for firmware controlled resource media, e.g., the optical or wireless bandwidth. Here, the logical channels can be created and deleted dynamically with little (or, minimal) effort (i.e., cost and delay). *Second*, with a localized traffic distribution across the network, and idle regions in the remaining segments of the network, the goal is to minimize allocation of channel resources to the links which need little (or, no) bandwidth, and maximize the allocation of bandwidth resource to the hot spot regions. This is done effectively by shrinking the cycle time, after deleting unused (time, wavelength) slots, and optimizing the TWDM TS. The first objective, stated above, is implemented using the 'extend' algorithm, while the second objective is implemented using the 'shrink' algorithm. Overall, the extend and shrink based cycle time management algorithm is presented using a finite state machine model, and the thresholds to trigger the extension, garbage collection and shrink steps are elaborated. We propose a network controller model for management of the optical network. Cut-through routing policy is adopted for multi-packet messages across multiple hops.

2   System Model and Analysis

In WDM-based all optical network, messages are multiplexed into several different wavelengths with a guard band between pairwise adjacent frequencies. A centralized controller (mentioned as CC later) for the network is assumed, which schedules the traffic in the network, allocates the bandwidth, and performs the admission control when a new message is generated. We assume that the wavelengths are classified into control and data transmission wavelengths. A control wavelength is used to transmit control packets between the centralized controller (CC) and the other nodes. This model of system description has been used in [12] by the authors. The data transmission channel on each WDM wavelength is multiplexed using time-division-multiplexed (TDM) technique, which divides each wavelength into fixed length time slots. A clock synchronization algorithm is assumed. The logical topology of the network, defining the network connectivity, is embedded on the TWDM media-access controller. Each duplex edge of the topology is embedded as two back-to-back simplex link, where each simplex link is assigned to one (or more) (time, wavelength) slot of the TWDM TS. Thus, we define the TS according to the time slot allocation for each data transmission wavelength in a cycle time based on the network topology.

System Behavior and Transmission Schedule: The system model operations are as follows. Whenever a source node of the network has to send a message, the source node will compute the optimum number of TWDM slots according to its message size, end-to-end deadline, and other system data. Then,

178

the source node will send a "New-Msg-Req" control packet to the CC with the computed result, priority of the message, and its routing path. The new TS will be broadcast to every node in the topology through the control wavelength, if a new message is admitted. At this time, all nodes freeze new message generation and keep on exhausting the packets in the existing message streams. When the existing message streams are all completely transmitted, the new TS is initiated simultaneously at all nodes. Figure 1 shows these steps using a finite state machine model, with respective control packets. Traffic scheduling algorithms, at each node, are implemented as micro-code to minimize call processing delays. The CC embeds the admission control, scheduling, and bandwidth allocation mechanisms into micro-coded execution format. The exchange of control packets and TS broadcast are done over control channels. Control channels are dedicated, i.e., set aside, resources, e.g., pre-allocated TWDM slots or token bus or other such protocols connecting the different nodes. Such separation of the control channels from the regular data channels can provide determinism in the network control operations.

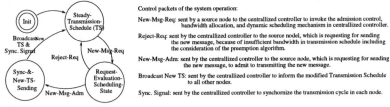

Control packets of the system operation:

New-Msg-Req: sent by a source node to the centralized controller to invoke the admission control, bandwidth allocation, and dynamic scheduling mechanism in centralized controller.

Reject-Req: sent by the centralized controller to the source node, which is requesting for sending the new message, because of insufficient bandwidth in transmission schedule including the consideration of the preemption algorithm.

New-Msg-Adm: sent by the centralized controller to the source node, which is requesting for sending the new message, to admit to transmitting the new message.

Broadcast New TS: sent by the centralized controller to inform the modified Transmission Schedule to all other nodes.

Sync. Signal: sent by the centralized controller to synchronize the transmission cycle in each node.

Fig. 1. System behavior of the TWDM MAC embedded network.

The CC is responsible for admission control and slot allocation for multihop messages, and in generating the overall co-ordination of the TWDM TS. An example with a simple network, three transmitted messages, and bandwidth allocation of the messages on the TS (In the example network topology, we use "$-e_j$" to denote the inversive direction of "e_j".) are shown in Figure 2. Figure 2a shows a simple network topology with directional edges. Figure 2b shows the routing paths of three messages. Figure 2c shows the bandwidth allocation of these three messages in the sample TS. Message m1 is allocated in wavelength W1 with two slots for transmission in each hop of its routing path. Message m2 is allocated in wavelength W2 and W3 with four slots for transmission in each hop of its routing path, and message m3 is allocated in W4 with three slots for each hop. Wavelength W5 is not included in the data transmission, as an example, since it is set aside for communication of the control packets.

We define the TS using the following notations. Let, the matrix, $S_{F \times \alpha}$, denote the TS. Let F be the number of total wavelengths. Define α to be the number of slots in a cycle time in one wavelength. Let $f \in \{0, 1, \cdots, F-1\}$ be the f-th wavelength. Define $t \in \{0, 1, \cdots, \alpha-1\}$ to be the t-th time slot within a cycle. There are n directional edges, $e_0, \cdots, e_{n-1}$, in the network topology. Let, $S_{f,t} = e_j$ indicate that the t-th time slot of the f-th wavelength is allocated to edge e_j. $S_{f,t}=0$ indicates that this slot is idle.

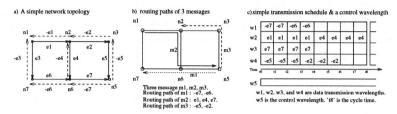

Fig. 2. An example topology on TWDM embedding system.

Computation of Optimal Bandwidth Allocation (OBA): We summarize the results of (single wavelength, single hop) and (multiple wavelength, multiple hop) topology cases, details can be found in [12]. Cut-through routing policy is adopted. Let D_i denote the end-to-end deadline requirement of message i. For (single wavelength, single hop) case, the best design goal is to find the q_i, optimal value of the number of slots for each message i, which will satisfy equation 1. τ is the time length of one slot, W_i is the number of packets of message i and p is the number of packets that can be transmitted in one slot.

$$\left\lceil \frac{W_i}{p \times (q_i - 1)} + 1 \right\rceil \times \tau \times \alpha > D_i \geq$$

$$\left\lceil \frac{W_i}{p \times q_i} + 1 \right\rceil \times \tau \times \alpha, \quad where \quad q_i \neq 1 \tag{1}$$

For (multiple channel, multiple hop) case, the best design goal is to find the $q_{i,min}$ satisfying equation 2, where $q_{i,min} = \text{minimum} \sum_{k=0}^{f-1} q_{i,j,k}$; where, $q_{i,j,k}$ is the number of slots in a cycle time for transmitting message i in edge j of wavelength k.

$$\tau \times \alpha \times \sum_{j=0}^{n-1} T_{i,j} + \left\lceil \frac{W_i}{p \times (q_{i,min} - 1)} \right\rceil \times \tau \times \alpha +$$

$$\frac{\alpha \times \varepsilon_1 \times W_i}{p \times q_{i,min}} + \frac{\varepsilon_2 \times W_i}{p \times q_{i,min}} + s'(\sum_{j=0}^{n-1} T_{i,j} - 1) > D_i \geq$$

$$\tau \times \alpha \times \sum_{j=0}^{n-1} T_{i,j} + \left\lceil \frac{W_i}{p \times q_{i,min}} \right\rceil \times \tau \times \alpha +$$

$$\frac{\alpha \times \varepsilon_1 \times W_i}{p \times q_{i,min}} + \frac{\varepsilon_2 \times W_i}{p \times q_{i,min}} + s'(\sum_{j=0}^{n-1} T_{i,j} - 1) \tag{2}$$

where, $T_{m \times n}$ is a matrix of the transmission topology, s' is the maximum intermediate node processing delay in the optical network, ε_1 is the interval between two successive TDM slots, and ε_2 is the interval between two successive TDM cycles. Let there be m messages in the network. Let $i \in \{0, \cdots, m-1\}$, and $j \in \{0, \cdots, n-1\}$. $T_{i,j}$, defined as follows, capture the effect of the routing path.

$$T_{i,j} = \begin{cases} 1 \text{ if message } i \text{ needs passing directed edge } j, \\ 0 \text{ otherwise} \end{cases}$$

Moreover, the maximum value of the total number of slots should be limited, because the total number of slots allocated to all the transmitted messages have to be less than or equal to the total number of slots in the transmission schedule of one cycle time, $\alpha \times f$.

$$\sum_{i=0}^{m-1} \sum_{j=0}^{n-1} \sum_{k=0}^{f-1} q_{i,j,k} \leq \alpha \times f \tag{3}$$

3 Adaptive Cycle Time

The dual of the cycle time extension (limited to a maximum threshold) process is manifested by garbage collection and cycle shrinking (limited to a minimum threshold) process. The idle slots in the TWDM TS are periodically (or, event such as arrival to completion of an existing message) collected, deleted and the cycle time is compacted. The process is termed as "garbage collection". Once the number of idle slots have been identified, the shrink algorithm makes precise estimation of how many slots are still required for most efficient utilization of the network bandwidth, and makes a corresponding reduction of the cycle time. As a result, the available bandwidth of each one of the existing channels is improved, and the network throughput is maximized. Figure 3 shows a finite state machine model to demonstrate the entire cycle time management process.

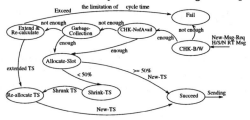

Fig. 3. A finite state machine for dynamic and adaptive cycle time of TWDM TS.

An input to the adaptive cycle time control process is the "New-Msg-Req" control packet. As the request arrives at the CC, the total allocated bandwidth is verified in state *Chk-BW*. If the necessary bandwidth, including the new message, exceeds the capacity of the network, the new message may be rejected by the CC. Thus, the new message is failed. On the other hand, if it does not exceed, then the control enters the *Chk-NofAvail* state, which computes the number of available slots in the current TS. Therefore, check the number of available (un-allocated) slots. If enough, then the necessary slots will be allocated to the new message at the state *Allocate-Slot*. Otherwise, the control enters the *Garbage-Collection* state, which collects the un-used, yet allocated slots (owned by the messages which have been completely transmitted), and releases their bandwidths. After releasing, a check is made to verify if there are adequate slots available to allocate the new real-time message. If adequate, then the control enters the *Allocate-Slot* state, where the new message is admitted for transmission. However, we introduce a bandwidth utilization check at this time. If due to the bandwidth release (by the garbage collection operation), more than θ% of the TWDM TS become empty (i.e., un-used) then the *Shrink-TS* state is invoked. (Figure 3 shows this with $\theta = 50$%.) At this state, the adjustment of the cycle duration, shrink algorithm, will be performed , and the new TS (including the existing messages, and allocation of slots for the new message) will be created and broadcast at the *Re-allocate-TS* state. Finally, the control returns to the *Succeed* state. Next, the available free slots are not enough after the *Garbage-Collection* state. The control will enter the *Extend-Re-calculate* state, which extends the cycle duration and re-computes the bandwidth requirement (modification of OBA) of all the current messages, due to the updated cycle duration to ensure that every message can still meet its deadline. If the extended TS can maintain all messages to meet their deadlines, then the new message is admitted, the TS is extended, and the control enters the *Re-allocate-TS* process. In the *Re-allocate-TS* state, slots are re-allocated to all the messages to fit the new cycle duration. Therefore, the new TS is constructed, and the control enters the *Succeed* state. All current messages and the new one can now commence transmission. The cycle time extension process cannot be allowed to repeat without restriction, as otherwise the cycle time may hurt the deadline satisfiability condition for even a single packet across a single hop. The worst case for deadline satisfiability arises for a single packet, across a single hop, where the deadline must be honored within two cycle (one to raise the message request, and the other to transmit). Thus, a design limitation follows in that the maximum cycle time cannot exceed twice that of the initial (start-up time) cycle time. To reflect this design decision, in the *Extend-Re-calculate* state, if the extended length of the cycle duration is greater than the half of the minimum deadline of the messages in the system, then the new message cannot be admitted and rejected by the CC.

Modification of OBA: When a new real-time message arrives, the extension process can normally create logical channel resource for it. However, the question remains as to how many TWDM (time, wavelength) slots must be created, at a minimum, to support the needs (both bandwidth, and deadline) of this newly arrived message. If the number of slots required is $\leq F$, then creating one extra time-slot could be adequate (since, 1 time slot across F wavelengths can give F extra slots). Likewise, if the number of extra slots required for this new message is $\leq 2F$, but $> F$, then the cycle time needs to increase by two. The implication of increasing (or, decreasing) cycle time, has compound effect on the deadline computation. As the cycle time changes, the relative proportion of the number of slots with respect to the updated cycle time will vary. The deadline satisfiability condition for each message will require to be re-computed. Following equation demonstrates that the variation proportion of cycle duration should equal to number of slots allocated, where $q'_{i,min}$ is the new optimal bandwidth allocation, and α_1 is the new number of slots in the new cycle duration of TS.

$$q'_{i,min} = \left\lceil q_{i,min} \times \frac{\alpha}{\alpha_1} \right\rceil \qquad (4)$$

3.1 Dynamic Control of Cycle Duration

The three algorithms which form the major modules of this process are *Garbage Collection*, *Shrink Algorithm*, and *Extend Algorithm*, described as follows.

Garbage Collection: releases the un-used and unavailable slots in the TS, to provide space to the new message requests. Selection of an appropriate interval to invoke the garbage collection process is a critical design step. Garbage collection can be invoked at every message completion, however, then the overhead can become large. Here, we propose a garbage collection process invocation every time a new message cannot find adequate bandwidth. This is shown in Figure 3, where the CC cannot find enough slots in the TS for a new message request. A pseudo code description of the algorithm is given in Figure 4.

Algorithm Garbage_Collection (in: TS, out: TS)
    /* TS: Trans. Sch. = $S_{f,t}$ matrix */
for $f \in \{0, \cdots, F-1\}, t \in \{0, \cdots, \alpha-1\}$ **do**
        if $S_{f,t}$ not allocated to active message then $S_{f,t} = 0$
Endfor

Fig. 4. Garbage Collection Algorithm.

Shrink Algorithm: The shrink algorithm is invoked when a large (greater than the threshold θ) number of idle slots have been detected, and the objective is to reduce the cycle time by creating compact allocation of the slots for the existing (active) messages. Naturally, the input to the shrink algorithm is the TS, and the cycle time (α). The output is an updated TS, and reduced cycle time α^1. The algorithm is in two steps: first, it counts the total number of free slots, and makes a corresponding reduction of the cycle time. Second, the allocated slots which fall beyond the shrunk cycle time, will be swapped to be allocated to free slots within the reduced cycle time range. Figure 5 shows the pseudo code.

Algorithm Shrink_TS (in: TS, α; out: TS, α^1)
    /* TS: Trans. Sch. = $S_{f,t}$ matrix */
count = 0;
for $f \in \{0, \cdots, F-1\}, t \in \{0, \cdots, \alpha-1\}$ **do if** $S_{f,t} = 0$ then count ++; **Endfor**
$\alpha^1 = \alpha - \lfloor \frac{\text{count}}{F} \rfloor$
for $f \in \{0, \cdots, F-1\}, t \in \{\alpha^1, \cdots, \alpha-1\}$ **do**
        if $S_{f,t} > 0$ then swap edge at $S_{f,t}$ to S_{f,t^1}, where $t^1 < \alpha^1$
Endfor

Fig. 5. Cycle Shrink Algorithm.

Extend Algorithm: The cycle time extension algorithm is invoked when a new arriving message can fit within the total available bandwidth of the optical passive star, yet cannot find adequate free transmission slots in the TS. Consequently, the cycle time may be extended. Note that extending the cycle time by one slot duration can provide F additional slots, since there are F wavelengths. The algorithm proceeds in three steps: first, from the bandwidth and deadline requirements of the new arriving message, we compute the minimum number of slots required. Refer Section 2 and modified OBA for details. Second, from the required (minimum) number of slots, we obtain the minimum extension of the cycle time (divide by F, and round up). Third, the effect of extending the cycle time must be checked with respect to each active message, since, it may so happen that some of the existing messages may begin to miss their respective deadlines due to such extensions of the cycle time. If so, such messages will be allocated extra slots (refer equation of modified OBA), and if needed the cycle time may have to be further extended. However, under no circumstances, the cycle time may exceed twice that of the minimum deadline of any message. Figure 6 shows the pseudo code.

Algorithm Extend_TS (in: TS, α; out: TS, α^1)
    /* TS: Transmission Schedule = $S_{f,t}$ matrix */
count = min_slots_required(new message deadline, bandwidth);
        /* using equations from Section 2.3 */
$\alpha^1 = \alpha + \lceil \frac{count}{F} \rceil$
allocate 'count' slots between $S_{f,\alpha}$ to S_{f,α^1}, $f \in \{0, \cdots F - 1\}$
for every active message **do**
    if ($\frac{\text{no. slots allocated to this message}}{\alpha^1}$ < deadline threshold)
        then no_slots_allocated ++;
            if no free slot, **then** further extend α^1
            if $\alpha^1 \times$ slot width > $\frac{min.deadline}{2}$ **then** exit;
    Endif
Endfor

Fig. 6. Cycle Extend Algorithm.

3.2 Efficient Cycle Time Management

The efficiency and control of the adaptive cycle time management process is discussed in the following. An early check mechanism is provided, which can help determine a necessary condition for new message admission control, and if this condition is not satisfied, then the network controller can avoid extensive bandwidth analysis altogether. Likewise, an outline of the incremental TS propagation approach is presented, which can minimize the control traffic.

Admission Control: The capacity (in bps, or packets per second) of the transmission media is a natural bandwidth limitation of the underlying network. Regardless of how adaptive, and flexible the TS co-ordination might be, under no circumstances, a set of messages can be admitted whose total bandwidth need (C, in bps) exceed that of the physical media. Our first idea is to devise a check to verify, upon a new message arrival request, if its inclusion is going to violate any such fundamental limitation, and if so, deny its admission right away, without having to go through expensive computation process. This can save significant computing workload for the network controller. Let, W_i, D_i and T_i be the size, deadline and periodicity of message i, where D_i is expressed as the time differential between the message arrival time and latest allowable completion time. Let $\text{LCM}(T_i)$ denote the least common multiple of all the T_i values, for all messages. During this $\text{LCM}(T_i)$ period, the number of (periodic) invocations of message i would be $= \frac{\text{LCM}(T_i)}{T_i}$. During each invocation, the worst case (slowest) rate of packet transmission to meet the deadline for message i would be $\lceil \frac{W_i}{D_i} \rceil$. Hence, the net capacity required for i-th message is $\frac{\text{LCM}(T_i)}{T_i} \times \lceil \frac{W_i}{D_i} \rceil$. This net capacity must be less than the media capacity, which is stated as a *necessary* condition for admission control.

$$\sum_{i=0}^{m-1} \frac{\text{LCM}(T_i)}{T_i} \times \lceil \frac{W_i}{D_i} \rceil \leq C \times \text{LCM}(T_i) \tag{5}$$

The generalized admission control equation, posed as a necessary condition (where the sufficient condition is manifested in the TS allocation algorithms, describe in Section 3.1), can be simplified by assuming that the cycle time and individual slot allocations for each one of the messages stay unchanged for the duration of our analysis. In such a case, the rate (in bps) of transmission of each message stay identical for each transmission cycle. If so, the summation of the individual bandwidth needs of each message in each cycle must meet the channel transmission capacity in one cycle. Hence, the admission control (necessary) condition is stated in equation 6. Equations 5 and 6 present the generalized and simplified admission control conditions that can be checked by the *CHK-BW* state in the state machine model of Figure 3.

$$\sum_{i=0}^{m-1} \lceil \frac{W_i}{D_i} \rceil \leq C \times \alpha \times \tau \tag{6}$$

Incremental TS Broadcast: Since, the TS gets updated every time an extend, garbage collection or shrink operation are invoked, the network controller would require to re-transmit the TS data structure to each node in the optical network. A brute force approach is to re-transmit the entire TS, including the slot allocations of the unperturbed messages, and the updated ones. However, if the size of the broadcast information becomes a bandwidth crunch, then an incremental TS transmission may be attractive. Our goal is to reduce the size of the broadcast message for new transmission schedule. This can be done simply by broadcasting the modified part of the TS only. However, in an advanced approach, one may also choose to modify the TS in a minimally changing fashion. This is particularly true when there are multiple choices in the way a TS can be updated to include new messages, or delete idle slots.

- With the *extend* algorithm, the incremental TS information is derived in a simple manner. Suppose, the initial cycle time is α, and the updated cycle time is α^1, with $\alpha^1 > \alpha$. The incremental TS is constituted by the (time, wavelength) entries between time slots α and $\alpha^1 - 1$. That is, the network controller needs only to transmit $S_{f,t}, \forall f, f \in \{0, \cdots, F - 1\}, \alpha \leq t < \alpha^1$
- With the garbage collection algorithm, the incremental TS information contains those slots which have just been marked 'idle' $(= 0)$ by the network controller. In other words, the incremental TS information would be a list $\{\forall f, f \in \{0, \cdots, F - 1\}, \forall t, t \in \{0, \cdots, \alpha^1 - 1\}, [S_{f,t}], \text{where}, \quad S_{f,t} = 0$

3.3 Network Control Manager

The CC allocates the bandwidth resource, performs traffic scheduling, and processes the new call requests (i.e., admission control). A large amount of control information may have to be transmitted during this process, and thus, it is important to design an efficient protocol in control channel. Our design avoids any collision instance by using a token bus alike protocol, as shown in Figure 7a. The participating nodes take turn in transmitting their control information, including report of new arrival messages and traffic characteristics. The network manager, either a special node, or one of the nodes elected to act as the network manager, is also connected to the logical token bus. Hence, an updated TS (decided by the network manager) will be transmitted by the network manager node using control packets on this token bus protocol. A state machine model of the network management protocol is shown in Figure 7b. The state *Circulating* refers to a steady network situation, i.e., existing messages have been successfully allocated with their respective (time, wavelength) slots and being currently transmitted - no new message has arrived, and none of the existing messages have terminated. When a new message arrives, it is reported in the circulating token from the node. The state *New Message* refers to the instance when a new message, along with its traffic requirements (bandwidth, deadline) are reported to the network controller. The state *Negotiation* refers to the entire decision making process, as to whether or not accept this new message request, to extend or not, to collect idle slots and/or shrink etc. This state essentially captures the entire flow in the state machine model shown in Figure 3. Once these decisions have been made, the network controller transits to the steady state *Circulating*. Figure 7c. shows the connection setup process. The sequence of steps, i.e., operations, invoked when a new connection request arises from a source node and delivered to the CC, are shown in a timeline diagram in this figure. The different control messages, used in the state machine model, are described below.

- "New-Msg-Req": indicates the arrival of a new message.

186

- "New-Msg-Adm": the new message is admitted by the CC.
- "Brct-Req": the CC notifies every node that a new (or, updated) TS will be broadcast shortly.
- "Brct-Req-Ack": each source node acknowledges the "Brct-Req" sent from the CC to indicate that the node is now ready to receive an updated TS.
- "Brct-New-TS": the CC broadcasts the new TS to all the nodes.
- "Brct-TS-Ack": all nodes acknowledge the "Brct-New-TS".
- "Sync-Sig": the CC broadcasts a signal to all nodes to inform that all nodes should begin to use the new transmission schedule.

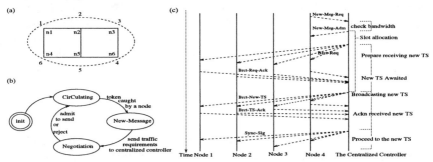

Fig. 7. a) A token bus protocol for network management and control. b) State machine for the network controller. c)Timing diagram of the connection establishment.

4   Simulation Performance

We report a steady state simulation based performance results. The simulation tool builds a (4 × 4) 2D mesh topology with 16 routers. One of the nodes is delegated to be the CC. The metric is "successful transmission rate", defined as the percentage of messages that are transmitted within deadline. The simulation results are analyzed and evaluated with adaptive control of the cycle duration. We compare the results with another network environment in which the cycle time is not adaptive, i.e., fixed. We focus on simulating the task of bandwidth allocation on the transmission schedule and dynamic scheduling behavior. The input data items, including message size (in packets), deadline requirement, and (source, destination)-pair, are randomly generated. The network traffic load is controlled by selecting the average deadline of messages and average message generation probability. The output metric, "successful transmission rate", is defined as the proportion of messages (compared to the total number of generated messages) that are transmitted following their respective deadlines.

Comparison Strategy: In the simulation, the objective is to compare the "successful transmission rate" between dynamic scheduling with "Extend-and-Shrink" algorithm and the naive scheduling (i.e., current technology). The approach without "Extend-and-Shrink" algorithm is a static scheduling method, which simply rejects the new message if the TWDM cycle time is not enough.

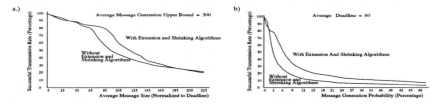

Fig. 8. a.) Performance with variation of the average message generation probability.
b.) Performance with variation of the average message size (nor malized to deadline).

The performance of the adaptive cycle time approach is expected to be much enhanced than the static cycle time approach. This is because the adaptive scheduling approach dynamically adjusts the cycle duration of the TS to more accurately fit the bandwidth requirements of the messages at each time interval. However, the price paid is in the complexity of the extend, shrink and garbage collect algorithms, and the overhead of the dynamic cycle time control messages. **Observations:** Figure 8 depicts the "successful transmission ratio" by varying the message generation probability and the average message size respectively. In each plot, the case with adaptive cycle time (marked as "with extension and shrinking algorithms") and static cycle time (marked as "without extension and shrinking algorithms") are shown. As can be readily observed, the proportion of messages that meet their respective deadlines is much higher when using the adaptive cycle time approach, as proposed in this paper. In Figure 8a., the curve with "Extend-and-Shrink" is close to the one without it when the message generation probability is low. This occurs because when the message generation probability is sufficiently low, the bandwidth is always available, and the availability of cycle time adaptiveness feature is really not adding any extra value. On the contrary, with increasing traffic load, the benefit of the adaptive cycle time approach becomes clear. Similar comment can also be made regarding Figure 8b., where for lower message size (deadline normalized) ranges the adaptive and static cycle time approaches perform nearly identical - since, not enough traffic load is present to bring forward the benefits of dynamic cycle time. As the message size increases, the adaptive cycle time approach depicts better performance than the static approach. However, with message size beyond a threshold, the cycle extend process cannot stretch the cycle time any longer, and hence the static and dynamic cycle time scheduling approach behaves similar.

5 Conclusion and Future Works

This paper proposes the real-time traffic scheduling over a TWDM based optical network. Unlike the existing approaches to preemption-based real-time traffic scheduling, which can impose ungraceful QoS degradation features, we propose an adaptive cycle time maneuvering approach that allows to keep the existing messages and allocate a new arriving real-time message on a newly created logical channel. This capability is implemented by dynamically changing the cycle time. Benefits of the propose approach include a near perfect communication load balancing, where the local traffic load impacts the global channels in a uniform speed slowdown manner, and hence, avoidance of channel hot-spots. We propose a range of state machine models for the network controller, the cycle time update process, and allocation of the control traffic bandwidth to the optical media. The extend, shrink and idle slot identification process (termed as "garbage collection") are presented in this paper. We report an early set of performance evaluation results using simulation. Our research discusses a new paradigm for real-time traffic scheduling for firmware controlled media (e.g., optical and wireless), namely the logical channel creation and deletion on-the-fly as needed by the traffic load (instead of preemption). Above and beyond, the price paid for dynamically controlling the cycle time is in added network management overhead (computation and/or bandwidth) and an accurate depiction of the price-performance benefit is in order.

References

1. Aly M., Dowd P., "A Class of Scalable Optical Interconnection Networks through Discrete Broadcas t-select Multi-domain WDM", *Infocom*, v.1, 1994, pp 392-399.
2. Borella M., Mukherjee B., "Efficient Scheduling of Nonuniform Packet Traffic in a WDM/TDM Local Lightwave Network with Arbitrary Tranceiver Tuning Latencies", *Infocom*, V.1, 1995, pp 129-137.
3. Chen M.S., Dono N., Ramaswami R., "A Media-Access Protocol for Packet-Switched Wavelength Division Multiaccess Metropolitan Area Networks" *IEEE Journal on Sel. Areas in Comm.*, vol.8,1990, p1048-p1057
4. Elby S., Acampora A., "Wavelength-based Cell Switching in ATM Multihop Optical Networks" *Infocom*, v.2, 1993, pp 953-p963.
5. Hluchyj M., Karol M., "ShuffleNet: An Application of Generalized Perfect Shuffles to Multihop Lightwave Networks", *Jo. of Light. Tech.*, v. 9, 1991, pp 1386-1397.
6. Ling T.L., Shroff N., "Scheduling Real-Time Traffic in ATM Networks", *Infocom* v.1, 1996, pp 198-20.
7. Mukherjee B., Ramamurthy S., Banerjee D., Mukherjee A., "Some Principles for Designing a Wide-Area Optical Network", *Infocom*, v.1, 1994, pp 110-119.
8. O'Mahony M., "Optical Multiplexing in Fiber Networks: Progress in WDM and OTDM", *IEEE Comm. Mag.*, DEC. 1995, pp 82-88.
9. Raha A., Kamat S., Zhao W., "Admission Control for Hard Real-Time Connections in ATM LANs" *Infocom* V. 1, 1996, pp 180-188.
10. Rouskas G., Sivaraman V., "On the Design of Optimal TDM Schedules for Broadcast WDM Networks with Arbitrary Transceiver Tuning Latencies", *Infocom*, v.3, 1996, pp 1217-1224.
11. Yan A., Ganz A., Krishna C., "A Distributed Adaptive Protocol Providing Real-Time Services on WDM-Based LANs", *Infocom*, v.3, 1996, pp 962-969.
12. Yu C.C., Bhattacharya S., "Dynamic Scheduling of Real-Time Messages over an Optical Network", Proc. *International Conference on Computer Communications and Networks*, 1997, IEEE Communication Society Press, pp 336-339.

A Comparative Characterization of Communication Patterns in Applications Using MPI and Shared Memory on an IBM SP2

Sven Karlsson and Mats Brorsson

Department of Information Technology,
Lund University, P.O. Box 118, SE-221 00 LUND, Sweden
email: Sven.Karlsson@it.lth.se

Abstract. In this paper we analyze the characteristics of communication in three different applications, FFT, Barnes and Water, on an IBM SP2. We contrast the communication using two different programming models: message-passing, MPI, and shared memory, represented by a state-of-the-art distributed virtual shared memory package, TreadMarks. We show that while communication time and busy times are comparable for small systems, the communication patterns are fundamentally different leading to poor performance for TreadMarks-based applications when the number of processors increase. This is due to the request/reply technique used in TreadMarks that results in a large fraction of very small messages. However, if the application can be tuned to reduce the impact of small message communication it is possible to achieve acceptable performance at least up to 32 nodes. Our measurements also show that TreadMarks programs tend to cause a more even network load compared to MPI programs.

1 Introduction

It has recently been quite popular to investigate the use of networks of workstations (NOWs) as parallel computing platforms with the motivation that they should be more cost-effective than multiprocessors with highly customized hardware and software. Since there is no hardware support in a NOW for shared memory, the programming model of choice has been message-passing. While message-passing is natural for some problems, it can be very cumbersome to use for applications with irregular communications patterns and many programmers feel that the shared memory programming model is a more natural approach to parallel programming.

The choice of programming model is, however, not merely a choice of convenience. It can also affect performance as well. Message-passing programs might suffer from extra calculations and memory overhead to partition the data in a regular manner in order to facilitate the programming of communication. Shared memory programs might suffer from the separation of synchronization and data communication and most importantly, in the case of a NOW, the lack of hardware support for shared memory. It is therefore important to understand the performance trade-offs in choosing one programming model over the other.

This paper characterizes the communication patterns for three different applications on the IBM SP2 coded in two different programming models: message-passing using MPI and shared memory using the TreadMarks DVSM package [1]. For this purpose, the IBM SP2 multiprocessor can be seen as a network of rs6000 workstations, albeit with a specialized and high-performance network switch. Compared to related work that compare these two programming models on platforms that do not support shared memory in hardware [4], we have used more processors and concentrate more directly on the characterization of communication patterns in the two programming paradigms.

To summarize, we have found that by using TreadMarks, there is a more even load on the network compared to the MPI versions of the applications which tend to have peaks of communication demanding very high bandwidth. On the other hand, TreadMarks inherent request/reply nature results in at least 50% very small messages leading to poor end-to-end bandwidth utilization. Moreover, when the number of processors increase, the MPI programs tend to result in a smaller fraction small messages while the situation is the opposite for Tread-Marks further reducing the performance of TreadMarks.

The rest of the paper is organized as follows: Section 2 presents the two programming models used in the study. This is followed by a description of the three applications and the differences in communication. In Sect. 4 we present results from measurements on an IBM SP2 and discusses the results before we conclude in Sect. 5.

2 MPI and Distributed Virtual Shared Memory

Different programming models will lead to different communication patterns even if the basic algorithm of the application is the same. We have used MPI (message passing) and TreadMarks (shared memory) and compare the resulting communication patterns.

2.1 MPI

The Message Passing Interface (MPI) standard was defined in a concerted effort by both high-performance computing vendors and research institutes [5]. The standard defines a variety of point-to-point send and receive primitives as well some collective communication primitives that involves more than two processing nodes. Table 1 lists the MPI routines used in the applications studied in this paper. In addition to the primitives listed in Table 1, there are primitives to find out the number of participating processors, and the rank, i.e. identity, of the local processor.

MPI primitive	Application	Meaning
MPI_SEND	Barnes	Standard point-to-point send of messages. Does not synchronize with the receiver.
MPI_RECV	Barnes	Standard blocking receive of message from a named sending node. When the program returns from this call, a message has been received.
MPI_BARRIER	FFT	Blocks execution until all processors have called MPI_BARRIER. Does not communicate data but is used to synchronize the program.
MPI_BCAST	Barnes, Water	A message is distributed from one processor to all other processors.
MPI_SCATTER	Water	A root node distributes its data across all the other nodes.
MPI_ALLGATHER	Water,FFT	All nodes fetches data from each node and stores it in a local array.
MPI_REDUCE	FFT, Barnes, Water	All nodes send a piece of data to the root node that performs a reduce operation, e.g. min., max or sum,on the collected data.
MPI_ALLREDUCE	Water	The same as MPI_REDUCE except that the result is distributed to all participating processors.

Table 1. MPI communication primitives used in the applications in this study.

2.2 Lazy Release Consistency shared memory

The other programming model we use for the SP2 is shared memory with the Lazy Release Consistency (LRC) memory model as found in TreadMarks [1]. In shared memory multiprocessors, communication occur implicitly based on what data is modified and when. Synchronization primitives such as locks for mutual exclusion and barriers are often used to ensure that only one processor at a time is modifying a particular shared data object.

The IBM SP2 does not implement shared memory in hardware and we therefore use TreadMarks, a Distributed Shared Virtual Memory (DVSM) system, to provide a shared memory programming model in software [1], using the existing virtual memory management system. Compared to a multiprocessor that implement shared memory in hardware, a DVSM system has a very high overhead to maintain a coherent shared memory. In order to overlap some of the shared memory communication with computation, TreadMarks uses a relaxed memory consistency model with a multiple-writer, invalidate protocol.

The main idea behind relaxed memory models is that write operations need not be conveyed to other processors immediately and that subsequent memory operations may bypass outstanding writes in order to increase the performance [3]. Since most shared memory programs are data-race free, i.e., updates to shared data are protected by critical regions, e.g. locks-unlocks, it is sufficient if information on updates are propagated to the other processors at the next synchronization operation. In TreadMarks this memory model has been further improved by delaying the time at which other processors are notified of memory updates until a processor acquires the lock that was used to protect the shared data. At the time of lock acquisition, all pages modified by the previous lock holder are invalidated. However, the update of the actual page contents is deferred to the time when it is actually needed.

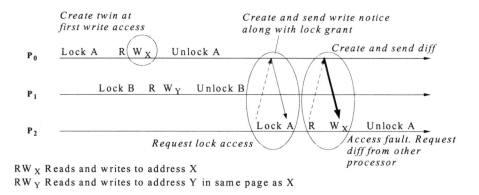

RW$_X$ Reads and writes to address X
RW$_Y$ Reads and writes to address Y in same page as X

Fig. 1. The Lazy Release Consistency protocol in TreadMarks defers the propagation of consistency information to the latest possible moment.

Figure 1 shows a scenario that exemplifies how TreadMarks maintains consistency. Processors 0 and 2 take turn in accessing a variable X protected by lock A. When processor 0 first modifies X, a copy of the page, in which this variable is located, is created. This copy is called a *twin*. The twin is later used to make an encoding, called a *diff*, of the changes made. The release of lock A will not result in any communication as long as no other processor has requested the lock. When processor 2 acquires the lock, it sends a message to the last holder of the lock (via a lock manager) and requests information on which pages the previous lock holder has modified. Processor 0 responds with a write notice for each modified page along with the lock grant message. Processor 2 invalidates these pages by removing the access privileges. Processor 2 will take an access fault at the first access to the page in which X is located. It then requests the changes, the diffs, from processor 0, the previous holder of lock A.

Note that during these operations, other processors can very well be accessing other locations within the same page as long as these memory locations do not overlap with X and they are protected by some other lock, e.g. lock B. This multiple-writer protocol effectively removes the issue of false-sharing from TreadMarks unless the same synchronization variable is used to protect an entire page.

The barrier operation, which is an important shared memory synchronization operation, can with respect to memory consistency be modeled as all processors performing a release followed by an acquire at the exit of the barrier. The effect is that all processors become updated on all changes made by all other processors and it is therefore a rather communication intensive operation.

Let us now describe the applications that we have used to characterize the differences in communication between MPI and Shared memory versions of the same algorithms.

3 Applications

Three different benchmark applications, that all are part of the TreadMarks application distribution, were used in the study. Barnes-Hut and Water originally from the SPLASH benchmark suite [7] and 3D FFT from the NAS benchmarks [2]. The MPI versions were written based on the corresponding TreadMarks versions.

3.1 Barnes-Hut

This application is a simulation of the motion of bodies interacting with gravitational forces. The bodies are hierarchically ordered in a tree where the internal nodes are called cells and represents collections of bodies in relatively close physical proximity. The algorithm loops over a number of time steps, in which the acceleration, velocity and position of each body are updated and the tree is reconstructed. Some system-wide parameters, e.g., total energy and system boundaries, are also calculated in each time step. All processors must have access to all of the database since the gravitational forces from all bodies on each body must be evaluated.

The TreadMarks version is directly taken from the TreadMarks distribution and uses shared memory for the bodies and the cells. At the beginning of each time step the root processor builds the tree and each processor processes its part of the bodies. The databases and system parameters are distributed using shared memory and the processors are synchronized using barriers.

The MPI version was developed from the shared memory version. It uses exactly the same algorithm but the root processor broadcasts the bodies and tree at the start of the time step and the slave processors send the updated bodies back to the root processor. The system wide parameters are collected by the root processor with reduction operations.

3.2 Water

Water simulates the dynamics of water molecules. Both intra- and inter molecule forces are evaluated. Similarly to Barnes-Hut this means that all processors must be able to read all of the database. However, unlike Barnes-Hut each processor not only update its own molecules but also those of others. In the original Tread-Marks version the race hazards are solved by using one lock per molecule. This approach proved to yield too much communication when directly ported to MPI so instead a different method was used. Each processor has a private copy of its modifications of all of the molecules. At the end of the time step all processor's "diffs" are merged and applied. This optimization proved to be effective in reducing the communication needed in the MPI version and it was therefore also used in the TreadMarks version used in this study. The TreadMarks version became more than twice as fast as a unmodified version when running on two nodes. When running on more nodes the difference was even higher due to the reduced communication.

The algorithm uses a couple of small global reduction operations in each time step. It also uses one large global sum for the "diffs" and a broadcast for the distribution of the database. The MPI version uses the specialized MPI operations for reduction etc. while the TreadMarks version uses shared memory protected by barriers and locks.

3.3 3D FFT

This application is a PDE solver using a three dimensional FFT. It solves the PDE by first doing a forward FFT and then stepping in time by updating the frequency space and doing inverse FFT back into the time space. The FFT and inverse FFT are done by allocating planes of the cube to the processors and then performing two one-dimensional transforms along the two axis in the plane. The cube is then transposed and a third one-dimensional transform is performed. The transpose is the main communication problem. It is solved in the TreadMarks version by simply using the shared memory and copying while in the MPI version each processor needs to build a partially transposed cube which is then broadcast to the other processors.

4 Results

4.1 Experimental test-bed

All measurements have been done on an IBM SP2 with 110 nodes using IBM's native MPI library and TreadMarks v0.10.1. TreadMarks was modified so that profiling data could be collected during program execution. The network switch of the SP2 has an end-to-end latency of about 40 μs using MPI [6] and measurements have shown that the corresponding UDP/IP latency is about 200 μs.

The programs were compiled using AIX's own C compiler using identical compile switches. They were executed on 1,2,4,8,16 and 32 node configurations. Two runs were done for each program, with and without profiling. The run without profiling measured the execution time while the profiling run gathered execution statistics, see below. Two runs had to be performed since the profiling code induces some overhead.

Sequential execution time, together with workload parameters, are listed in Table 2. The sequential execution time is the execution time of the parallel version running on a single processor and is the same for both the MPI and the TreadMarks version of the applications. The measured time does not include the startup phase since the timing is started after the first iteration. This to ensure a true speedup is calculated, i.e. the speedup of the parallel section of the application.

The MPI versions were profiled using IBM's own trace format and the Tread-Marks versions by profiling code inserted into TreadMarks itself. Unless otherwise stated, all profiling data were collected from all of the execution phases, i.e. even the startup phase. During the profiling runs communication and processor usage statistics were obtained. Profiling was done at the MPI API layer for the MPI versions and at the TreadMarks API layer and at the UDP/IP socket API layer for the TreadMarks versions. The execution times of all MPI and Tread-Marks functions respective were measured as well as all socket read and write calls in the TreadMarks library. Using these data the execution time of the applications could be broken down into busy time, communication time, i.e. time spent sending or waiting for messages, and time spent in the TreadMarks library, i.e. time spent ensuring consistency.

Application	Workload	Time (s)
Barnes-Hut	65536 bodies, 6 time steps	279
Water	1728 molecules, 5 time steps.	400
3D FFT	64 * 64 * 64 Cube, 64 iterations	54

Table 2. Application workloads and sequential execution times

4.2   Overall performance characterization

Figure 2 shows the speedup of the MPI and TreadMarks versions of the applications. As seen, there is a great variation in speedup among the applications and implementations. In general, the MPI versions do relatively well in terms of speedup, while the TreadMarks versions of FFT and Barnes perform very poorly for large configurations. Let us examine the communication characteristics in more detail.

Figure 3 displays the execution times of the applications subdivided into *busy time, communication time* and *TreadMarks time*. The busy time for both MPI and TreadMarks programs is the fraction spent executing useful code in the algorithm. The Communication time in the TreadMarks versions is the time spent blocking in socket calls while for the MPI programs it is the time spent in MPI calls. The TreadMarks time is the time spent inside the TreadMarks

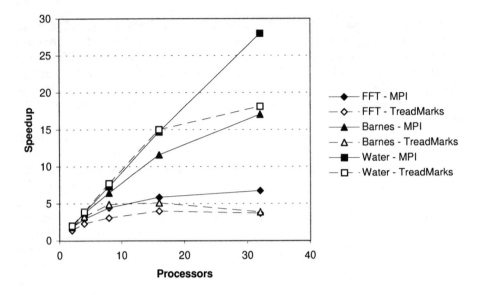

Fig. 2. Application speedups.

library itself, i.e. everything that is not in the algorithm and not in the socket communication protocol.

Figure 3 shows that the relative importance of the communication time for FFT and Barnes increases with the number of processors. In fact, it also increases in absolute time. Water, on the other hand, which has been tuned to aggregate changes, displays a behavior for the TreadMarks version which is much more similar to the MPI version.

Tables 3 and 4 show the aggregate number of messages and the total amount of data communicated in the MPI and TreadMarks versions of the applications respectively. The MPI versions generally communicate more data than the corresponding TreadMarks versions. However, since this is done in fewer but larger messages, the overall effect is a better speedup.

no.	FFT			Barnes			Water		
procs.	Mbytes sent	Msgs sent	kbytes/ message	Mbytes sent	Msgs sent	kbytes/ message	Mbytes sent	Msgs sent	kbytes/ message
2	260.0	194	1372.4	68.76	108	652.0	14.0	108	174.9
4	780.0	972	821.7	178.0	324	562.5	38.8	286	139.0
8	1820.0	4088	455.9	381.2	756	516.3	88.0	934	96.5
16	3900.0	16560	241.2	781.7	1620	494.1	186.2	3190	59.8
32	8060.0	66464	124.2	1579.7	3348	483.1	382.6	11542	34.0

Table 3. MPI program communication characteristics

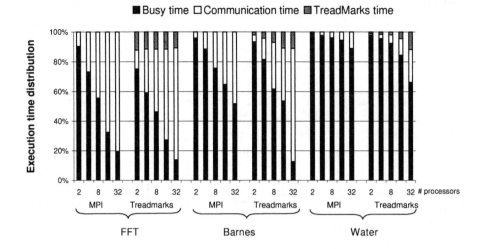

Fig. 3. Execution time distribution for the different applications.

no.	FFT			Barnes			Water		
procs.	Mbytes sent	Msgs sent	kbytes/ message	Mbytes sent	Msgs sent	kbytes/ message	Mbytes sent	Msgs sent	kbytes/ message
2	136.5	35478	3.9	47.5	20508	2.4	10.7	3572	3.1
4	208.3	55536	3.8	141.4	91570	1.6	22.8	8381	2.8
8	246.5	71582	3.5	282.5	275965	1.0	47.8	18256	2.7
16	523.2	165960	3.2	533.9	856078	0.6	100.5	39936	2.6
32	1088.8	402504	2.8	976.4	2502602	0.4	222.4	92283	2.5

Table 4. TreadMarks program communication characteristics

4.3 Results and discussion

We will now further investigate the reasons to poor speedup for applications using TreadMarks. From the communication statistics collected we have built histograms on the size of the messages sent during the course of execution. These show that TreadMarks distribution of message sizes differ radically from MPI's. MPI's distribution is polarized, i.e. the messages sent are either very small or very large, while TreadMarks' are much more evenly distributed. A typical distribution is shown in Fig. 4 for Water. The figure shows the cumulative distribution of the fraction of sent messages. The last value, corresponding to a message size of 8192 bytes, in the distribution is the fraction of messages larger than or equal to 8 k-bytes.

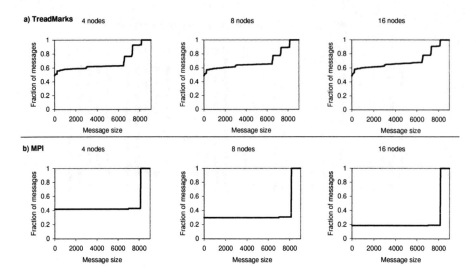

Fig. 4. The distribution of message sizes for Water, a) TreadMarks, b) MPI.

A general trend that we have observed for all three applications is that the fraction of small messages tends to decrease for the MPI versions when the number of processors increases, see Fig. 4. Although difficult to discern from Fig. 4, the opposite situation, i.e. the fraction of smaller messages increases, tends to be the case for the TreadMarks versions. This will of course further reduce the performance of TreadMarks as the number of processors increases. There are a number of reasons to this difference in message size distribution. First there is a difference in how the message size is measured. The communication data for MPI is collected at the MPI API layer which means that no acknowledgment messages that MPI itself might need are shown. Since TreadMarks' communication data is collected at the socket layer all TreadMarks' messages are shown. Thus the fraction of small messages in the MPI's distributions could in fact be higher! By running the FFT application on the free MPI implementation MPICH we have seen that each MPI message produces roughly 3 to 4 network messages. These additional messages are acknowledge and control messages. However, since IBM's native MPI implementation is supported by the hardware in the network interfaces of the SP2 nodes, it should produce fewer explicit control and acknowledgment messages than MPICH.

Secondly, while an MPI version of a program can use arbitrarily large messages and thus optimize the program to a given network, a TreadMarks program relies on the TreadMarks system for communication. Since TreadMarks uses the virtual memory system, the maximum message size is limited by the virtual memory page size. This can partly be alleviated by using larger page sizes in the TreadMarks code [4], but the optimal page size is application dependent and not always easy to estimate.

Furthermore, due to the request/reply technique used in TreadMarks at least 50% of the total number of messages are small, i.e., requests.

Interestingly enough, the overhead of TreadMarks LRC protocol itself is relatively small for Water and Barnes (up to eight nodes, see Fig. 3). For FFT it is much more significant. A closer examination reveals that the diffs in FFT's case are three times as large as those in Barnes and Water. The diff generation and application is the single largest component in TreadMarks overhead.

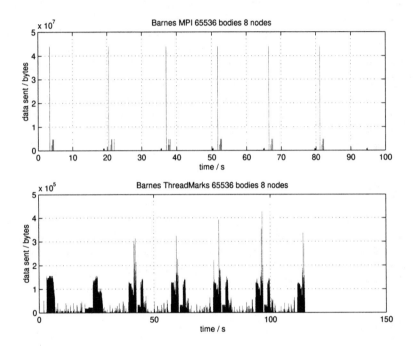

Fig. 5. Message traffic vs time for Barnes. Note the difference in scale on the y-axis.

We have also measured the network load induced by the different applications. A typical example of how many bytes sent per time interval is shown for Barnes in Fig 5. The other applications displayed similar characteristics. Note that MPI sends up to 100 times as much data as TreadMarks per time interval. Also note the more even distribution of messages caused by TreadMarks as opposed to MPI's discrete distribution. The difference in the distribution of communication over time indicates that TreadMarks might do better than MPI on a network with limited bandwidth but low latency.

5 Conclusions

We have studied and compared the communication patterns of three applications under two different programming models executing on the IBM SP2, message-passing using MPI and shared memory using TreadMarks. The results show that, for the applications studied, both programming models can be used with acceptable performance using up to eight processors. However, for large configurations, the fraction of small messages inherent in TreadMarks leads to poor performance.

TreadMarks causes a more even distribution of communication over time which suggests that it is not as prone to congestion in the network as are MPI applications. However, for the type of network used in the SP2, where the bandwidth is not a problem, and if the message latency is still high the message overhead will outweigh the potential benefits from less bandwidth demand.

We can therefore conclude that in order to improve the performance of a DVSM system work should be done to reduce the latency of the network system, decrease the number of sent packets and increase the size of sent network packets. This can be done by using network drivers that implement more functionality in hardware and by incorporating prefetch and producer push techniques into the DVSM protocols.

6 Acknowledgments

The research in this paper was in part supported by the Swedish National Board for Industrial and Technical Development (NUTEK) under project number P855. It was also supported with computing resources by the Swedish council for High Performance Computing (HPDR) and Center for High Performance Computing (PDC), Royal Institute of Technology.

References

1. C. Amza, A.L. Cox, S. Dwarkadas, P. Keleher, H. Lu, R. Rajamony, W. Yu and W. Zwaenepoel.: *Tread Marks: Shared Memory Computing on Networks of Workstations*, IEEE Computer, Vol. 29, no. 2, pp. 18- 28, February 1996.
2. D. Bailey, T. Harris, W. Saphir, R vd Wijngaart, A. Woo, and M. Yarrow, *The NAS Parallel Benchmarks 2.0*, Report NAS-95-020, Nasa Ames Research Center, Moffett Field, Ca, 94035, USA. December, 1995.
3. K. Gharachorloo, D. E. Lenoski, J. P. Laudon, P. Gibbons, A. Gupta, and J. L. Hennessy. *Memory Consistency and Event Ordering in Scalable Shared-Memory Multiprocessors.* In Proceedings of the 17th Annual International Symposium on Computer Architecture, pp. 15-26, May 1990.
4. H. Lu, S. Dwarkadas, A. L. Cox, and W. Zwaenepoel, *Quantifying the Performance Differences Between PVM and TreadMarks*, Journal of Parallel and Distributed Computing, Vol.43, No. 2, pp. 65-78, June 1997.
5. Message Passing Interface Forum, MPI: *A Message-Passing Interface Standard*, version 1.1, June 12, 1995.

6. J. Miguel, A. Arruabarrena, R. Beivide and J. A. Gregorio, *Assessing the Performance of the New IBM SP2 Communication Subsystem*, IEEE Parallel & Distributed Technology, Winter 1996, pp. 12-22.

7. J. P. Singh, W.-D. Weber, and A. Gupta. *SPLASH: Stanford parallel applications for shared-memory.* Computer Architecture News, 20(1):5-44, March 1992.

Characterization of Communication Patterns in Message-Passing Parallel Scientific Application Programs

JunSeong Kim and David J. Lilja

Department of Electrical and Computer Engineering
University of Minnesota, 200 Union St. SE, Minneapolis, MN 55455
{jskim, lilja}@ece.umn.edu

Abstract. This paper examines the communication patterns of parallel scientific programs, including some of the NAS benchmarks and the Miami Isopycnic Coordinate Ocean Model (MICOM), that use explicit message-passing. *Communication locality*, including communication event locality, message destination locality, and message size locality, is proposed and studied in addition to the widely accepted metrics of message size, destination, and generation distributions. We find that the locality metrics are relatively insensitive to system and problem size variations making them robust metrics for characterizing the communication patterns of parallel applications. We observe that the communication patterns of the benchmark programs are consistent with those of the actual application. The results of this study will be useful for understanding parallel applications' communication behavior and for designing more realistic synthetic benchmarks.

1 Introduction

Clusters of workstations have become popular for both scientific computing and general-purpose applications. In these environments, communication is a significant performance factor when executing an application in parallel since the communication overhead makes only coarse-grained parallelism feasible, which thereby limits the number of applications that can be usefully parallelized. A proper understanding of the communication patterns of parallel applications is important for determining how to maximize their performance within a given environment, and for designing better architectures in the future.

While computer network performance evaluation has been a widely researched topic [2], [3], [5], [8], [9], communication performance still is not well understood for scientific computing applications in network-based computing environments. This paper quantifies the communication patterns of a wide range of scientific applications. These patterns are characterized using the traditional metrics of message destination, size, and frequency distributions, but we also extend this characterization to *message locality*. Specifically, we extend the concept of memory access locality based on the Least Recently Used (LRU) stack model [8] to determine the locality of message destinations, sizes, and consecutive runs of send and receive operations.

These locality metrics provide good complements to traditional communication metrics. They allow, for example, more realistic synthetic message generation for communication network testing [9]. Furthermore, they can help in designing better communication protocols to improve performance by providing a means to predict the communication patterns of an application. We also examine the impact of different problem sizes and different numbers of processors on these metrics, and the impact of communication overhead relative to computation time when using several different types of communication networks.

In the remainder of the paper, Section 2 describes the system configuration and benchmarks used in the measurements. Section 3 then presents the measurement methodology, while Section 4 characterizes the communication patterns of the test programs. Finally, Section 5 summarizes our results and conclusions.

2 System Configuration and Benchmarks

2.1 System Configuration

A distributed cluster of four Silicon Graphics Challenge Series servers was used to measure the communication traffic in this study. One node in this system contains eight R10000 processors with the other three nodes each containing four R10000 processors. The processors run at 196 MHz and communicate via a shared bus within a node. All nodes run version 6.2 of the IRIX operating system. As shown in Figure 1, the nodes can communicate with each other via three different physical networks - Ethernet, Fibre Channel, and HiPPI.

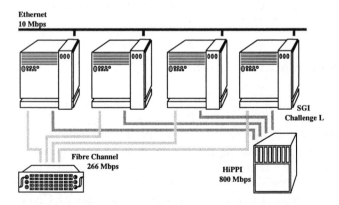

Fig. 1. System configuration used in the experiments.

The Ethernet is a 10 Mbps contention bus network that uses Carrier Sense Multiple Access with Collision Detect (CSMA/CD) technology for distributed access control. Fibre Channel (FC) [6] is a high-performance serial link supporting various topologies, such as point-to-point, loop, or switch. We use Ancor FCS 250 VME/64 adapters within each node. The nodes are networked together with an Ancor CXT 250 16 Fibre Channel Port Switch running at 266 Mbps. Each machine in the cluster is also equipped with an SGI HiPPI adapter that connects directly to a NetStar HiPPI Switch running at 800 Mbps. HiPPI [4], [13] is a connection-oriented, circuit-switched transport network linked by two 50-pair copper cables.

2.2 Programs Tested

We evaluated the communication patterns of several different types of parallel scientific application programs, as summarized in Table 1. The *CG, MG*, and *IS* programs from the Numerical Aerodynamic Simulation (NAS) parallel benchmarks suite [1], plus six other benchmarks, *Filter, Gauss, Hough, Kirsch, TRFD*, and *Warp* [14], are used as examples of kernel benchmarks. We also evaluate the *BT, LU*, and *SP* computational fluid dynamics (CFD) applications from the NAS suite. Finally, we include the *Miami Isopycnic Coordinate Ocean Model (MICOM)* [12] program as an example of a large, complete application program. The 127x127 problem size with *MICOM* version 2.6 is run for one simulated day.

Any consistency in communication behavior between *MICOM* and the other benchmarks will give us some indication of how well the benchmark programs characterize the communication patterns of a real application program. While any experimental study is limited to drawing specific conclusions for only those applications actually measured, it is felt that these test programs are representative of the types of parallel program kernels one might expect to find running on a typical networked parallel processing system. Figure 2 shows the communication intensity of the test programs in terms of the number of send events per processor and the average number of bytes transferred per send event.

3   Experimental Methodology

All of the application programs had been previously parallelized using either the Parallel Virtual Machine (PVM) [7] or the Message Passing Interface (MPI) [11] message-passing libraries, as shown in the last column of Table 1. The message-passing programming model used in these applications is based on just two primitives - SEND and RECEIVE. The SEND routines in this experiment are always asynchronous so that computation on the sending process resumes as soon as the message is written to the send buffer. The RECEIVE routine, on the other hand, blocks the receiving process until a message has arrived.

To measure the communication patterns, we extend the parallelized versions of the test programs by inserting monitor operations at points in the programs where message-related activities occur. The MONITOR operation consists of some arithmetic operations to calculate the appropriate characterization metrics.

Programs	Description	Parallel Lib.
CG	Uses a conjugate gradient method to compute an approximation of the smallest eigenvalue of a large, sparse, symmetric, positive-definite matrix.	PVM
MG	Solves a 3-D Poisson partial differential equation. This program is a simplified multigrid kernel with constant coefficients, and is a good test for both short- and long-distance data communication.	PVM
IS	Tests a sorting operation that is important in particle method codes. In this benchmark, no floating point arithmetic is involved, but significant data communication is required.	PVM
Filter	Smoothing (averaging) filter that calculates the value of an input image element as the weighted sum of up to 36 neighboring pixel elements in the input image.	MPI
Gauss	Gaussian elimination with back substitution. This program is very communication intensive, requiring several point-to-point, broadcast, and reduction operations.	PVM
Hough	Detects straight lines in the input image, according to the general Hough transform, by finding points of intersections between lines. This algorithm uses both nearest neighbor and global communications.	MPI
Kirsch	Calculates magnitude and direction gradients of an input image.	MPI
TRFD	Simulates a two-electron integral transformation using a fourth-order tensor equation. This algorithm is a series of matrix multiplications and transpositions requiring several point-to-point communication operations.	PVM
Warp	Spatial domain image restoration algorithm that aligns an input image along a given axis. This program exhibits very irregular communications.	MPI
BT	Simulated CFD application. The block tridiagonal benchmark solves multiple independent systems of non-diagonally dominant, block tridiagonal equations with a 5x5 block size.	PVM
LU	Simulated CFD application. The lower-upper diagonal benchmark employs a symmetric successive over-relaxation numerical scheme to solve a regular, sparse, block 5x5 lower and upper triangular system.	PVM
SP	Simulated CFD application. The scalar pentadiagonal benchmark solves multiple independent systems of non-diagonally dominant, scalar pentadiagonal equations with a 5x5 block size.	PVM
MICOM	Miami isopycnic coordinate ocean model [12]. A highly parallel ocean circulation application code characterized by hydrostatic balance in the vertical dimension and a near-geostrophic equilibrium between pressure and Coriolis forces in the horizontal dimension.	MPI

Table 1. Parallel benchmark programs tested.

206

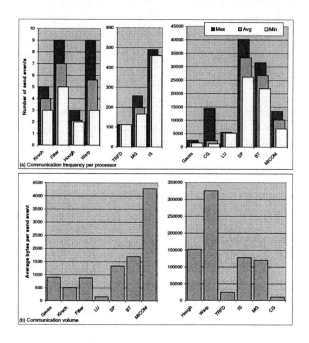

Fig. 2. Communication intensity in terms of communication frequency and volume.

This monitoring does not affect the communication patterns of the test programs since they are not a function of time, but rather are counts of the occurances of an event. This monitoring can affect the temporal behaviors of the messaging routines, however. To compensate for this perturbation, we insert time-stamps before and after each MONITOR operation. This allows us to subtract the monitoring overhead from the time measurements. In this way, the execution time of each parallel program is divided into send time, receive time, and computation time. The send time is defined to be only the time required to execute the SEND instruction and to move data into the sending buffer on the sending process, since we use an asynchronous send routine. The receive time, however, includes both the receiving overhead and the time the receiver is blocked waiting for a message. The send and receive times can vary since three different types of networks can be used. The computation time will be constant, however, since the processors remain the same.

4 Communication Patterns and Characteristics

This section presents the measurements of the communication patterns observed with these test programs. These observations include message size and destination distribution, communication localities, the effect of the problem size and

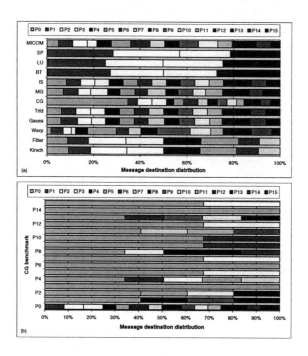

Fig. 3. Overall message destination distribution for the test programs and the message destination distribution for each processor in the CG benchmark.

the system size on those metrics, and the performance effect of the different networks.

4.1 Traditional Message Size and Destination Distributions

Traditionally, the communication requirements of a parallel application have been characterized by three attributes - the *temporal*, *spatial*, and *volume* components [2]. Spatial behavior is characterized by the distribution of message destinations. The common assumption is that the destinations of messages are evenly distributed among all of the processors. Figure 3 (a) appears to verify this assumption for our test programs since the overall destinations are uniformly distributed among all of the processors. However, we find that destinations are not uniformly distributed from the viewpoint of the individual processors. Figure 3 (b) shows the message destinations of each individual processor for the *CG* benchmark. Except for P0, which is the favorite destination of all of the processors, each processor prefers one to five distinct processors out of the 15 available destinations as their communication partners. The other programs also show favored communication partners except for the *IS*, *TRFD*, and *Gauss* programs, which communicate equally among all processors. We find that this pattern is

208

consistent within an application when varying both the number of processors used to execute the application and the problem size.

The volume of data transferred is characterized by the distribution of message sizes and the average number of messages. In this section, we focus only on the size of the messages transferred, measured in bytes and ignoring header information, since the number of messages is dependent on the number of processors. For message-passing primitives, some amount of overhead is unavoidable, since the data transfered must be combined with an appropriate header. This header contains source and destination information, and, for reliable communication, a sequence number, an acknowledgment field, and so on. In this study, we do not consider the size of this header information focusing instead on the amount of data sent in each message.

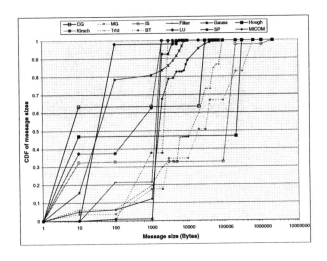

Fig. 4. The cumulative distribution of message sizes in the test programs.

Figure 4 shows the distribution of message sizes in the test programs, giving a more detailed view of the volume behavior of the applications than in Figure 2. The horizontal axis in this figure represents the message size plotted on a logarithmic scale with the vertical axis showing the cumulative distribution of message sizes. Most benchmarks show two or three clear steps in the distribution indicating that all of the messages within an application have only two or three distinct sizes. Furthermore, some fraction of all the messages within an application tend to be very large while the remainder tend to be very small. For example, about 64% of the messages in the *CG* program are 8 bytes in length whereas the remainder are around $28K$ bytes. Similarly, in the *IS* program, about 33% are 4 bytes and the remainder are around $130K$ bytes. Thus, the distribution of the sizes of the messages sent by these applications is sharply bimodal with two widely-separated peaks.

The temporal behavior of the applications' messages is characterized by the distribution of the message generation rate. Figure 5 shows cumulative distribution functions (cdf) of the computation time, the send time, and the receive time of the *CG* and *Gauss* benchmarks when they are executed using different networks. As is often assumed in analytic studies of network performance, the temporal behavior of message-sending appears to be exponentially distributed [2], [9]. There is little difference in the temporal behavior when using Fibre Channel or HiPPI, while the Ethernet shows more delay for send and receive operations. This difference occurs because the Ethernet uses a contention bus while the other two networks use a switched topology.

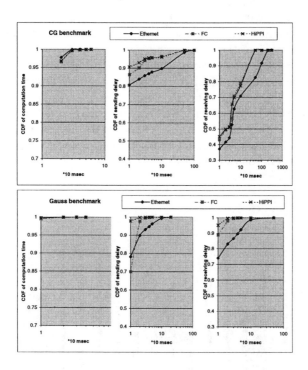

Fig. 5. The cumulative distribution function of the computation and communication times.

4.2 Communication Localities

While these measurements tend to confirm both previous studies and intuition of communication characteristics, we extend this standard characterization to investigate the *localities* of communication behavior. Specifically, we quantify patterns and repetitions in types of communication events (i.e. send or receive), message size, and message destination using the Least-Recently Used (LRU) stack model of memory access locality. For example, this model assumes a stack window of size n for each node that contains the processor number of the n most recent message destinations or the size, in bytes, of the n most recent messages sent. If the next message's destination (or size) is in the window stack, we count a hit. Otherwise, we count a miss. We then define the *locality* of the particular type of event to be $\#\ hits/(\#\ hits\ +\ \#\ misses)$. The window size for the locality of message destinations varies from one to the total number of processors. Various window sizes are used to examine the locality of message sizes.

In addition to localities of message destinations and sizes, the *locality of communication events* is a metric that shows the repetition of send and receive events. For example, completely alternating send and receive events will produce zero locality with a window size of 1. It is interesting to see in Figure 6 that many applications have high (greater than 80%) communication event locality. This means that 80% of the time a send operation is followed by another send operation, or a receive is followed by another receive. We notice in the programs' source code that there are often communication phases alternating with computation phases. During the communication phase, a bundle of send or receive operations are executed consecutively. This pattern may be due to the nature of the application itself or due to the preference of the programmer. However, this pattern can have a large impact on performance, since overlapping send and receive operations becomes difficult.

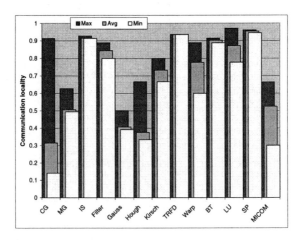

Fig. 6. Communication event (i.e. send/receive) locality.

While Figure 3 showed that the overall distribution of message destinations is uniform, the *message-destination locality* measurement in Figure 7 shows that in most of the applications, processors have only a small number of favored communication partners. For example, the line representing the MICOM program shows a 1% hit ratio when the window size is 1, meaning that only 1% of the time, when it sends a message to one processor, it sends its next message to that same processor. When the window size is expanded to 2, however, we find that 25% of the time when a processor sends message, it is sent to one of the two processors to which it has most recently sent messages. Continuing to expand the window size, we find that nearly 99% of the time, this program sends its messages to one of the four processors to which it has most recently sent messages.

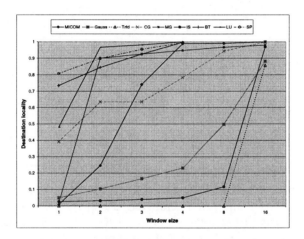

Fig. 7. Message destination locality.

Figure 7 shows that this type of communication locality is common among the applications tested. Although it is not shown in these figures, we find that the processors tend to communicate with relatively disjoint sets of destination processors. As a result, even though an individual processor communicates with only a small subset of those in the system, the overall distribution of message destinations tends to appear uniformly distributed.

Figure 8 shows *message size locality*, extending the message size distribution results in Figure 4 to include a temporal component. It is clear from Figure 8 that, since the message size locality of most programs with window size two or three is more than 90%, there are just two or three distinct message sizes used in applications. The exception is the *IS* benchmark which shows message size locality of only around 33% for window sizes of 1 to 20. However, as shown in Figure 4, this benchmark has 67% of its messages clustered around $130K$ bytes with only small differences. Since we count only messages with exactly the same size as LRU hits, this program shows poor locality. If we counted messages sizes

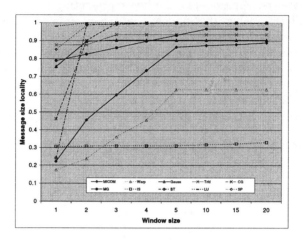

Fig. 8. Message size locality.

that were *close* in size as hits, though, this program would show similar behavior as the others.

4.3 Effect of Problem Size and System Size Variations

We next examined the impact of varying the problem size and the number of processors on the communication characteristics of the test programs. Two to sixteen processors and three different problem sizes were considered for most of the test programs. In general, when additional processors are used to execute an application, the communication frequency tends to increase while the average size of each message decreases. These changes occur since, as more processors share the same data set, each processor handles a smaller fraction of the total data. Also, when the problem size increases, the communication frequency remains roughly the same. However, the average size of each message increases since there is more total data. Thus, larger problem sizes produce *larger* messages instead of *more* messages.

While the size and number of messages varies with the problem size and the number of processors, the localities are quite unaffected. As shown in Figure 9, only communication event locality increases as the number of processors increases. That is, any change in the number of processors produces a change in communication frequency. As the communication frequency increases, there are longer runs of consecutive send or receive events during a given communication phase. This change in communication behavior is shown by the increase in communication event locality as the number of processors, n, increases in Figure 9. Since the other locality parameters are relatively insensitive to changes in the number of processors or the problem size, they should be very useful to characterize an application's communication patterns.

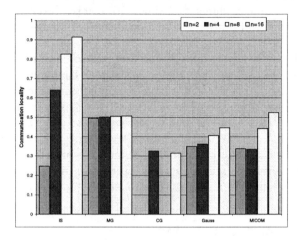

Fig. 9. Changes in communication event (i.e. send/receive) locality as the number of processors is changed.

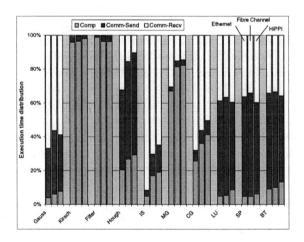

Fig. 10. Execution time distributions for the different communication networks.

4.4 Performance Effect of Network Type

Another interesting issue is the application-level performance of these benchmarks. Figure 10 shows the execution time of the programs divided into send, receive, and computation time when they are executed using the Ethernet, Fibre Channel, and HiPPI networks. It is surprising to find that communication time dominates the computation time for most of these applications to such a large degree. For many of the applications, the fraction of communication time is significantly larger than the computation time so that it would be impossible to completely overlap communication time with computation time. As a result, communication time will continue to be a bottleneck in the performance of these applications.

There is little difference in application-level performance when using the different networks even though their differences in peak bandwidth are quite large. This is because the applications are latency-limited not bandwidth-limited. In these measurements, the system is dedicated to the experiment to avoid any interference from other applications or networks. In this environment, high-bandwidth does not necessarily translate to low-latency. To overcome this high communication overhead, more fundamental methods are needed to directly reduce the communication latency, such as using low-overhead communication protocols or using multiple networks simultaneously [4], [9], [10].

5 Summary and Conclusion

This study has evaluated the communication characteristics of several scientific application programs that have been explicitly parallelized using the PVM and MPI message-passing primitives. We have studied these applications on a cluster of Silicon Graphics multiprocessor workstations interconnected with Ethernet, HiPPI, and Fibre Channel communication networks. Our results have confirmed earlier studies [2], [3], [8], [9] that have used traditional communication characterization metrics. Specifically, we found that the overall distribution of message destinations appears to be uniform, and that the distribution of the size of messages tends to be bimodal. That is, the messages sent by the processors executing the application tend to be either very large or very small, and each processor has an equal likelihood of being the destination of a send operation.

To dig deeper into the characteristics of the communication behavior of these parallel application programs, however, we extended these traditional metrics to incorporate the concept of the *locality of communication events*. Based on a technique derived from the LRU stack model of memory reference locality, we come to the following conclusions.

- Send and receive operations typically occur in runs of consecutive sends or runs of consecutive receives. In fact, approximately 80% of the time, a send operation is followed by another send, or a receive is followed by another receive.
- Using the *destination locality* metric, we found that, instead of message destinations being uniformly distributed as previously assumed, each processor tends to have only a small number of favored destination processors for the messages it sends. These destinations tend to be relatively disjoint, however, so that the overall *cumulative* distribution of message destinations does tend to appear uniform.
- The *message size locality* metric confirms that most application programs have only two or three distinct message sizes that processors send.

– While the *frequency* of communication events tends to increase as the number of processors used to execute an application increases, and the sizes of the messages tend to increase as the problem size increases, the values of the locality metrics are relatively insensitive to changes in both the number of processors and the problem size.

We also found that, from the application performance point-of-view, the communication time severely dominates the computation time. This characteristic holds true even as the peak bandwidth of the communication network is dramatically increased. Even if the communication time of the applications could be completely overlapped with the available computation time, there would still be "leftover" communication time that could not be hidden by the computation time. Thus, this communication time is the major performance bottleneck.

Based on these measurements, we conclude that the proposed locality metrics could be very useful in characterizing the communication behavior of message-passing parallel application programs. We further conclude that, even with significant increases in raw network bandwidth, communication delays continue to be an important limitation in using networked clusters of workstations to speed-up the execution of scientific application programs.

Acknowledgments

We thank Steven VanderWiel and Aaron Sawdey for all their help with the test programs. This work was supported in part by the National Science Foundation under grant no. CDA-9414015.

References

1. Bailey, D., Barszcz, E., Barton, J., Browning, D., Carter, R., Darum, L., Fatoohi, R., Fineberg, S., Frederickson, P., Lasinski, T., Schreiber, R., Simon, H., Venkatakrishnan, V., Weeratunga, S.: The NAS Parallel Benchmarks. NAS Report RNR-94-007. (March 1994)
2. Chodnekar, S., Srinivasan, V., Vaidya, A., Sivasubramaniam, A., Das, C.: Towards a Communication Characterization Methodology for Parallel Applications. High-Performance Computer Architecture. (1997)
3. R. Cypher, A. Ho, S. Konstantinidou, and P. Messina, Architectural Requirements of Parallel Scientific Applications with Explicit Communication. International Symposium on Computer Architecture. (1993) 2–13.
4. Hsieh, J., Du, D., Troullier, N., Lin, M.: Enhanced PVM Communications over a HIPPI Networks. Proceedings of the Second International Workshop on High-Speed Network Computing. (April 1996)
5. Fatoohi, R., Weeratunga, S.: Performance Evaluation of Three Distributed Computing Environments for Scientific Applications. Supercomputing'94. (1994) 400–409
6. Frymoyer, E.: Fibre Channel Fusion: Low Latency, High Speed. Data Communications Magazine. (February 1995)

7. Geist, A., Beguelin, A., Dongarra, J., Jiang, W., Manchek, R., Sunderam, V.: PVM: Parallel Virtual Machine - A Users' Guide and Tutorial for Networked Parallel Computing. The MIT Press. (1994)
8. Hsu, J., Banerjee, P.: Performance Measurement and Trace Driven Simulation of Parallel CAD and Numeric Applications on a Hypercube Multicomputer. International Symposium on Computer Architecture. (1990) 260–269
9. Kim, J., Lilja, D.: Exploiting Multiple Heterogeneous Networks to Reduce Communication Costs in Parallel Programs. Heterogeneous Computing Workshop, International Parallel Processing Symposium. (April 1997) 83–95
10. Kim, J., Lilja, D.: Utilizing Heterogeneous Networks in Distributed Parallel Computing Systems. International Symposium on High Performance Distributed Computing. (August 1997) 336–345
11. Message Passing Interface Forum: MPI: A Message-Passing Interface Standard. Version 1.1 (June 1995)
12. Sawdey, A.: Using the Parallel MICOM on SGI Multiprocessors and the Cray T3D. The MICOM User's Group Meeting. (February 1995)
13. Tolmie, D., Flanagan, D.: HIPPI: It's Not Just for Supercomputers Anymore. Data Communications Magazine. (May 1995)
14. VanderWiel, S., Nathanson, D., Lilja, D.: Complexity and Performance in Parallel Programming Languages. International Workshop on High-Level Parallel Programming Models and Supportive Environments, International Parallel Processing Symposium. (April 1997) 3–12

Cross-Platform Analysis of Fast Messages for Myrinet*

Giulio Iannello, Mario Lauria, and Stefano Mercolino

Dipartimento di Informatica e Sistemistica
Università di Napoli Federico II
via Claudio, 21 – 80125 Napoli – Italy
{iannello, lauria, merco}@grid.unina.it

Abstract. Designing high performance communication software requires an in-depth understanding of the role of the components of the underlying machine/network architecture and their reciprocal interactions. The task is complicated by the continuing technological advances in the machine architectures. In this paper we analyze the performance of the Fast Messages (FM) high performance messaging layer on three platforms as different as a Sparc 5, a Ultra 1, and a PentiumPro PC. Using a characterization in terms of the LogP model, we expose how the differences in the machine architectures are reflected in the way the different parts of a communication library like FM behaves and how their reciprocal interaction is affected. Our work shows that the FM implementation is "robust", tolerating large variations of machine performance while preserving the basic balances of its design. It also shows that a properly extended LogP model can be an invaluable architectural analysis tool.

1 Introduction

Networks of workstations are becoming an increasingly attractive alternative to massively parallel processors for high performance computing. The remarkable growth in the computational performance of workstations and high-end PCs is reducing the computational performance gap between commodity and proprietary processors. Beside a very favorable price/performance ratio, network of workstations have a number of additional advantages, like the abundance of applications, the availability of a number of operating systems and development environments, a large choice of software and hardware vendors.

But the decisive factor in making workstation cluster attractive for high performance computing has been the advent of new network technologies, with much improved raw performance with respect to traditional networks. These "killer networks" include ATM, FDDI, 100 Base-T Ethernet, Fibrechannel, Myrinet, with physical bandwidths ranging from 100 Mbits/s to 1.2 Gbits/s.

Unfortunately the advent of this new technology has not been accompanied by a corresponding advancement in the communication system software, and

---

* This work has been partially supported by MURST under funds 40% and 60%, by TELECOM Italia, and by NATO under a Collaborative Research Grant.

legacy protocols have been shown not to be able to deliver the unprecedented level of performance made available [8].

A number of high-performance communication projects have been started to reduce the gap, like U-Net [12], and SHRIMP [3]. This has also been the objective of the Fast Messages (FM) project [7, 9, 11, 10]. In such project a highly optimized, low latency messaging layer providing a virtual interface to the hardware was developed for the Myrinet network [4].

The design of FM addresses the critical issues found in building a low level messaging layer: division of labor between the host and the network coprocessor, management of the input/output (I/O) bus, and buffer management. Implemented entirely in user space, FM avoids the high overhead of system calls. FM achieves a short message latency of only 14 μs and a peak bandwidth of 17.6 MB/s on Sparc 20s, with an Active Messages style interface.

Developed originally mainly on Sparc 20s, FM is routinely used on a variety of other workstations, and is being ported to radically different platforms, like the Pentium PC under Windows NT [10]. Every new architecture represents an opportunity to further improve performance, but it also requires an evaluation of how the balance between FM components has changed as a result of the change in the hardware. Examples of critical aspects that are likely to be affected are the division of labour, given that the host processors evolve much more rapidly than the interface processor, and the management of the I/O bus, which can have substantially different features on different systems.

An accurate performance characterization of FM has been an important design tool since the very beginning of the project [9]. It helped in improving the performance delivered at the application level by the first version of the library [7]. However, only very simple benchmarks measuring the round trip time and the bandwidth have been used so far to this purpose.

By presenting a detailed performance characterization of FM for Myrinet on three different platforms, the goal of this work is to expose how the differences in the machine architectures are reflected in the way the different parts of a communication library like FM behaves and how their reciprocal interaction is affected.

We have used a series of communication microbenchmarks to measure the parameters of the LogP model. These specialized benchmarks are similar to those employed by Culler et al. [6] to characterize the network interfaces of three different parallel architectures running the Active Messages communication library [13]. What differentiates our work is the focus on the interaction between the messaging layer and the underlying network architecture.

2 Background

Fast Messages for Myrinet. Myrinet is a high speed LAN interconnect which uses bidirectional byte-wide copper links to achieve physical bandwidth of nearly 160 MB/s in each direction [4]. The network interfaces are connected to crossbar switches by point-to-point links; the switches can be interconnected to form arbitrary topologies. The network use wormhole routing, which allows the packets to be switched with a latency of about half a microsecond.

The network interface consists of a custom VLSI chip (the *LANai*), 256 KB of SRAM, differential line drivers/receivers for the link, and the I/O bus control logic. The LANai contains a link interface, a processor and three DMA engines (one each for the incoming link, outgoing link, and the I/O bus). The SBus and the PCI bus versions of the Myricom interfaces employed in the tests belong to the same product generation, with a LANai processor version 4.1. The processor is clocked at 1.5 times the I/O bus clock on the Sun (37.5 MHz), and at the same clock on the PPro (33 MHz).

Host-LANai interaction is achieved by mapping the interface memory into the host address space. While the host can read/write the interface memory with load/store operations, it cannot start the DMAs. Single word accesses to the LANai memory are rather expensive, because they cross the SBus. As in most systems, DMA transfers to/from the host must be performed through a pinned-down DMA buffer in the kernel address space.

FM [10] differs from a pure message passing paradigm in that there is a send operation but there is no corresponding receive. Rather, each message includes the name of a handler, which is a user-defined function that is invoked upon message arrival, and that will process as required the carried data. The FM interface is a generalization of the Active Messages model [13], in that there are no restrictions on the communication operations that can be carried out by the handler. (The user is responsible for avoiding deadlock situations.)

By providing a few key services – buffer management, reliable and in-order delivery – the FM programming interface allows a leaner, more efficient implementations of the higher level communication layers. For our experiments we used the version 2.01 of the library which is characterized by the ability to assemble and disassemble arbitrary size messages on the fly, using a *stream* abstraction. For example, on the receive side an arbitrary number of FM_receive(...) calls within an handler can be used to copy fragments of the incoming message directly into user-defined buffers.

The notification mechanism on the receive side is of the polling type. The FM_extract() primitive checks for incoming messages and starts the executions of the corresponding handlers. The user needs to call this primitive frequently to ensure the prompt processing of incoming communication.

Given its limited programming interface, the FM library is targeted to language and library developers rather than to end users. The range of applications being considered for development on FM, or already in the works, is testimonial of the flexibility of its interface. Besides the MPI message passing library, these are the BSD socket interface, the Orca Project parallel object language [2], the Shmem Put/Get interface [10].

FM is composed of two parts, the host program and the LANai control program. The division of labour between the host and the interface processor is critical for performance because of the potential for parallelism in protocol processing but also for bottlenecks if the load is not properly balanced. The relative difference in the speeds of the two processors and the modest performance of the LANai in absolute terms, suggests assigning most of the work to the host, and keeping the LANai control program as simple as possible.

One of the main tasks of the hosts program is the fragmentation of messages in fixed size packets, and the reassembly on the receive side. FM use a fixed packet format because this streamlines the queue management in the LANai control program. It also allows the overlapping of the send, network and receiver protocol processing in the transfer of a message. A potential drawback is the increased complexity of the assemble/disassemble operations.

The choice of the size of the packet was the result of a tradeoff between contrasting benefits. A small packet size gives better latency, increases pipelining through the network, and gives potentially better network utilization. A larger size reduces the overheads, and thus gives better bandwidth. The size of 256 bytes adopted for FM 2.01 has been found to be the best compromise on the Sun architectures. Messages longer than 256 bytes are segmented and then reassembled within FM.

To send a packet, the host processor writes the data directly into the LANai memory, one double-word at a time (programmed I/O). This procedure saves the double cost of copying the data into the DMA buffer, plus synchronizing with the LANai to get it to start the DMA. Since programmed I/O cannot take advantage the faster burst transfer mode of the SBus, this solution improves latency at the expense of bandwidth.

When a packet arrives at a node, the LANai moves it into host memory (DMA buffer) with a DMA transfer. This procedure ensures good bandwidth, quick delivery of the packet, and prompt draining of the network, even when the host program is busy or not available (i.e., descheduled). The packets are deposited into a receive queue in the DMA buffer, from which they will be dequeued and processed by the FM_extract() primitive.

The LogP model as used in the analysis. LogP is a model for parallel algorithm design proposed by Culler et al. in [5]. It is intended to serve as a basis to develop fast, portable parallel algorithms and to offer guidelines to machine designers.

The LogP model is based on four parameters: the number P of processor-memory pairs in the machine, the *gap g* representing a lower bound on the time between the transmission of successive messages, or the reception of successive messages, at the same processor, the *latency L* representing the maximum delay associated with delivering a message from its source processor to its target processor, the *overhead o* representing the amount of time for which a processor is busy during the transmission or reception of a message.

LogP has been successfully used to design and tune new parallel algorithms in several fields, and it served as a basis for further extensions addressing specific issues in algorithm design like the use of bulk-data transfers [1]. Less attention has been given to the model as a tool to drive architectural choices and evaluate the different components making up a parallel system.

Recently, Culler et al. [6] have used the model to compare network interfaces. They measured the LogP parameters using microbenchmarks on three parallel machines characterized by different network architectures. This way they obtained a much more detailed performance characterization than the traditional one based on round-trip time and bandwidth.

In the following sections we present a similar approach to the performance analysis of the Fast Messages library. Like in the Culler's paper we use a slightly modified LogP model that distinguishes between the overhead o_s at the send side and the overhead o_r at the receive side, and that recognizes that for bulk-data transfers, L, o and g depend on message size.

In FM, o_s is the host overhead on the send side, which includes the transfer across the SBus. The o_r parameter describes the host overhead on the receive side, which is due to the buffer management in the kernel DMA region, handler startup and packet overheads. The L parameter includes the LANai processing time on both sides, the latency over the Myrinet links, plus the DMA transfer into the host memory on the receive side. Finally, the g parameter is the time needed to process one message by the slower stage of the communication pipeline.

3 Measurements

Description of the benchmarks. We carried out three tests each involving two homogeneous machines. The machines used in the tests were SPARC 5s, Ultra 1s, and Pentium Pro PCs respectively. The Sun workstations used for the first two tests were connected to a same Myrinet switch, and were part of a cluster at the Dip. di Informatica e Sistemistica of the "Federico II" University of Naples. The PPro PCs were part of the 64-node DAS cluster at the Mathematics and Computer Science Dept. of the Vrije Universiteit of Amsterdam[2].

For each of the three configurations we measured round trip time and bandwidth as a function of message size. We then performed the additional benchmarks needed for the measurements of the LogP parameters.

Two simple tests were employed for the basic round-trip/bandwidth characterization. In the first we measured latency incurred by one message to go from one node to another, from the moment the send is started to the time the messages reception is acknowledged at its destination. The test was performed by timing the round trip between the two machines, i.e. the time it takes for a message to go and to be bounced back.

In the second, the bandwidth was measured by sending a continuous sequence of messages, and dividing the total time by the number of bytes sent. The timer is stopped when the last message is acknowledged, so to measure the actual bandwidth and not the bandwidth as seen by the sender alone.

The measurements of the LogP parameters has been carried out as follows. The round-trip time measured with the basic tests gives the quantity $2\,(o_s + L +$

---

[2] The DAS measurements were realized by one of the authors (Lauria) while visiting the Computer Systems group at the Vrije Universiteit, during the Summer of 1997.

222

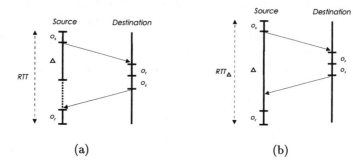

Fig. 1. Modified ping-pong test: (a) Small Δ; (b) Large Δ

o_r). We then performed two microbenchmarks. The first one gives the values of o_s and g, and the second one gives the quantity $o_s + o_r$. From all these results we can easily derive the values of L, o_s, o_r and g.

The first microbenchmark measures the time needed to send a sequence of N messages of size M in a row (i.e. like in the bandwidth benchmark). Since the communication channel between two processors works as a pipeline, at the beginning of the sequence the sender is speed limited by just the first stage. Thus for small values of N the completion time of the microbenchmark divided by N gives the time the first stage takes to handle the message, i.e. o_s. As N increases the pipeline fills up reaching its steady-state, in which the slowest stage is pacing the entire pipeline. Thus for large values of N the completion time of the benchmark divided by N does correspond to g.

The second microbenchmark measures the round-trip time when a delay of Δ μs is inserted between the send call and the loop of FM_extract calls on the node that starts the test. When $\Delta < L + o_r + o_s + L$, the completion time of the microbenchmark corresponds to the round-trip time (Figure 1-(a)). For sufficiently large values of Δ the completion time of the microbenchmark becomes $o_s+\Delta+o_r$ (Figure 1-(b)). Since Δ is known one can obtain the quantity $o_s + o_r$.

Platform #1: SPARCstation 5. The Sun workstation used for this setup are a pair of SPARCstation 5 (SS5) running Solaris 2.5.1. The SPARCstation 5/110 has a MicroSparc2 processor clocked at 110 MHz, a 16KB/8KB instruction/data internal cache, no external cache, and is rated at 1.37/1.88 SPECint-base95/SPECfp-base95. The SBus is clocked at 22 MHz.

Figures 2-(a) and 2-(b) show latency and bandwidth. For the latency, two versions of the test were used, one in which the received data is untouched and the other in which data is copied into a preallocated buffer (on both sides). Given that in the current version of FM messages are sent in 256-byte packets, the additional overhead of the copy (the gap between the two curves) keeps growing until the 256-byte mark is reached, and then it remains constant. Such constant value (approximately 15 μs) represents the time spent for the copy of the first packet, the subsequent copies being completely overlapped with the reception of the next packet. The minimum one-way latency with copy is 21.5 μs. For short messages the curve can be approximated with the line $35 + 0.090\,M$ μs. For long messages the curve is $42.5 + 0.063\,M$ μs.

Figure 2-(b) shows the results of the bandwidth test. The peak bandwidth is 15.25 MB/s, with 14.29 MB/s already for 256-byte messages. Here the bandwidth is not affected by the copy of the message out of the kernel memory because messages are sent back-to-back, making possible the overlapping between messages in addition to the one between packets.

Figure 2-(c) shows the completion time of the first microbenchmark versus N, Fig. 2-(d) of the second microbenchmark versus Δ for several small message lengths.

Let's examine what happens when message size is varied. For messages of length M up to 64 bytes, the graphs of Fig. 2-(c) give different values for o_s and g – i.e. there are a transient and a steady-state region. Moreover while g turns out to be basically independent of M, the overhead at the send side grows linearly as $o_s = 2.3 + 0.057\,M$ μs. Such dependence comes from the copy through the SBus which takes a time proportional to the message size. Since g is larger than o_s, for small messages the bottleneck must be elsewhere.

The situation is quite different for larger message sizes. Fig. 2-(e) shows that o_s and g coincide and grow linearly with M. This means that for messages longer than 128 bytes, the copy through the SBus at the send side becomes the actual bottleneck, and it determines the value of g. For messages longer than 256 bytes it is $o_s = g = 0.063\,M$ μs. The difference in the growth rate of o_s for small and large messages is due to the additional cost per packet due to the packetization overhead.

A similar dual slope graph can be observed for o_r. Combining the data shown in Figs. 2-(d) and 2-(f) and the values found for o_s, we found $o_r = 6 + 0.040\,M$ μs for messages up to 256 bytes, and $o_r = 0.063\,M$ μs for large M (Fig. 3-(a)). For messages up to 256 bytes the only dependence from M is given by the memory-to-memory copy. For longer messages the cumulative effect of per-packet overheads (due to packetization and streaming interface management) adds to the global cost per byte represented in Fig. 3-(a).

For what L is concerned, its value does not scale with message size, and is approximately constant. For messages shorter than 256 bytes, always an entire packet is transferred, and the corresponding delay entirely contributes to the round trip time. This delay is approximately 14.5 μs as measured for messages of 16 bytes. For messages longer than 256 bytes, the payload is packetized and pipelined through the network. Hence the delay incurred by any packet other than the first one within the network is completely masked by the SBus transfer time on either the send or receive side (these costs are very close in this setup).

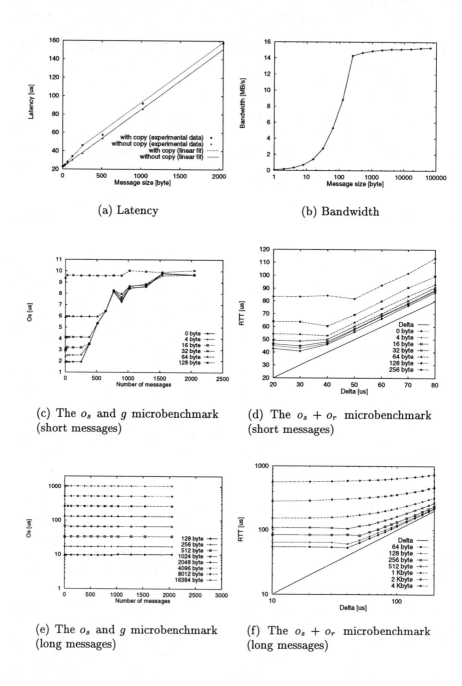

(a) Latency

(b) Bandwidth

(c) The o_s and g microbenchmark (short messages)

(d) The $o_s + o_r$ microbenchmark (short messages)

(e) The o_s and g microbenchmark (long messages)

(f) The $o_s + o_r$ microbenchmark (long messages)

Fig. 2. Platform #1 (Sparc5).

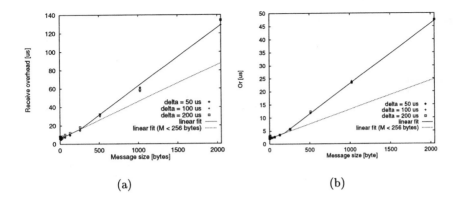

Fig. 3. o_r versus message size; (a) on the Sparc 5, (b) on the Ultra 1/170.

Platform #2: Ultra 1. The Sun workstations used for this setup are a Ultra 1/170 and a Ultra 1/140 running Solaris 2.5.1 (a Ultra 1/140 has been used for lack of a second Ultra 1/170). Both machines have a 16KB/8KB instruction/data internal cache, a 512 KB external cache, and their SBus is clocked at 25 MHz. The Ultra 1/170 processor is clocked at 167 MHz, and is rated at 5.26/8.45 SPECint-base95/SPECfp-base95. The Ultra 1/140 processor is clocked at 143 MHz, and is rated at 4.52/7.73 SPECint-base95/SPECfp-base95.

With this setup we have measured a minimum latency of 15 μs (Fig. 4-(a)). The peak bandwidth (with copy) is 34.7 MB/s when the faster machine is on the receive side, 33 MB/s otherwise (Fig. 4-(c)). The bandwidth difference between the two configurations is observed only in the copy version of the test, suggesting that the slower memory hierarchy of the Ultra 1/140 becomes the communication bottleneck for messages larger than 128 bytes. All the other graphs of Figure 4, when not specified, are relative to measurements with the faster machine on the receive side.

Figure 4-(e) shows a marked oscillations of the value of o_s for number of messages greater than ≈ 1000. The period of the oscillation is 512, which is the size of the FM receive queue in the Myrinet interface. By changing the size of the queues and repeating the measurements, we have confirmed the dependence of the period from the queue length. Some additional comments on this issue will be given in Section 4.

The qualitative behavior of o_s, o_r and g in this setup is quite similar to the one described in the previous one and we do not report the corresponding graphs. The quantitative results are reported in Table 1. In the linear approximations given for messages greater than 256 bytes the constant part is neglected because i) difficult to measure with accuracy and ii) hardly significant.

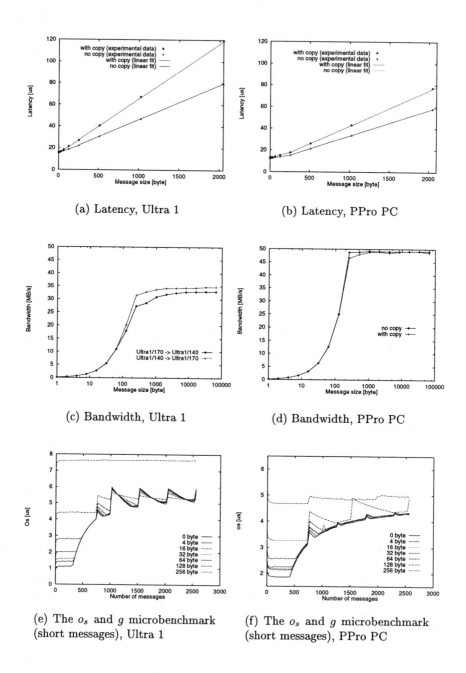

(a) Latency, Ultra 1

(b) Latency, PPro PC

(c) Bandwidth, Ultra 1

(d) Bandwidth, PPro PC

(e) The o_s and g microbenchmark (short messages), Ultra 1

(f) The o_s and g microbenchmark (short messages), PPro PC

Fig. 4. Platforms #2 (Ultra1, on the left) and #3 (PPro PC, on the right).

Platform #3: Pentium Pro PC. The DAS cluster of the Vrije Universiteit has 64 nodes connected in a torus topology. Each node is a 200 MHz Pentium Pro PC with a 32 bit, 33 MHz PCI bus and 64 MB of RAM, running BSDI's BSD/OS (version 3.0). The Pentium Pro has a 8KB/8KB instruction/data level 1 cache, a 256KB level 2 cache, and a similar motherboard (Intel Alder) is rated at 8.09/5.99 SPECint-base95/SPECfp-base95. The FM library required only marginal modifications to run on the DAS.

Figures 4-(b) and 4-(d) show latency and bandwidth. For the latency, two versions of the test were used, one in which the received data is untouched and the other in which data is copied into a preallocated buffer (on both sides).

The minimum one-way latency with copy is 12.5 μs. For short messages (i.e. less than the packet size) the curve can be approximated with the line $12.5 + 0.02 M$ μs. For long messages the curve is $9 + 0.033 M$ μs.

Figure 4-(d) shows the results of the bandwidth test. The peak bandwidth is 49.1MB/s, with 24.85 MB/s already for 128-byte messages.

Figure 4-(f) shows two sets of oscillations of the value of o_s starting from a number of messages of 768. For one set the period is 768, for the other it is 512. These numbers correspond to the size of the receive queue alone (512), and to the sum of the send and receive queues in the Myrinet interfaces. These oscillations are discussed in Section 4.

The qualitative behavior of o_s, o_r and g on the DAS is quite similar to what already seen for the the other two machines and we do not report the corresponding graphs. The quantitative results are reported in Table 1.

4 Discussion

In this section, we discuss the experimental results presented in the previous sections to derive some insight into key design issues like the overall performance bottleneck, the packetization and streaming overhead, the role of the size of the packet, how tolerant is FM to system performance variations. We also point out how some differences in the machines architecture influence the library performance.

The bandwidth bottleneck. The results reported in Fig. 2-(c) confirm that the transfer of data across the SBus on the send side is the bandwidth limiting factor on older generation Sparcs. The o_s cost of 63 ns per byte does correspond to a bandwidth of 15.8 MB/s which is only marginally higher than that measured directly with the bandwidth test.

The present generation of Sun workstations has a much improved SBus: 25 MHz operation independent of processor clock, 64-bit wide data bus, transfer sizes up to 64 bytes (in burst mode). All these improvements brought forth a doubling in the FM peak bandwidth with respect to the original platform, the Sparc 20. Nevertheless, the SBus remains the communication bottleneck, and only a more advanced bus architecture like the PCI can break this barrier.

On the DAS a value for o_s of 0.019 μs per byte corresponds to about 52.6 MB/s, which is in good agreement with the 49 MB/s found by direct measure-

Parameter		Sparc 5	Ultra 1/170	DAS
L		14.5	12	8
o_s	$M \leq 256$	$2.3 + 0.057M$	$1.1 + 0.025M$	$1.9 + 0.011M$
	$M > 256$	$0.063M$	$0.028M$	$0.019M$
o_r	$M \leq 256$	$6 + 0.040M$	$2.2 + 0.011M$	$3 + 0.009M$
	$M > 256$	$0.063M$	$0.023M$	$0.013M$
g	$M > 256$	$0.063M$	$0.028M$	$0.019M$

Table 1. The FM LogP parameters (in μs) on the different machines, as a function of the message size M (in bytes).

ment. The write-combining feature of the PCI design is what is benefiting FM, by speeding the programmed I/O transfer of the send side. Bandwidths in excess of 70 MB/s have been achieved on a carefully tuned implementation under WinNT [10].

Packetization and pipelining. The result concerning o_s is even more interesting when compared with that found for o_r. When received data are copied out of the kernel memory in the Sparc 5, the cost per byte at the receive side is 63 ns, i.e. the same as the send side (Table 1). This explains why the copying of the received data does not affect the bandwidth test: the copy at the receive side is completely overlapped with the SBus transfer at the send side. The same happens on the PPro PC and on the Ultra, where the cost per byte on the receive side is even smaller than on the send side.

The streaming interface overhead. The cost per packet of the streaming interface can be estimated in about 1 μs on the Pentium Pro PC. This is because the cost per byte at the receive side is 9 ns for message sizes up to 256 bytes and 13 ns for longer messages. Since for message sizes up to 256 bytes only one packet is sent, the variable part of o_r is entirely due to the copy out of the kernel memory, and the cost for managing the single packet is included in the constant costs. For long messages, the variable part of o_r is due to both the memory-to-memory copy and the costs of managing packetization and streaming. (Streaming overhead derives mainly from maintaining stream state across handler invocations.) The latter contributions therefore correspond to 4 ns per byte that leads to the above estimate considering a packet of 256 bytes. The same calculation for the Ultra 1/170 leads to an estimate of about 3.1 μs/packet. A possible explanation of such difference is the highly cache-unfriendly nature of the context switching mechanism, which puts at a disadvantage the Ultra more RISC-oriented processor.

The packet size. The effect of the packet size on the balance of the communication pipeline can be seen in Fig. 2-(c) and Fig. 4-(e) where is evident that the g for short messages is higher than the send overhead o_s. This result can be explained by remembering that for M up to 256 bytes, always a packet of 256 bytes is injected into the network and DMAed through the SBus into the kernel memory at the the receiving node. The message length at which the send overhead becomes the bottleneck is between 64 and 128 bytes on the Sparc 5, and between 128 and 256 bytes on the Ultra and on the PPro. This result can be used to evaluate the impact of the packet size on the bandwidth achievable with short (less than 256 bytes) messages.

The queues' size. The marked oscillations of o_s on the Ultras (Fig. 4-(e)) and on the PPro (Fig. 4-(f)) are much less evident on the slower SS5 (Fig. 2-(c)). Their period is equal to the length of the receive queue alone (512 packets), or to the sum of both the send (256 packets) and receive queues' lengths in the interface memory, pointing to the wrap-around overhead incurred by the interface code as the main cause of the oscillations. On the faster machines this overhead is exposed by the increased speed of the host relative to the interface processor.

The amplitude of the oscillations tapers off as the message size grows, so they do not affect peak bandwidth. Still, they have an effect on the shape of the bandwidth curve, degrading performance for short messages. The simplified queue handling scheme used in the interface control program can result in a momentary block of the input network link at each wrap-around. Modifying the code to reduce this block as much as possible we have been able to improve bandwidth for short messages (by as much as 4 MB/s for messages of 128 bytes in one test). However we found these results difficult to reproduce for reasons not yet clear to us.

Robustness of the implementation One of the issues facing the communication software architect is the variety of system configurations on which his/her software is going to be run. The present version of FM was developed mainly on Sparc 20s, and a lot of care went into balancing the load of the different parts of the system – host processor, interface processor, I/O bus. Our measurements show that on the Suns, the dramatic change in peak bandwidth across machine with a 4:1 CPU performance ratio is not accompanied by substantial changes in the internal qualitative behavior of the messaging layer. Moreover, FM maintains its internal balance across machine, like the Pentium Pro PC and the Sun Ultra 1/170, which have substantially different processor, I/O bus and memory architectures.

5   Related work

As previously mentioned, our characterization of FM uses the approach described in [6] for the measurement of the LogP parameters. The aspect that differentiates our measurements is that we used two microbenchmarks instead of one. In [6] all the data is derived from a bandwidth test augmented with artificial delays between sends. This choice has been induced by the request-reply Active Messages communication mechanism.

Taking advantage of the greater flexibility of the FM interface, we chose to disjoin the measurements of o_s and g on one hand, and of $o_s + o_r$ on the other. The advantage of this approach is that it can also be used with libraries that do not conform to the Active Messages paradigm, like, for instance, MPI. Although two different microbenchmarks must be used, we gain the ability to show in a single graph the dependence of the parameters on the message size. In other words, we bring a new variable into the analysis, and we do so in a way that provide additional valuable information. So for instance, from Fig. 2-(c) is immediately apparent that $o_s < g$ for messages up to 64 bytes, and from Fig. 2-(e) that o_s linearly depends on message size for messages longer than 256 bytes.

6 Conclusions

In this paper we have presented an analysis of the FM library for Myrinet based on the LogP model. This modelization provides information at a level of detail that cannot be obtained with the traditional latency and bandwidth tests.

One of the objectives of this work was the use of such a detailed modelization to analyze the impact of machine architecture differences on FM. We have employed LogP to study how the balance between the different parts composing FM changes when the library is run unmodified on machines as diverse as a Sparc 5, a Ultra 1/170, a PentiumPro PC. We have shown that a low level messaging layer can be very sensitive to differences in just one critical component, which alone can bring about dramatic variations in the overall performance. In the case of FM, the critical component was the I/O bus.

Despite the large variations observed in the overall performance across the three platforms, a carefully designed communication software like FM can preserve the basic balances of its design remarkably well. Within FM, the host/interface load balance and the relative weight of the sender and receiver overheads didn't change substantially on all the tested machines.

A collateral result is that a properly extended LogP model can be an invaluable tool for architectural analysis. It achieves the right balance between model simplicity, ease of model parameters evaluation, and accuracy. By explaining the behavior of the LogP parameters in terms of specific FM features we were able to provide some insight on key design issue – like the overall performance bottleneck, the influence of packet size on the bandwidth curve, or the amount of packetization and streaming interface overhead. The analysis also exposed an area susceptible of further optimization in the queue management on the receive side.

7 Acknowledgments

The authors wish to acknowledge the contribution of all the people that made possible this work. Among them are Henri Bal and Koen Langendoen, for their kind invitation for M. Lauria to visit the Computer Systems group at the Vrije Universiteit. Kees Verstoep's help was essential in carrying out plenty of productive work on the DAS. We are indebted to Andrew Chien for allowing the source of FM to be used by a few selected groups outside the University of Illinois.

References

1. A. Alexandrov, M. Ionescu, K.E. Schauser, and C. Scheiman, "LogGP: incorporating long messages into the LogP model - one step closer towards a realistic model of parallel computation", In *Procs. of the 7th Annual ACM Symp. on Parallel Algorithms and Architectures*, pp. 95–105, July 17-19 1995.

2. H. E. Bal, M. F. Kaashoek, and A. S. Tanenbaum, "Orca: A language for parallel programming of distributed systems", *IEEE Transactions on Software Engineering*, 18(3), pp. 190–205, March 1992.

3. M. A. Blumrich, K. Li, R. Alpert, C. Dubnicki, E. W. Felten, and J. Sandberg, "Virtual memory mapped network interface for the SHRIMP multicomputer", in *Proceeding of the International Symposium on Computer Architecture*, April 1994, pp. 142-153.

4. N.J. Boden, D. Cohen, R.E. Felderman, A.E. Kalawik, C.L. Seitz, J.N. Seizovic, and W.-K. Su, "Myrinet–a gigabit-per-second local-area network", *IEEE Micro*, 15(1), February 1995.

5. D.E. Culler, Karp, D.A. Patterson, A. Sahay, K.E. Schauser, E. Santos, R. Subramonian, and T. von Eicken, "LogP: towards a realistic model of parallel computation", *Procs. of the 4th SIGPLAN Symp. on Principles and Practices of Parallel Programming*, ACM, May 1993.

6. D.E. Culler, L.T. Liu, R.P. Martin, C.O. Yoshikawa, "Assessing Fast Network Interfaces", *IEEE Micro*, 16(1), pp. 35–43, Feb. 1996.

7. Mario Lauria and Andrew Chien, "MPI-FM: High performance MPI on workstation clusters", *Journal of Parallel and Distributed Computing*, vol. 40(1), January 1997, pp. 4–18.

8. M. Liu, J. Hsieh, D. Hu, J. Thomas, and J. MacDonald, "Distributed network computing over Local ATM Networks", In *Supercomputing '94*, 1995.

9. S. Pakin, M. Lauria, and A. Chien, "High performance messaging on workstations: Illinois Fast", Messages (FM) for Myrinet, In *Supercomputing '95*, December 1995.

10. S. Pakin, M. Lauria, M. Buchanan, K. Hane, L. Giannini, J. Prusakova, A. Chien, "Fast Messages Documentation", Available from: http://www-csag.cs.uiuc.edu

11. S. Pakin, V. Karamcheti, and A. Chien, "Fast Messages: Efficient, Portable Communication for Workstation Clusters and MPPs", *IEEE Concurrency*, vol. 5(2), April-June, 1997, pp. 60–73.

12. T. von Eicken, A. Basu, V. Buch, and W. Vogels, "U-Net: A user-level network interface for paralle and distributed computing", in Proceedings of the 15th ACM Symposium on Operating Systems Principles, December 1995.

13. T. von Eicken, D. Culler, S. Goldstein, and K. Schauser, "Active Messages: a mechanism for integrated communication and computation", In *Proceedings of the International Symposium on Computer Architecture*, 1992.

Performance of a Cluster of PCI Based UltraSparc Workstations Interconnected with SCI

Knut Omang

Department of Informatics, University of Oslo, Norway
Email: knuto@ifi.uio.no

Abstract. SCI is based on unidirectional point-to-point links forming ringlets that can be connected with switches to allow further scaling. This paper presents performance results from running on a number of differently configured SCI clusters. The SCI technology used is Dolphin's second generation PCI/SCI adapter based on the LC-2 LinkController chip as well as a new 4 port, LC-2 based switch. Nodes are UltraSparcs running Solaris 2.5.1 as the operating system. Results show latencies down to 2.9 μsec for remote stores, and bandwidths up to 80 Mbytes/s into a single system. Network throughput of more than 270 Mbytes/s (8 node system) is demonstrated. Results indicate that the new LC-2 eliminates a number of problems with the earlier LC-1 chip in addition to increasing peak performance. With its flexible building blocks this technology should also make it possible to construct systems with a large number of nodes, pushing I/O adapter based SCI interconnects forward as a promising system area network technology.

1 Introduction

SCI (Scalable Coherent Interface)[16] is an IEEE interconnect standard based on unidirectional point-to-point links and switches. Dolphin adapters and switches are built up around the B-link bus, a split-transaction 64-bit bus that can support up to 8 devices. The LinkController (LC-2) chip from Dolphin Interconnect Solutions implements the SCI standard, being Dolphin's 3rd generation SCI interface chip. The LC-2 is connected to the PSB-1, Dolphin's new PCI to B-link bridge. The LC-2 runs a 500 Mbytes/s SCI link on the SCI side. On the PCI side, the PSB-1 supports 33 MHz, 32 bits PCI implementations. A simple view of internals of the PCI/SCI adapter is shown in figure 1. This paper presents an early low level performance study of LC-2 based clusters. A number of two-node measurements shows PCI-to-SCI throughput of the adapter and minimal latency of remote stores. For these measurements a single two node ring without switch is used. Measurements for the larger configurations are done for a couple of different configurations using rings and switches with up to 8 nodes. A few characteristic communication patterns is used to reveal bottlenecks and worst case performance as well as demonstrating performance under optimal conditions.

1.1 Testbed hardware

The PSB-1 based adapters studied in this paper differs from the older FPGA based implementation for the Sbus[12] in several ways:

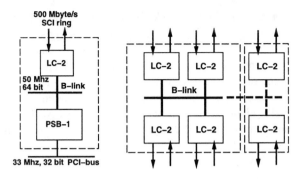

Fig. 1. Internals of the SCI to PCI adapter(left) and the 4 port switch(right). The switch can be extended with an optional mezzanine card with two additional ports (dotted right box) to enable cascading.

- The ASIC implementation of the PSB-1 enables higher speeds than possible with a firmware based implementation as in the older Sbus adapters.
- The PSB-1 has a different model of operation and more functionality, which both complicates optimal usage and performance measurements with the increased number of parameters to control, but also opens up a range of new possibilities for usage, with features as card-atomic fetch/add, pull DMA, 64 byte load, prefetching and write gathering.
- The LC-2 runs a higher link speed and has a number of other improvements and fixes compared to the LC-1 used in the Sbus and the old PCI/SCI implementation.

The PCI/SCI card can in principle be run on any type of node hardware having a PCI bus. Full driver support currently exists for the operating systems Solaris (Sparc, x86), NT and UnixWare. However, unfortunately currently most low end PC hardware will severely limit the achievable throughput performance due to CPU speed, memory subsystem performance or PCI implementation limitations. This paper uses the more powerful Sun UltraSparcs as nodes. This is both because of availability in Dolphin's lab and their much better memory subsystem performance, which we discuss more closely in section 3.

1.2 System software setup

Almost all measurements are carried out using the LC-2 version of the card with an experimental, portable device driver, the Interconnect Manager (ICM), developed for the PCI/SCI adapter at the University of Oslo[13]. Exceptions from this rule was required due to heavy multiplexing of usage of the lab equipment: The 8 node configuration was run with LC-2 based adapters using Dolphin's driver, and the lock performance numbers were collected using the older LC-1 based PCI adapter. Performance of the locks is mostly dependent on the PSB-1 which is the same for both adapters, the difference in overhead on the SCI side is almost ignoreable[1]. The ICM driver has been particularly

---

[1] On a two node ring, latency numbers for ordinary remote stores on the LC-1 based adapter differs from the slightly faster LC-2 based version by 50 ns

designed for performance by limiting the kernel initiated driver activity to a minimum, with a focus on providing maximal parallelism inside the driver and between driver and hardware by using a fine grained resource protection scheme. In addition performance has been put in focus when designing the driver interface that is seen by user processes, to minimize the number of system calls necessary to carry out communication. The driver also provides user level abstractions that are independent of operating system, thus allowing (nearly) identical code to run on all platforms. With respect to the programmed I/O numbers measured with Dolphin's driver in this paper, differences should be minimal. The protocol used (the LLM) operates entirely in user space, without any system calls once the connection is set up.

1.3 Options for remote memory mapping

Upon initialization the PSB-1 require the system to provide two continuous ranges of PCI addresses for mapping remote memory. An address translation table (ATT) in the PSB can then be used to map SCI addresses into local PCI addresses to be offered as remote memory segments to the kernel or the user. The PSB uses 512K pagesize when mapping remote memory, so for user level mappings of smaller regions the unused parts of the ATT must be protected by the driver to avoid accesses to illegal addresses on the remote node. One of the PCI address ranges is denoted I/O space (not to be confused with the I/O space from the PCI specification which is not used by the PSB). Accesses to mappings set up through this address space will be handled by the PSB as consistent accesses, that is, all load or stores are processed immediately by the PSB and forwarded to the link controller (over the B-link). The other address range is called prefetch space. Stores to legal (ATT mapped) addresses within this space are (somewhat simplified) kept by the PSB unless the end of the address range is 64 byte aligned. Consecutive accesses within the same 64 byte block will thus be gathered and flushed, that is forwarded to SCI with as large transactions as possible. This happens either as a result of a buffer timeout or as a result of arrival of another access that is not aligned with the previous data and that "needs" the same buffer (these buffers are often denoted *streams*). In addition a number of special mappings can be set up by setting special ATT entry bits. Interrupt enabled maps allows a write to a remote memory location in certain cases to generate an interrupt on the remote node. Fetch-and-add maps can make a read to a remote location trigger a fetch-and-add in the remote PSB on the particular memory location. This functionality is abstracted by the ICM to allow a number of features such as locks (described more closely in section 5) and selective remote thread wakeup or remote user process signaling.

2 Overview of experiments

The following sections presents measurements obtained with the following locally developed microbenchmarks:

- The membw benchmark. Simple measurements of the memory and memory to I/O bandwidth on the host systems involved, to eliminate the host's memory system as the bottleneck. Uses memset and memcpy.

- The `pingpong` benchmark, latency of remote stores between nodes in different configurations. Latency is measured for pingpong between two nodes in an otherwise idle system and for multiple, simultaneous pingpongs between different pairs of nodes.
- The `mutest` benchmark shows the improved performance of cluster wide mutual exclusion locks on the new PCI/SCI adapter. The PCI/SCI adapter has now been extended with a hardware mechanism similar to the one we proposed at last year's CANPC workshop [10]. With this mechanism, mentioned above as fetch-and-add maps, mutual exclusion can be achieved with a single remote operation independent of the support for atomic operations on PCI implementations.
- The `ctp` benchmark program (described more closely in [12]) is used to measure unidirectional and bidirectional throughput of messages of different sizes in different configurations. Larger blocks of data can be moved by setting up DMA engine on the SCI adapter, or by the CPU itself using programmed I/O to do remote stores or loads.

3 Node memory bandwidth

Memory bandwidth (single access – memory write and dual access, memory copy) is the limiting factor of many end systems when considering network performance. The `membw` microbenchmark measures internal memory bandwidth by

1. writing zeros into a 4 Mbytes region using memset
2. copying 2 Mbytes from one half to the other of a 4 Mbytes buffer using memcpy.

A few memory bandwidth results are shown in table 1. The two leftmost columns are obtained with the `membw` microbenchmark, measuring the local memory subsystem only. The three rightmost columns are from running the `ctp` throughput measurement benchmark (described in more details in section 6). SCI 2-copy is the full LLM protocol used for all measurements in sec.6. On the sender side each message is copied from the user buffer directly across SCI using remote stores. On the receiver side, memory is copied from the receive buffer into the user buffer. This is the typical communication pattern needed to support the protocol requirements that many MPI[2] programs would demand. The SCI 1-copy just skips the receive end copying step, that is, the receiving node no longer competes with the incoming remote stores on memory bandwidth in the receiver. For LLM this of course makes the protocol useless for anything but examining the load of each suboperation on the memory interconnect. SCI 0-copy is an even more extreme variant. Instead of copying out on SCI useful data from a user buffer in the sender, the sender just uses memset to write directly across SCI, thus eliminating half of the memory bus accesses on the sender side. All the SCI numbers in table 1 are obtained using a 64K message size.

For reference table 1 also includes a few DMA numbers to show that this is not a CPU utilization issue. With the full protocol (SCI 2-copy) we get comparable numbers for DMA on the 166 MHz Pentium, thus obviously we have a memory bandwidth bottleneck on the receiving end. On the sender side we get a certain effect of relieving the CPU of work (comparing the SCI 1-copy numbers for programmed I/O with the

236

numbers for DMA). Obviously SCI 0-copy is impossible with DMA since the DMA controller is designed for copying. All systems used for the measurements in table 1 were running Solaris. As is evident from the table, these three different "protocols" give considerable difference in throughput on standard PCs, making memory bandwidth a limiting factor. Other corresponding PC results can be found in [18, 14]. Consequently,

Platform	memset	memcpy	SCI 2-copy	SCI 1-copy	SCI 0-copy
166 MHz Intel Pentium	83.73	43.94	21.60	37.25	64.52
– using DMA			21.53	41.97	N/A
248 MHz UltraSparc-II	409.96	211.77	75.38	76.64	76.72

Table 1. Memory bandwidth in Mbytes/s obtained with the membw benchmark compared to measured SCI bandwidth

the rest of the measurements in this paper are carried out on UltraSparc-II workstations (prototypes) running at 248 MHz. The UltraSparcs with its memory bandwidth from table 1 and a good PCI implementation is the for us currently available platform that is best capable of utilizing the potential of the SCI interconnect.

4 Latency of remote stores

Latency is measured between a pair of nodes as the round trip time of sending a message using remote stores and for the receiver to send an equally sized response back, divided by two. All communication across SCI is done by the sender using remote stores into the receiver's memory. The pingpong benchmark uses the single program multiple data model and can be set up to run a number of simultaneous "ping-pong"s between the nodes configured in the system. The pingpong benchmark uses the prefetch space for remote mappings. Since transactions may get reordered on SCI, multi-store messages must use a store barrier to ensure that the full message has arrived before it is replied. The store barrier is implemented as load of a special CSR register that does not return until all outstanding store transactions have completed. The ICM exports a read only mapping of this register to user space to save the overhead of a system call. For single store "messages" no store barrier is needed, but all locations used for such "independent" stores must be end aligned on a 64 byte boundary, otherwise latency will be incremented by the timeout value for the PSB buffer (stream).

Table 2 shows the results from running a single pingpong test in three different configurations. Configuration 2 is done between two nodes in a single two node ring. Configuration 4x1 shows a run between two nodes in a 4-node system where there is a single node on each switch port. Configuration 6 shows performance of of a single pingpong between two nodes in a 6 node ring. The 4x1 result tells us that a 4 byte crossing of a single 4-port switch building block adds to the latency an average of less than 400ns for a 4-byte message. Each node on the ring adds an average of another 25ns of bypass latency (in the 6 case, four extra nodes must be bypassed, adding a total of 100ns).

Config.	Latency in μs for msg.sz.(bytes)				
	4	8	64	1K	64K
2	2.90	3.02	4.08	20.94	811.56
4x1	3.31	3.44	4.73	22.46	814.18
6	3.00	3.12	4.18	21.42	811.99

Table 2. Pingpong latency between two nodes in an otherwise idle system in different configurations

5   Mutual exclusion

Fast mutual exclusion between multiple nodes is important to control access to shared resources in a distributed environment. Different synchronization issues with SCI is more thoroughly discussed in [10].

As mentioned earlier, the PCI/SCI adapter hardware has been modified to include a way to get atomic operations even when the PCI bus implementation in the nodes does not support such operations (PCI locks). A special bit in the SCI address translation table can be set to indicate a special remote shared memory mapping, a fetch-and-add mapping. When an address within this mapping is read, the PCI/SCI adapter will send a SCI fetch-and-add lock transaction which on the remote side will perform a load, an increment and a store operation towards the local memory. The original load operation will in turn get back the old value. These operations are not atomic seen from the local memory bus, but all following accesses to the same location through the SCI adapter will block waiting for the complete fetch-and-add to complete. Thus if all accesses to these locations are through an SCI mapping (even from the local node) atomicity is ensured.

Using this functionality, mutual exclusion locks can be implemented using a set of ordinary memory locations in one of the nodes. Acquiring the lock will involve reading the lock's memory location through the special fetch-and-add mapping. If a zero was returned, the lock is held, otherwise repeat the operation. A release of a lock is done by writing a zero through a consistent ordinary SCI mapping of the same memory location. Making this access go through SCI is necessary to ensure that the lock release is not intervening any ongoing fetch-and-add. Such an intervening access that gets in between the fetch and the add could create a lost update situation where nobody owns the lock. Thus even the adapter local to the memory must access the lock variables solely through SCI. This makes a local lock acquire/release slower than a remote. Transactions on the lock from the owner of the lock memory must make a full loop around the SCI ring.

Memory location is:	local	remote
Acq./rel. time(μs)	12.7	11.7

Table 3. Average time in μs to acquire and release a cluster-wide mutual exclusion lock

238

As mentioned earlier, a complicating factor with SCI is the possibility of load and store reordering. Thus in addition a lock implementation need to ensure sequential consistency between the lock operations and ordinary loads and stores. This is accomplished by issuing store barriers as part of the lock operations. The implemented functionality is exercised through the simple `mutest` benchmark, which repeatedly acquires and releases a lock. Table 3 shows the average time to acquire and release a lock with no contention, depending on where the lock memory is situated with respect to the involved process. As explained above we see that a local acquire is slightly more costly than a remote due to the increased distance these transactions must travel. The costly alternatives without hardware support is discussed more thoroughly in [10], the least expensive being Lamport's[7] algorithm, which for this testbed will cost more than 50 μs due to the many store barriers needed in presence of no ordering[2].

6 Overview of throughput measurements

Node-to-node throughput as well as aggregate interconnect bandwidth measurements are collected using the `ctp` multithreaded performance tester. The `ctp` program can be set up to run any number of producer and/or consumer threads to/from any number of other nodes using the SCI user level programming interface or standard socket based communication. This enables comparison with IP based interconnect technologies. A comparison of the previous Sbus based generation of SCI interfaces with Ethernet and ATM was presented in [11]. The `ctp` program uses the SPMD (single program multiple data) model and is started with identical parameters as one process on each node. Each such process can be set up to use a number of read and/or write threads. Each node measure the rate of incoming data, and data from all nodes are collected at the end using a simple SCI shared memory protocol. The `ctp` program requires a configuration setup file where each node in the configuration is given a unique number (rank value) between 0 and $N - 1$ where N is the number of nodes configured in the system. In this paper `ctp` is used with three patterns of communication:

1. Unidirectional: All odd node numbers are sending on a single thread and all even node numbers are receiving on a single thread.
2. Neighbour Send Ring (NSR): All nodes are receiving from a neighbour and sending to another neighbour. Two notions of neighbours are used, the best possible and the worst possible.
3. Hot receiver: Node 0 runs one receiving thread for each of the other nodes. All the other nodes run a single sender thread.

The unidirectional case can be seen as a restricted NSR where only every second of the threads around the logical ring is started. Thus also the unidirectional case has a "ring-like" structure where each node is either sending or receiving instead of doing both.

---

[2] The PCI/SCI board offer a configuration option to force ordering of loads with respect to stores and other loads, but the ICM operates with this feature off for optimal performance of pull based communication

6.1 Support for bulk messages

The PCI/SCI adapter has an on board DMA controller with a 256 entries scatter/gather list and can be set up to do both push and pull DMA. Push DMA will translate into 80 byte SCI write64 requests over SCI and end up as 64 byte stores into the remote memory located at the node corresponding to the upper part of the 64 bit SCI DMA target address. Similarly pull DMA will translate into a 16 byte SCI read64 request which will result in a 64 byte load on the remote source side and a 80 byte read64 response packet carrying the SCI data back to the requesting DMA engine which will forward the data into the appropriate local target address.

DMA setup has a high initial cost and involves kernel activity, but once setup, relieves the CPU of work. Programmed I/O (PIO) can be issued without kernel intervention once a connection to the remote shared memory segment is set up. In this paper, the UltraSparc's 64 byte loads/stores[9] are used for programmed I/O whenever feasible. For the throughput measurements, the simple LLM (Low Latency Messages) protocol is used. LLM uses a simple ring buffer and a write and read pointer placed in the reader of the pointer's memory. Since SCI transactions can arrive out of order, in LLM a store barrier must be issued by the sender before proceeding with the remote pointer update to allow the reader to process the message. As discussed in [10] the store barrier functionality on the PCI/SCI adapter is less expensive than on the SCI/Sbus-2 adapter, where a store barrier was accomplished by issuing a remote load, which would stall in the adapter until all previous stores had completed. On the PCI/SCI adapter, store barrier semantics is achieved by reading a particular CSR register. This read will stall until all previous writes are completed, but saves the roundtrip latency of the dummy remote load. However, for small messages even this store barrier is relatively expensive. Better performance can be achieved by using 63 byte messages with a valid flag in the 64th byte as discussed in detail in [10].

The current user level access path to the DMA controller in the Solaris port of the Interconnect Manager (ICM) is through the UNIX `pwrite` system call. The `pwrite` call is similar to a write call, but takes an additional offset parameter. The driver translates this offset into a an offset into a particular shared memory segment. This way `ctp` can use the same user space flow control implementation with DMA as with PIO. An advantage of using `pwrite` with autonomously established shared memory segments is that most of the receive activity is done in user space, with less user-to-kernel context switch overhead. Thus no corresponding read system call is needed for each write. Instead the ICM supports pull based DMA through the `pread` system call. Dolphin's implementation of read/write uses a kernel controlled ring buffer in the receiver.

A higher peak unidirectional throughput is measured with programmed I/O than with DMA, but in case of bidirectional tests, PIO loses to DMA in our test cluster, since the test nodes are only single CPU. Since PIO requires the CPU to do the remote stores, and the CPU is shared between the reader and writer thread, write stalls due to a full pipeline in the PCI/SCI system will hurt the reader process too. Thus to give the full picture, in the following, when appropriate both DMA and PIO throughput is measured.

7 Two-node measurements

The left graph of figure 2 shows the throughput of the two different transfer methods (DMA or PIO) of a single producer and a single consumer in an otherwise idle two node system. With a measured peak throughput of 77 Mbytes/s using PIO this is considerably better than in the Sbus case where node-to-node throughput peaks at around 31 Mbytes/s[12]. To illustrate the change from the LC-1 to the LC-2 based PCI adapter, LC-1 curves are included. DMA results for small packets are hurt by the setup cost

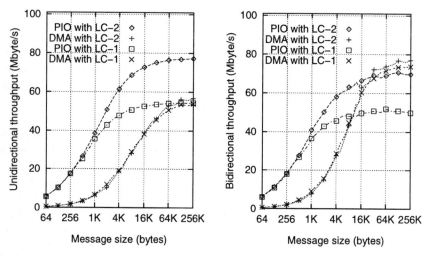

Fig. 2. Unidirectional(left) and bidirectional (right) throughput between two nodes in a "back-to-back" connection (two-node ring)

(kernel context switch etc.) for small packets. For large messages we believe that we are experiencing the peak performance limit of the DMA controller. The DMA controller has the disadvantage over PIO in that each transfer operation needs two crossings of the PCI host bridge, one for the request and one for the data, while for PIO only one I/O boundary crossing is needed, however this cannot possibly explain the whole difference. Comparing unidirectional performance with LC-1 and LC-2 we see that there is only a small difference in DMA performance, that is, no gain (using the same DMA controller on the PSB-1 chip) from LC-1 to LC-2 with the higher link speed. For programmed I/O however, the LC-2 version performs significantly better for larger messages.

Bidirectional throughput (each of the two nodes running two independent threads, a producer and consumer) is presented in the right graph of figure 2. Bidirectional throughput in the two node case is the special case of the NSR communication pattern used for larger clusters. Bidirectional DMA peaks at around 77 Mbytes/s while PIO degrades slightly from the unidirectional case. As suggested earlier, since the test uses multithreading to achieve the bidirectionality, a reader thread which only processes messages from local memory will have to compete for CPU cycles with the writer thread doing the remote stores. The writer thread will spend a lot of the CPU's cycles in stalls waiting for remote stores to complete. Thus multi CPU nodes are expected to perform bidirectional PIO in the same range as for DMA for large messages, and also somewhat better for smaller messages.

8 Interconnect bandwidth for different topologies

This section presents result from measuring performance of the unidirectional, bidirectional(NSR) and hot receiver communication pattern for four different multiple node cluster configurations, 4 and 6 node rings (figure 3(right)), a 4x1 configuration with a 4-port switch with 1 compute node on each port (each port on the switch makes the second SCI node on a two node SCI ring), and finally on a dual-switched 8 node configuration as shown to the left in figure 3.

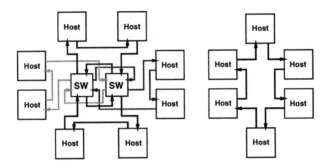

Fig. 3. A dual-switched 8-node configuration(left) and a 6 node ring configuration(right)

8.1 Ring configurations

Figure 4 shows two different runs of `ctp` with the NSR downstreamcommunication pattern. The left graph shows a run where all nodes are sending to their physical neighbour downstream on the ring and receiving from the upstream node. Thus the length (number of ring subsegments) data packets need to travel is always 1. In the right graph the direction of communication is reversed, thus data packets will have to travel $N - 1$ subsegments to get to their destination. The SCI protocol includes echo, sync, and response traffic in addition to the larger packets carrying (64 byte) data. We have computed the approximate maximal possible user bandwidth as a function of the number of nodes (n) and the raw SCI link bandwidth (B) assuming the NSR communication pattern:

$$NTE(n) = 8Bn/(5n + 8) \tag{1}$$
$$NTE(n) = 8Bn/(13n - 8) \tag{2}$$

Equation (1) gives the never-to-exceed bandwidth of NSR in the downstream (shortest path) case and equation (2) for the similar upstream (longest path) case. The functions are also plotted in the graphs of figure 4. Details of how to arrive at this formula can be found in [12]. Thus as is clear from figure 4, LC-2 based interconnects perform well for the NSR pattern independent of how the traffic is going for up to 6 nodes on a ring, but the useful number of nodes on a ring (looking at the NTE curve) is much higher if data can be organized in a way that limits the number of subsegments the data traffic will have to travel. Thus with applications with well known and adaptable communication patterns it should be possible to get good performance beyond 10 nodes, while for less controllable communication we may see a substantial drop in performance already for 8 nodes.

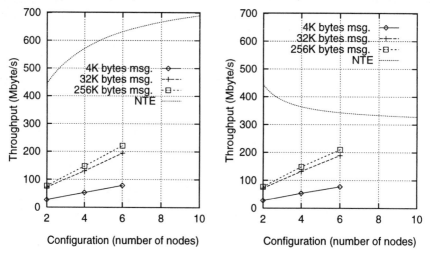

Fig. 4. DMA performance of the NSR communication pattern for different topologies related to theoretical never-to-exceed value for this pattern. Left: Data packets going . Right: Data packets going upstream

8.2 Using a switch versus a 4-node ring

As is evident from the two graphs in figure 4, the upstream and downstream cases for the 4 node ring are practically identical. We have omitted the 4-node switch throughput numbers which appeared to be almost identical to the ring numbers. Consequently, a 4-node ring is more cost effective than a switch based configuration, since the switch is needed in addition to the adapter boards. The ring also provides somewhat lower latencies, however, the switch is more fault tolerant in that one node may fail without bringing the whole interconnect down, so if fault tolerance is a goal, the switched solution is better.

8.3 A dual-switched 8 node configuration

The idea of the dual-switched setup is to double the switch bandwidth by connecting 2-node rings to one port on each switch (making 4 doubly connected 4-node rings).

The switches are set up to forward only half of the packets, thus diving the individual switch load by two. This configuration is an alternative to the 8-node configuration with switches using the optional mezzanine board to enable cascading by connecting the switches by another layer of SCI rings. The setup illustrates the many possibilities for combining SCI components to improve scalability of a system. The mezzanine boards were not available at the time of these experiments. Also resource allocation constraints did not allow comparison between this 8-node configuration and the standard 4x2 configuration (just removing one of the switches). NSR throughput performance of this configuration using PIO is shown to the left in figure 5 with a peak aggregate performance of 221 Mbytes/s. As discussed earlier, using PIO for bidirectional traffic does not give optimal performance due to contention between reader and writer for CPU cycles. Unfortunately DMA was not an option in the available environment. In figure 5(left) half of the connections are within a ring and half across the switch. With four unidirectional streams all going across the switch and using 64K buffers, a total of 278 Mbytes/s has been measured, compared to 297 Mbytes/s if all four unidirectional streams are going within the rings. Thus with double bandwidth across the switch system, an 8-node configuration can be run without much degradation in performance even in bad traffic pattern scenarios. With respect to latencies, traffic on the dual switched system will at most cross 1 switch and bypass up to 4 nodes (the other node and the other switch port on both involved rings) It remains to be seen how the 8-node ring and the single switch, 8-node case as well as the cascaded, fully switched 8-node case behaves in comparison.

9   Hot receiver

A hot receiver situation where one node is receiving from all the other nodes sending at full speed is a particularly demanding communication pattern that also often occur in applications (e.g. the reduce operation in MPI[2]). Work on the LC-1 based Sbus boards in [12] demonstrated that this pattern was particularly bad for multinode rings due to a too simple implementation of the SCI A/B retry protocol. The A/B retry protocol's purpose is to ensure fairness and forward progress of all nodes. The right graph of figure 5 shows performance of a hot receiver situation in three configurations. As opposed to LC-1 results where bandwidth on ring topologies were halved for as small hot node situations as two nodes sending to one, we see that the LC-2 performs as it should in this sense, with a slight increase in input for from a one-to-one situation, suggesting that a node is able to input data from SCI slightly faster than it can output. The 4-node ring actually behaves slightly better than the 4-node switched configuration, which is in contrast to results on the LC-1 where the 4-node switched configuration was the only configuration that behaved well in a hot node situation.

10   Related work

A number of other groups are working on SCI interconnects. Ibel et al.(University of California, Santa Barbara) discusses the mapping of programming models as active messages and remote queues onto an Sbus based SCI cluster in [6]. Simon and

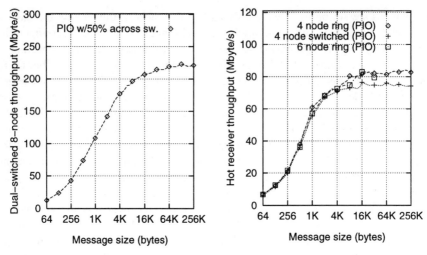

Fig. 5. Left: Aggregate network bandwidth of NSR communication in an 8-node dual-switched system. Right: Input bandwidth of a hot receiver situation in three configurations.

Heinz [18](University of Paderborn) looks at performance of PCs with Windows NT clustered with the LC-1 based PCI/SCI adapter.

A number of papers address SCI performance through simulation. Scott [17] analyses the performance of SCI rings. SCI performance in loaded rings has been investigated by simulations in [19]. A detailed simulation study of switch architectures and how the size of link buffers affect performance is presented in [8]. They also mention the problem with hot receivers, as well as looking at ways of improving the switch architecture.

The only other commercially available high speed I/O adapter based interconnect we are aware of that has support for remote stores is DECs Memory Channel[1]. Memory Channel uses a different memory mapping model with read only and write only mappings of pages. A page that is mapped by multiple nodes will exist in one copy on each node. A write to a writable mapping will be reflected into all these copies, thus making reads as inexpensive as local reads, but at the cost of more memory usage and probably less scalability, since an amount of local memory equal to the combined sizes of all remote memory mappings must be reserved on each node.

Tandem's ServerNet[3, 4] has a similar memory model as SCI, allowing direct remote memory access, but does not offer remote load/stores, only DMA based communication. On the hardware side, ServerNet uses links that run at 50 Mbytes/s and packets propagated using wormhole routing as opposed to the cut-through routing used in SCI. Their focus is also scalable systems. Tandem has provided our lab at University of Oslo with ServerNet boards to enable comparison with Dolphin technology. However we have so far not been able to do a fair comparison due to less intimate knowledge of hardware features.

11 Conclusion and further work

Performance of Dolphin's new LC-2 based PCI/SCI adapter as well as behavior of the LC-2 itself has been studied. using up to 8 PCI based UltraSparc-II systems. The SCI interconnect provides low latency and high throughput, with flexible options for scaling. The new hardware supported fetch+add has been used to implement cluster wide mutual exclusion locks, much more efficient than possible with the Sbus/SCI adapters, which have no hardware supported atomic transactions.

This is the first study of clusters using the LC-2 based PCI/SCI adapter. Introduction of the LC-2 improves bandwidth of the PSB-1 based PCI/SCI adapter by more than 10 Mbytes/s, and also removes a couple of bottlenecks like the documented retry problem of the LC-1. This makes systems with several nodes on each ring more attractive than with the LC-1. Showing end system bandwidths of up to 80 Mbytes/s scaling to a moderate number of nodes on a ring (6) we have demonstrated that smaller systems with very good capacity and very low latencies for user program message passing can be built. The 8 node dual switched configuration shows that scalability to larger systems should be achievable, at least by doubling the switch capacity, however work on larger configurations is needed to make sure that there are no significant hidden problems with these systems.

To make the picture complete, this paper should ideally have included a study of pull based algorithms, however we felt that at this stage it would be more interesting to see results for the new LC-2 based adapters, rather than a more complete picture of the "old" LC-1 based SCI implementation for PCI. Another part left for future work is measurements of real applications. Considering the amount of work needed to keep simple applications updated to use the latest hardware features for optimal performance, getting for instance MPI with applications to work on top of this was out of question within the timeframe available for this paper. However, we believe that using a full protocol stack with flow control and buffering for the throughput measurements, at least we have done what is possible within a microbenchmark study to demonstrate what could be expected user application performance.

Other further work include larger configurations and combined ring/switch configurations. The new device driver, the Interconnect Manager has been used as a basis for a very high performance MPI implementation by Scali Computer[15]. This implementation will provide a basis for running off-the-shelf scientific application benchmarks as well as more highly tuned applications like the very high performance FFT application used in [5]. Department of Informatics at University of Oslo is also building up a lab for network demanding multimedia and web applications in which SCI interconnected systems will play a central role.

12 Acknowledgments

The experiments were carried out using Dolphin Interconnect Solution's lab equipment. Stein Jørgen Ryan implemented the membw benchmark. Thanks to Ola Tørudbakken, Morten Schanke and a lot of others at Dolphin for discussing hardware details and for lending out the sparse test equipment during busy periods. Thanks also to Øystein Gran Larsen for reading and providing comments on the last draft on very short notice.

References

1. Richard B. Gillett and Richard Kaufmann. Experience Using the First-Generation Memory Channel for PCI Network. In *Proceedings of Hot Interconnects IV*, pages 205–214, August 1996.
2. William Gropp, Ewing Lusk, and Anthony Skjellum. *Using MPI, Portable Parallel Programming with the Message-Passing Interface*. MIT Press, 1994.
3. Robert W. Horst. TNet: A Reliable System Area Network. *IEEE Micro*, February 1995.
4. Robert W. Horst and David Garcia. ServerNet SAN I/O Architecture. In *Proceedings of Hot Interconnects V*, July 1997.
5. Lars Paul Huse and Knut Omang. Large Scientific Calculations on Dedicated Clusters of Workstations. In *Proceedings of International Conference on Parallel and Distributed Systems, Euro-PDS'97*, June 1997.
6. Maximillian Ibel, Klaus E. Schauser, Chris J. Scheiman, and Manfred Weis. High-Performance Cluster Computing Using SCI. In *Proceedings of Hot Interconnects V*, July 1997.
7. Leslie Lamport. A Fast Mutual Exclusion Algoritm. *ACM Transactions on Computer Systems*, 5(1):1–11, February 1987.
8. Manfred Liebhart, André Bogaerts, and Eugen Brenner. A Study of an SCI Switch Fabric. In *Proceedings of IEEE International Symposium on Modeling, Analysis and Simulation of Computer and Telecommunication Systems, Haifa*, January 1997.
9. Sun Microsystems. *UltraSparc Programmer Reference Manual*. SPARC Technology Business, 1995. Part No.:STP1030-UG.
10. Knut Omang. Synchronization Support in I/O adapter based SCI Clusters. In *Proceedings of Workshop on Communication and Architectural Support for Network-based Parallel Computing, San Antonio, Texas*, February 1997.
11. Knut Omang and Bodo Parady. Performance of Low-Cost UltraSparc Multiprocessors Connected by SCI. In *Proceedings of Communication Networks and Distributed Systems Modeling and Simulation, Phoenix Arizona*, January 1997. Also available at http://www.ifi.uio.no/~sci/papers.html.
12. Knut Omang and Bodo Parady. Scalability of SCI Workstation Clusters, a Preliminary Study. In *Proceedings of 11th International Parallel Processing Symposium (IPPS'97)*, pages 750–755. IEEE Computer Society Press, April 1997.
13. Stein Jørgen Ryan. The Design and Implementation of a Portable Driver for Shared Memory Cluster Adapters. Research Report 255, Department of Informatics, University of Oslo, Norway, December 1997. Available at http://www.ifi.uio.no/~sci/papers.html.
14. Stein Jørgen Ryan and Haakon Bryhni. Eliminating the Protocol Stack for Socket Based Communication in Shared Memory Interconnects. In *Proceedings of International Workshop on Personal Computer based Networks Of Workstations (at IPPS'98)*, April 1998.
15. Scali Computer. http://www.scali.com.
16. IEEE Standard for Scalable Coherent Interface (SCI), August 1993.
17. Steven L. Scott, James R. Goodman, and Mary K. Vernon. Performance of the SCI Ring. In *Proceedings of 19th International Symposium on Computer Architecture*, volume 20(2) of *Computer Architecture News*, pages 403–414, May 1992.
18. Jens Simon and Oliver Heinz. SCI Multiprocessor PC Cluster in a Windows NT Environment. In *Proceedings of ARCS/PARS Workshop*, September 1997.
19. Bin Wu and Haakon Bryhni. Effectively Using Your Fast SCI Links. In *Proceedings of Second International Workshop on SCI-based High-Performance Low-Cost Computing*, pages 19–24, March 1995.

Author Index

Lecture Notes in Computer Science

For information about Vols. 1–1281

please contact your bookseller or Springer-Verlag

Vol. 1318: R. Hirschfeld (Ed.), Financial Cryptography. Proceedings, 1997. XI, 409 pages. 1997.

Vol. 1319: E. Plaza, R. Benjamins (Eds.), Knowledge Acquisition, Modeling and Management. Proceedings, 1997. XI, 389 pages. 1997. (Subseries LNAI).

Vol. 1320: M. Mavronicolas, P. Tsigas (Eds.), Distributed Algorithms. Proceedings, 1997. X, 333 pages. 1997.

Vol. 1321: M. Lenzerini (Ed.), AI*IA 97: Advances in Artificial Intelligence. Proceedings, 1997. XII, 459 pages. 1997. (Subseries LNAI).

Vol. 1322: H. Hußmann, Formal Foundations for Software Engineering Methods. X, 286 pages. 1997.

Vol. 1323: E. Costa, A. Cardoso (Eds.), Progress in Artificial Intelligence. Proceedings, 1997. XIV, 393 pages. 1997. (Subseries LNAI).

Vol. 1324: C. Peters, C. Thanos (Eds.), Research and Advanced Technology for Digital Libraries. Proceedings, 1997. X, 423 pages. 1997.

Vol. 1325: Z.W. Ras´, A. Skowron (Eds.), Foundations of Intelligent Systems. Proceedings, 1997. XI, 630 pages. 1997. (Subseries LNAI).

Vol. 1326: C. Nicholas, J. Mayfield (Eds.), Intelligent Hypertext. XIV, 182 pages. 1997.

Vol. 1327: W. Gerstner, A. Germond, M. Hasler, J.-D. Nicoud (Eds.), Artificial Neural Networks – ICANN '97. Proceedings, 1997. XIX, 1274 pages. 1997.

Vol. 1328: C. Retoré (Ed.), Logical Aspects of Computational Linguistics. Proceedings, 1996. VIII, 435 pages. 1997. (Subseries LNAI).

Vol. 1329: S.C. Hirtle, A.U. Frank (Eds.), Spatial Information Theory. Proceedings, 1997. XIV, 511 pages. 1997.

Vol. 1330: G. Smolka (Ed.), Principles and Practice of Constraint Programming – CP 97. Proceedings, 1997. XII, 563 pages. 1997.

Vol. 1331: D. W. Embley, R. C. Goldstein (Eds.), Conceptual Modeling – ER '97. Proceedings, 1997. XV, 479 pages. 1997.

Vol. 1332: M. Bubak, J. Dongarra, J. Was´niewski (Eds.), Recent Advances in Parallel Virtual Machine and Message Passing Interface. Proceedings, 1997. XV, 518 pages. 1997.

Vol. 1333: F. Pichler. R.Moreno-Di´az (Eds.), Computer Aided Systems Theory – EUROCAST'97. Proceedings, 1997. XII, 626 pages. 1997.

Vol. 1334: Y. Han, T. Okamoto, S. Qing (Eds.), Information and Communications Security. Proceedings, 1997. X, 484 pages. 1997.

Vol. 1335: R.H. Möhring (Ed.), Graph-Theoretic Concepts in Computer Science. Proceedings, 1997. X, 376 pages. 1997.

Vol. 1336: C. Polychronopoulos, K. Joe, K. Araki, M. Amamiya (Eds.), High Performance Computing. Proceedings, 1997. XII, 416 pages. 1997.

Vol. 1337: C. Freksa, M. Jantzen, R. Valk (Eds.), Foundations of Computer Science. XII, 515 pages. 1997.

Vol. 1338: F. Plás˘il, K.G. Jeffery (Eds.), SOFSEM'97: Theory and Practice of Informatics. Proceedings, 1997. XIV, 571 pages. 1997.

Vol. 1339: N.A. Murshed, F. Bortolozzi (Eds.), Advances in Document Image Analysis. Proceedings, 1997. IX, 345 pages. 1997.

Vol. 1340: M. van Kreveld, J. Nievergelt, T. Roos, P. Widmayer (Eds.), Algorithmic Foundations of Geographic Information Systems. XIV, 287 pages. 1997.

Vol. 1341: F. Bry, R. Ramakrishnan, K. Ramamohanarao (Eds.), Deductive and Object-Oriented Databases. Proceedings, 1997. XIV, 430 pages. 1997.

Vol. 1342: A. Sattar (Ed.), Advanced Topics in Artificial Intelligence. Proceedings, 1997. XVII, 516 pages. 1997. (Subseries LNAI).

Vol. 1343: Y. Ishikawa, R.R. Oldehoeft, J.V.W. Reynders, M. Tholburn (Eds.), Scientific Computing in Object-Oriented Parallel Environments. Proceedings, 1997. XI, 295 pages. 1997.

Vol. 1344: C. Ausnit-Hood, K.A. Johnson, R.G. Pettit, IV, S.B. Opdahl (Eds.), Ada 95 – Quality and Style. XV, 292 pages. 1997.

Vol. 1345: R.K. Shyamasundar, K. Ueda (Eds.), Advances in Computing Science - ASIAN'97. Proceedings, 1997. XIII, 387 pages. 1997.

Vol. 1346: S. Ramesh, G. Sivakumar (Eds.), Foundations of Software Technology and Theoretical Computer Science. Proceedings, 1997. XI, 343 pages. 1997.

Vol. 1347: E. Ahronovitz, C. Fiorio (Eds.), Discrete Geometry for Computer Imagery. Proceedings, 1997. X, 255 pages. 1997.

Vol. 1348: S. Steel, R. Alami (Eds.), Recent Advances in AI Planning. Proceedings, 1997. IX, 454 pages. 1997. (Subseries LNAI).

Vol. 1349: M. Johnson (Ed.), Algebraic Methodology and Software Technology. Proceedings, 1997. X, 594 pages. 1997.

Vol. 1350: H.W. Leong, H. Imai, S. Jain (Eds.), Algorithms and Computation. Proceedings, 1997. XV, 426 pages. 1997.

Vol. 1351: R. Chin, T.-C. Pong (Eds.), Computer Vision – ACCV'98. Proceedings Vol. I, 1998. XXIV, 761 pages. 1997.

Vol. 1352: R. Chin, T.-C. Pong (Eds.), Computer Vision – ACCV'98. Proceedings Vol. II, 1998. XXIV, 757 pages. 1997.

Vol. 1353: G. BiBattista (Ed.), Graph Drawing. Proceedings, 1997. XII, 448 pages. 1997.

Vol. 1354: O. Burkart, Automatic Verification of Sequential Infinite-State Processes. X, 163 pages. 1997.

Vol. 1355: M. Darnell (Ed.), Cryptography and Coding. Proceedings, 1997. IX, 335 pages. 1997.

Vol. 1356: A. Danthine, Ch. Diot (Eds.), From Multimedia Services to Network Services. Proceedings, 1997. XII, 180 pages. 1997.

Vol. 1357: J. Bosch, S. Mitchell (Eds.), Object-Oriented Technology. Proceedings, 1997. XIV, 555 pages. 1998.

Vol. 1361: B. Christianson, B. Crispo, M. Lomas, M. Roe (Eds.), Security Protocols. Proceedings, 1997. VIII, 217 pages. 1998.

Vol. 1362: D.K. Panda, C.B. Stunkel (Eds.), Network-Based Parallel Computing. Proceedings, 1998. X, 247 pages. 1998.